QUESTIONS & ANSWERS:
INTELLECTUAL PROPERTY

QUESTIONS & ANSWERS:
INTELLECTUAL PROPERTY

Multiple-Choice and Short-Answer Questions and Answers

SECOND EDITION

Gary Myers
Dean and Earl F. Nelson Professor of Law
University of Missouri School of Law

Lee Ann W. Lockridge
David Weston Robinson Professor of Law and the McGlinchey Stafford Professor of Law
Louisiana State University Paul M. Hebert Law Center

ISBN: 978-1-6304-3598-1

eBook ISBN: 978-1-6304-3599-8

> **NOTE TO USERS**
> To ensure that you are using the latest materials available in this area, please be sure to periodically check the LexisNexis Law School web site for downloadable updates and supplements at www.lexisnexis.com/lawschool.

Editorial Offices

121 Chanlon Rd., New Providence, NJ 07974 (908) 464-6800

201 Mission St., San Francisco, CA 94105-1831 (415) 908-3200

www.lexisnexis.com

MATTHEW◆BENDER

INTRODUCTION

The questions and answers in this book are designed to cover the broad subject of "intellectual property" in a comprehensive way. All of the major subjects in this fascinating area of law are included in this book — including copyrights, patents, trademarks, trade secrets, the right of publicity, and unfair competition. The key aspects of each of these areas of law are addressed in a systematic way — subject matter and validity, ownership and duration of rights, infringement and remedies, and defenses and limitations. Aside from this legal framework, however, it is important to know that intellectual property covers an amazing array of varied creative endeavor. That is because intellectual property law has an impact on the most dynamic activities and enterprises in today's interconnected world — movies, music, the Internet, social media, inventive activity, business franchises, and entrepreneurship. If you can answer or at least understand the questions and answers in this book, you are ready to begin a journey into the most interesting area of law available to us today.

Each of the questions in this book has an answer that we believe — based on many years of study, practice, teaching, writing, and consulting work in the field — is superior to the other possible answers. We hope that our explanation of each question will shed some light on the reader's understanding of this field. But keep in mind that intellectual property is one of the most debated areas of law that you will ever encounter. Strong opinions run deep in this field, but we have endeavored to offer a clear statement of the law as it exists today.

The book begins with 173 multiple-choice and short answer questions, followed by detailed answers and explanations. The remainder of the book includes a 55-question sample final examination, again followed by complete answers.

A few words about citations and editing: Most legal propositions in the "answer" portion of this book are supported by at least one or two citations to statutes, case law, books, or articles. We have attempted to provide these important citations without cluttering the book with long string citations. All quotations have had internal citations and footnotes omitted without specific reference to these changes in the citations. Once again the goal is to have a readable but authoritative introduction to the law of intellectual property.

This second edition of this book is current as of January 1, 2014. If you encounter any development after this date, please keep in mind that the law is ever-changing. This disclaimer is more important in the field of intellectual property than it is in most areas of law because there are few fields in which changes are so dramatic and so frequent. It is this dynamic feature which convinces us that there is no more exciting area of law than intellectual property in which to study, write, or practice.

Best regards,

Gary Myers
Columbia, Missouri

Lee Ann W. Lockridge
Baton Rouge, Louisiana

PREFACE TO THE SECOND EDITION

This study guide uses over 170 multiple-choice and short-answer review questions, as well as an additional 55-question "practice final exam," to test — and expand — your knowledge and understanding of basic concepts in U.S. intellectual property law. The guide covers copyright, patent, and trademark, as well as both trade secret law and the right of publicity, with breadth and depth geared for an introductory, or survey course in intellectual property. To make the guide easy to use during the semester, the review questions are organized by subject area, and for most subject areas, the questions are further divided into four sub-categories: subject matter & validity; ownership & duration; infringement & remedies; and defenses & limitations. All subject areas and topics are combined for both a final overview section and the practice final exam. The authors have provided a detailed answer for each multiple-choice question that explains which of the four possible answers is correct, and why, and they have paired each short-answer question with a brief but thorough response. For ready reference, the guide's index includes a detailed list of topics indexed to the various questions.

ABOUT THE AUTHORS

Gary Myers is Dean and Earl F. Nelson Professor of Law at the University of Missouri School of Law. Before being named Dean at Missouri, he was a member of the faculty at the University of Mississippi School of Law for 23 years. He has also practiced law in Atlanta and served as a law clerk to Judge Gerald Tjoflat of the United States Court of Appeals for the Eleventh Circuit. Lee Ann W. Lockridge is the David Weston Robinson Professor of Law and the McGlinchey Stafford Professor of Law at the Louisiana State University Paul M. Hebert Law Center. She has also taught at the University of Cincinnati College of Law, practiced law in Dallas, and served as a law clerk to Judge Eugene E. Siler of the United States Court of Appeals for the Sixth Circuit. Dean Myers and Professor Lockridge, along with Professors David Lange (Duke University) and Mary LaFrance (University of Nevada at Las Vegas), are co-authors of an intellectual property case book, INTELLECTUAL PROPERTY, CASES AND MATERIALS (4th ed. West 2012).

TABLE OF CONTENTS

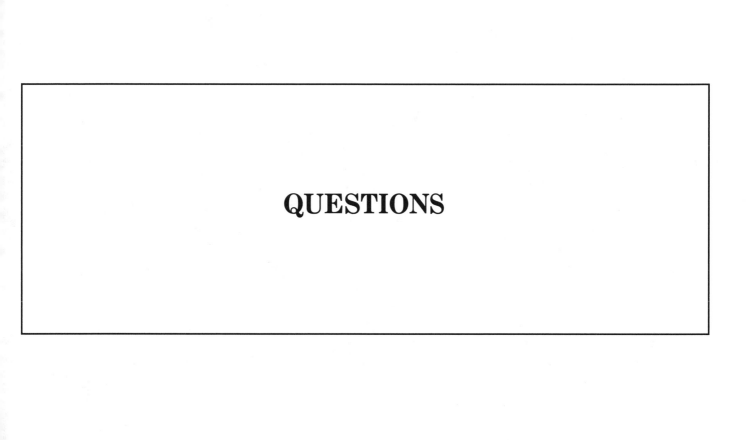

QUESTIONS

1. Which of the following is *not* protected by copyright?

    (A) literary works

    (B) musical works

    (C) ideas

    (D) architectural works

2. A work is "fixed in a tangible medium of expression" for copyright law purposes when it is:

    (A) handwritten on paper, recorded on film, stored on a hard drive, or even stored in a computer's random access memory (RAM — i.e., memory that would be lost if the computer lost power)

    (B) handwritten on paper, recorded on film, stored on a hard drive, but not when stored on a computer's random access memory (RAM — i.e., memory that would be lost if the computer lost power)

    (C) recorded on film, stored on a hard drive, or even stored on a computer's random access memory (RAM — i.e., memory that would be lost if the computer lost power), but not merely handwritten on paper

    (D) recorded on film or stored on a hard drive, but not when it is merely on a computer's random access memory (RAM — i.e., memory that would be lost if the computer lost power) or handwritten on paper

3. Professor Myers has assembled a great deal of information on Louisiana attorneys over the years, including through various roles with the Louisiana Bar Association. He has created, and makes available via his LAlaw.com website, two lists: (a) a directory containing (in alphabetical order) the names, addresses, and telephone numbers of all lawyers who are members of the Louisiana Bar (the "directory"), and (b) a guide called "Professor Myers's Guide to the 50 Best Lawyers in Louisiana," which lists 50 lawyers' names, addresses, and telephone numbers, as well as explanations of those lawyers' practices and relative merits (the "guide"). Consider the minimum standard of creativity for copyright protection as set forth in *Feist Publications, Inc. v. Rural Telephone Service Co.*, 499 U.S. 340 (1991). Under the Court's analysis in that case, which of the following is most accurate?

    (A) Both the directory and the guide are copyrightable.

(B)   Neither the directory nor the guide is copyrightable.

(C)   The directory is not copyrightable, but the guide is copyrightable.

(D)   The directory is copyrightable if it is maintained and updated, and the guide is copyrightable in any event.

4.   A law student takes photographs during a trip to Europe, making use of a fully automatic digital camera. Which of the following is most accurate?

(A)   The law student has a valid copyright on the images captured by the camera, assuming they are minimally creative or involve some judgment.

(B)   The law student has a valid copyright, as there is no minimum level of creativity required and courts do not assess the artistic merit of works.

(C)   The law student does not have a valid copyright, because photographs are not copyrightable subject matter.

(D)   The law student does not have a valid copyright, because only artistic and creative works of recognized stature are protected by copyright law.

5.   A famous celebrity meets a friend for a casual lunch. Unbeknownst to the celebrity, the "friend" has surreptitiously audio-taped the conversation (the celebrity did most of the talking). What claim or claims can the celebrity bring to prevent publication of the conversation in the tabloids?

(A)   state law copyright only

(B)   federal copyright only

(C)   both federal and state law copyright claims

(D)   neither federal nor state law copyright claims

6.   The first copyright law in the United States, enacted in 1790, did not protect which category of works?

(A)   books

(B)   charts

(C)   sculptures

(D)   maps

7.   What is the "sweat of the brow" theory for copyright protection and what is its status under current law?

ANSWER:

8.   Copyright registration for U.S. authors is:

   (A)   required in order to recover any compensatory damages for copyright infringement (i.e., no compensatory damages for infringement occurring before registration)

   (B)   required in order to obtain injunctive relief (i.e., no injunctive relief for infringement occurring before registration)

   (C)   required as a condition precedent to filing suit

   (D)   entirely optional and has no consequence for copyright litigation

9.   Which of the following most accurately describes the current importance of a copyright notice for a work written and *published in* 1980?

   (A)   Copyright notices are required and works published without the copyright notice fall into the public domain.

   (B)   Copyright notices are required and works published without the copyright notice fall into the public domain unless "cured" under the Copyright Act of 1976.

   (C)   Copyright notice is no longer required in light of the Berne Convention.

   (D)   Copyright notice is no longer required under the Sonny Bono Copyright Term Extension Act.

10.   How does the above — notice for works published in 1980 — compare to the copyright notice requirement under the 1909 Act?

ANSWER:

11.   How does above — notice for works published in 1980 — compare to the copyright notice requirement under present law?

ANSWER:

12.   What is the so-called "poor man's copyright" and what is its significance under copyright law?

ANSWER:

13.   The Visual Artists Rights Act of 1990 *does not* protect limited-edition or single copies of:

   (A)   sculptures

   (B)   prints

(C)   architectural plans

(D)   photographs

14.   Which of the following statements best characterizes the availability of copyright protection for the design of a utilitarian article, such as an attractive, original design for a large trash can for use in public parks?

(A)   The design is protectable if the original, aesthetic features are physically separable from the utilitarian aspects of the trash can.

(B)   The design is protectable if the original, aesthetic features are either physically or conceptually separable from the utilitarian aspects of the trash can.

(C)   The design is protectable if the original, aesthetic features show a modicum of creativity and if the look and feel of the trash can is aesthetically pleasing as a whole.

(D)   The design is not protectable because the article is useful, and copyright law does not protect functional articles.

15.   What is the copyright doctrine of "scenes a faire"?

ANSWER:

16.   What is the idea/expression distinction as it relates to copyright law?

ANSWER:

17. The United States government can own which of the following types of copyrights?

    (A) works of U.S. government employees acting in the scope of their duties

    (B) rights to works assigned to it by non-governmental authors

    (C) rights to meticulously maintained factual databases

    (D) both (B) and (C) above

18. A student is hired to do research for a professor and provides 10 pages of material, which the professor copies verbatim into a 30-page article. Which of the following is most accurate?

    (A) The professor and student are joint authors under the Copyright Act, given that each has contributed copyrightable expression.

    (B) The professor and student are joint authors under the Copyright Act, because the professor stole the work from the student, who would share any proceeds and rights.

    (C) The professor is the sole author of the work under the Copyright Act, given that there was no intent to form a joint work.

    (D) The professor is the sole author of the work under the Copyright Act, given that the professor wrote more than 50% of the work.

19. If two coauthors specifically wish to have joint authorship of the copyright in their work, what do most courts require in order to reach such a conclusion?

ANSWER:

20. If (for whatever reason) one person is sole author of a work, but desires to allow a second person to have an equal ownership interest in that work, how can this result be accomplished under applicable law?

ANSWER:

21. Assume that a famous author writes a new novel in the year 2010. The novel is written in his or her own name (i.e., not anonymously or under a pseudonym) and is not a work made

for hire. What is the current term of copyright protection for this work?

(A) ninety-five years from the date of publication or 120 years from the date of creation, whichever comes first

(B) ninety-five years from the date of creation or 120 years from the date of publication, whichever is longer

(C) life of the author plus 50 years

(D) life of the author plus 70 years

22. What is the copyright duration for a joint work?

(A) ninety-five years from the date of publication or 120 years from the date of creation, whichever comes first

(B) ninety-five years from the date of creation or 120 years from the date of publication, whichever is longer

(C) life of the last surviving author plus 50 years

(D) life of the last surviving author plus 70 years

23. Assume that a movie is produced in the year 2003. The movie is a "work made for hire." What is the current term of copyright protection for this work?

(A) seventy-five years from date of publication, or 100 years from date of creation, whichever term is shorter

(B) ninety-five years from date of publication, or 120 years from date of creation, whichever term is longer

(C) ninety-five years from date of publication, or 120 years from date of creation, whichever term is shorter

(D) life of the author plus 70 years

24. Your client runs across an old poem, originally written and published in Latin by an American author in the year 1915, and translated into English in 1935. Your client wishes to copy the poem, in its entirety, for a web site containing poetry. The client has the original 1915 text and the 1935 translation in his library. What is your advice?

(A) You can freely use either the Latin or the English version of the poem, as any copyright has necessarily expired and the poem is in the public domain.

(B) You can freely use the Latin version, as the copyright has necessarily expired and the poem is in the public domain, but the English version may still be protected by copyright.

(C) You cannot use either version as the copyrights have not necessarily expired.

(D) You can freely use either version because of the fair use defense.

25. What is a "work made for hire" under copyright law?

ANSWER:

26. What test has the Supreme Court adopted for defining a "work made for hire" by an employee under copyright law?

(A) contractual right to control

(B) actual control

(C) common law agency

(D) formal, salaried employee

27. Which of the following is required to be in writing under the Copyright Act?

(A) an exclusive license

(B) a non-exclusive license

(C) an assignment of copyright

(D) both (A) and (C) above

28. What are terminations of transfers under the Copyright Act?

ANSWER:

29. What is the duration for rights under the Visual Artists Rights Act ("VARA") for a sculpture created in 1995?

(A) life of the author

(B) life of the author plus 50 years

(C) life of the author plus 70 years

(D) the rights are perpetual

30. Your client wishes to record and make 1000 copies of a cover version of a copyrighted song (like Lenny Kravitz's cover version of the Guess Who's "American Woman"). The easiest way to do this is to:

    (A) obtain a public performance right from BMI, ASCAP, or SESAC

    (B) obtain a mechanical (reproduction) license from the Harry Fox Agency

    (C) obtain a distribution right from the songwriter

    (D) obtain a public display right from the songwriter

31. Sally's Hair Salon wants to hook up a CD player to its telephone system so that people placed on hold can hear music being played on the CD player in the store. Which of the following is most accurate:

    (A) Sally has not engaged in an unlawful public performance under the Copyright Act as long as her store is small enough to fit within the "safe harbor" for small businesses.

    (B) Sally has not engaged in an unlawful public performance under the Copyright Act as long as she purchased lawful copies of the CDs.

    (C) Sally has not violated the Copyright Act because playing CDs does not constitute a public performance in any situation.

    (D) Sally has violated the Copyright Act by publicly performing copyrighted works.

32. If Bob were to turn a published and copyrighted novel into a movie and release the movie on DVD, all without authorization, he would likely violate which right(s) of the author or other copyright owner of the novel?

    (A) derivative works

    (B) reproduction

    (C) distribution

    (D) all of the above

33. If Sally were to sell or rent a bootleg movie DVD (which she purchased from an anonymous seller who had the bootleg DVDs in the back of his van) she would likely violate which right of the copyright owner of the movie on the DVD?

(A) derivative works

(B) reproduction

(C) distribution

(D) all of the above

34. A public performance takes place when a copyrighted work is performed by:

(A) being played on CD in a semipublic place

(B) being played live in a place open to the public

(C) being transmitted beyond the place it is located by electronic means

(D) all of the above

35. Under present law, the owner of a copyright in a sound recording possesses which of the following rights:

(A) reproduction and distribution, but not public performance or public display

(B) reproduction, distribution, and public performance by digital transmission, but not general public performance or public display

(C) reproduction, distribution, and full public performance rights, but not public display

(D) reproduction, distribution, full public performance rights, and public display

36. Identify the types of moral rights protected under the Visual Artists Rights Act ("VARA").

(A) attribution

(B) integrity

(C) divulgation

(D) both (A) and (B)

37. The Digital Millennium Copyright Act ("DMCA") provides copyright owners with rights regarding which of the following acts?

(A) circumventing access controls on a copyright-protected work

(B) selling products for circumventing access controls

(C) violating the moral rights of an author in a copyright-protected work

(D) both (A) and (B)

38. The Copyright Act preempts state law when that law is:

    (A) equivalent to rights under copyright law

    (B) within the general scope of copyrightable subject matter

    (C) involving works of authorship fixed in a tangible medium of expression

    (D) all of the above must be shown to establish preemption

39. Which of the following statements most accurately describes the approach taken by federal copyright law to questions of remedies?

    (A) The presumptive form of relief is actual monetary damages and profits, and injunctions are rarely available.

    (B) The presumptive form of relief is injunctive relief, and actual monetary damages and profits are rarely available.

    (C) Injunctive relief is frequently granted, and actual monetary damages and profits are available only upon a showing of bad faith.

    (D) Injunctive relief is frequently granted, and actual monetary damages and profits are available upon a showing of bad faith or actual harm.

40. A successful copyright plaintiff can recover:

    (A) actual damages only

    (B) statutory damages only

    (C) either statutory or actual damages

    (D) both statutory and actual damages

41. Statutory damages can be:

    (A) increased or decreased based on the bad faith or good faith of the defendant

    (B) increased based on the bad faith of the defendant but not decreased

    (C) decreased based on the good faith of the defendant but not increased

    (D) specified by statute with no consideration of the good faith or bad faith of the defendant

42. Which of the following is *not* a complete defense to a copyright infringement action?

    (A) independent creation

    (B) common source

    (C) innocent copying

    (D) consent or license

43. Public performances of an audiovisual work in a classroom are permitted so long as:

    (A) the copy of the work being performed is lawfully made

    (B) the instructor provides notice to the copyright owner

    (C) the educational institution registers with the copyright office

    (D) both (A) and (B) above

44. The traditional "homestyle" exemption for public performances requires:

    (A) receipt of a radio or television broadcast (or the equivalent cable/satellite)

    (B) compliance with requirements regarding the number and type of receiving apparatus

    (C) no direct charge for admission

    (D) all of the above

45. Internet service providers are immune from copyright liability for user-generated material they store for their customers unless they:

    (A) have actual knowledge of the infringement

    (B) fail to take down infringing material after sufficient notice and opportunity

    (C) have control of and receive substantial financial benefit from the infringement

    (D) any of the above can extinguish the immunity

46. An undergraduate student buys one copy of a commercial outline. The student sells the book (in its original form) to another student the next semester, and that student sells it

the semester after that. The first student:

(A) has violated the right of distribution

(B) has violated the right to create derivative works

(C) has violated the right of reproduction

(D) has not violated any copyright, because of the first sale doctrine

47. Assume that a professor at a state college copies an entire textbook and distributes the copies to the professor's class of 30 students. The professor charges the students only for the actual cost of making the copies. What is the college's best defense in a suit brought by the publisher of the textbook?

(A) Sovereign immunity under the Eleventh Amendment bars suits against the state college.

(B) There is no respondeat superior or vicarious liability under the Copyright Act.

(C) The fair use defense precludes recovery, given that educational uses are protected under the fair use provision.

(D) The copying did not violate the Copyright Act because no profit was made by the professor or the college.

48. Which of the following statements most accurately describes the fair use defense under federal copyright law?

(A) The scope of fair use is broader for factual works (i.e., fair use is more likely to be found when the taking is from a fact work), and the commercial purpose of the defendant's taking is but one factor in the analysis.

(B) The scope of fair use is broader for factual works (i.e., fair use is more likely to be found when the taking is from a fact work), and if the defendant's taking is for a commercial purpose, the taking is presumed not to be a fair use.

(C) The scope of fair use is broader for fictional works (i.e., fair use is more likely to be found when the taking is from a fictional work), and the commercial purpose of the defendant's taking is but one factor in the analysis.

(D) The scope of fair use is broader for fictional works (i.e., fair use is more likely to be found when the taking is from a fictional work), and if the defendant's taking is for a commercial purpose, the taking is presumed not to be a fair use.

49. Which of the following statements most accurately describes the fair use defense under federal copyright law?

(A) The qualitative and quantitative amount taken in relation to the plaintiff's copyrighted work is relevant, and good faith (or bad faith) is taken into account.

(B) The qualitative and quantitative amount taken in relation to the defendant's alleged infringing work is relevant, and good faith (or bad faith) is taken into account.

(C) The qualitative and quantitative amount taken in relation to the plaintiff's copyrighted work is relevant, and good faith (or bad faith) is irrelevant.

(D) The qualitative and quantitative amount taken in relation to the defendant's alleged infringing work is relevant, and good faith (or bad faith) is irrelevant.

50. Which of the following statements most accurately describes the fair use defense under federal copyright law?

(A) A legitimate parody is protected and is per se fair use.

(B) A legitimate parody is presumed to be fair use, but this presumption can be rebutted using the factors on a case-by-case basis.

(C) A legitimate parody is taken into account in analyzing the fair use factors on a case-by-case basis.

(D) Whether a work is a legitimate parody does not affect the analysis of fair use, and courts simply analyze the fair use factors on a case-by-case basis.

51. Which of the following statements most accurately describes the fair use defense under federal copyright law?

(A) Unpublished works are not protected under the copyright laws, so fair use is irrelevant.

(B) Whether a work is published or unpublished is irrelevant under a fair use analysis.

(C) Whether a work is published or unpublished is a factor in a fair use analysis, and fair use is more likely to be found if a work is published rather than unpublished.

(D) Whether a work is published or unpublished is a factor in a fair use analysis, and fair use is more likely to be found if a work is unpublished rather than published.

52. Which of the following copyrighted works are not eligible for commercial rental under the first sale doctrine?

(A) audiovisual works, e.g. DVD movies

(B) computer programs, e.g. CD-ROMs containing software

(C) sound recordings of musical works, e.g. music CDs

(D) both (B) and (C)

53.   What are the three fundamental requirements for a utility patent on a process?

    (A)   novelty, nonobviousness, and ornamentality

    (B)   novelty, nonobviousness, and distinctness

    (C)   novelty, nonobviousness, and usefulness

    (D)   novelty, concreteness, and usefulness

54.   What is prior art?

ANSWER:

55.   What is PHOSITA?

ANSWER:

56.   What is constructive reduction to practice?

ANSWER:

57.   For applications containing only claims effectively filed before March 16, 2013, lack of novelty precludes patentability of an invention when:

    (A)   the device is either known or used, or patented or described in a printed publication, in the U.S. before the date the patent applicant invents the device

    (B)   the device is patented or described in a printed publication in the U.S. before the date the patent applicant invents the device

    (C)   the device is either known or used, or is patented or described in a printed publication, anywhere in the world before the date the patent applicant invents the device

    (D)   the device is known or used in the U.S., or is patented or described in a printed publication anywhere in the world, before the date the patent applicant invents the device

58. For applications containing claims effectively filed after March 16, 2013, lack of novelty precludes patentability of an invention when:

(A) the device is either publicly used or sold, or patented or described in a printed publication, in the U.S. before the date the patent applicant files the patent application

(B) the device is patented or described in a printed publication before the date the patent applicant files the patent application

(C) the device is either publicly used or sold, or is patented or described in a printed publication, anywhere in the world before the date the patent applicant files the patent application

(D) the device is publicly used or sold in the U.S., or is patented or described in a printed publication anywhere in the world, before the date the patent applicant files the patent application

59. A business method, such as a method of matching bidders and sellers in an online reverse auction, is:

(A) precluded from patentability under the "business methods" exception

(B) patentable, but only as a design patent

(C) patentable if it is novel, nonobvious, and ornamental

(D) patentable if it is novel, nonobvious, and useful

60. What form of patent protection is available for a functional feature of a product?

(A) a utility patent only

(B) a design patent only

(C) both a design patent and a utility patent

(D) neither a design patent nor a utility patent

61. A utility patent can protect a:

(A) new product

(B) new process

(C) improvement of an existing product or process

(D) all of the above

62. Which of the following is ineligible for patent protection?

(A) an abstract idea

(B) a mathematical algorithm

(C) printed matter

(D) all of the above

63. A genetically modified, asexually reproduced plant is eligible for protection under the:

(A) Plant Patent Act

(B) traditional utility patent

(C) none of the above

(D) either (A) or (B)

64. In early 2009, Bob Builder, an inventor working out of his garage, develops an innovative new machine that inexpensively makes pure fresh water out of salt water. In April 2009, Builder begins selling his machine on the Internet. In July 2010, Builder files a patent application on his machine. What is the result?

(A) Builder will obtain a patent on his machine.

(B) Builder will be precluded from patenting his machine because of the prior sale.

(C) Builder will be precluded from patenting his machine because of the statute of limitations.

(D) Builder will be precluded from patenting his machine on grounds of suppression of the invention.

65. In early 2013, Bob Builder, an inventor working out of his garage, develops an innovative new machine that inexpensively makes pure fresh water out of salt water. In April 2013, Builder begins selling his machine on the Internet. In July 2014, Builder files a patent application on his machine. What is the result?

(A) Builder will obtain a patent on his machine.

(B) Builder will be precluded from patenting his machine because of the prior sale.

(C) Builder will be precluded from patenting his machine because of the statute of limitations.

(D) Builder will be precluded from patenting his machine on grounds of suppression of the invention.

66. Do experimental uses of an invention affect an inventor's ability to later obtain patent protection for the invention? Explain.

ANSWER:

67.   What is the test for nonobviousness?

ANSWER:

68.   What are the Supreme Court's so-called "secondary considerations" and what role do they play in determining patent validity?

ANSWER:

69.   What is the written description requirement?

ANSWER:

70.   Green Co. is about to enter a bid for a construction project. The bidding is done by secret bid, with the contract going to the lowest bidder. If an employee of Green Co. "leaks" information about the amount of Green Co.'s bid to a competitor, who then undercuts Green Co. and gets the contract, does Green Co. have any legal remedy in one of the 47 states using the Uniform Trade Secrets Act (UTSA)?

(A)   Probably yes, against both the employee and the competitor, because the bid is protected as a trade secret under the UTSA as providing an actual or potential advantage.

(B)   Probably yes, but only against the employee, because the bid is protected as a trade secret under the UTSA; the competitor, however, can freely make use of this information.

(C)   Probably no, because the bid is not protected as a trade secret under the UTSA — it violates the rule that "one time" pieces of information do not qualify as trade secrets.

(D)   Clearly no, because the bid is not protected as a trade secret under the UTSA, which protects only formulas and other technical information.

71.   Can a customer list, consisting of names, addresses, telephone numbers, and the name and title of the primary sales contact, be protected as a trade secret? Why or why not?

ANSWER:

72. Who is an "inventor," and how does inventorship affect patent prosecution?

ANSWER:

73. When an employee in a research and development department creates an invention during the normal course of employment, to which of the following do the rights to the invention belong?

    (A) the employee

    (B) the employer

    (C) the rights are shared under the "shop right" doctrine

    (D) ownership depends upon the specific terms of the employment contract

74. In the scenario set forth in the question above, explain in whose name the patent will be sought and then who will ultimately own the rights to that patent.

ANSWER:

75. Inventor A conceives of an invention in January 2011, and reduces it to practice in April 2012. Inventor B independently conceives of the same invention in July 2011, and reduces it to practice in March 2012. Who gets the patent rights under *then-applicable* U.S. law?

    (A) Inventor A is entitled to the patent, assuming that she acts diligently in reducing the invention to practice.

    (B) Inventor A is entitled to the patent, regardless of diligence.

    (C) Inventor B is entitled to the patent, assuming that he acts diligently in reducing the invention to practice.

    (D) Inventors A and B are joint inventors, and both have an undivided interest in the patent rights.

76. Two competing inventors, A and B, independently develop an invention. Here is the time line for the inventors' activities:

Inv.	Conceives of Invention	Reduces to Practice	Files Patent Application
A	March 2005	March 2006	July 2006
B	January 2006	February 2006	April 2006

Who will own the patent rights under *then-applicable* U.S. law?

(A) B, because the first to reduce an invention to practice gets the rights, absent abandonment, suppression, or lack of diligence.

(B) B, because the first to file a patent application gets the rights, as long as no statutory bar applies.

(C) B, because A's one-year delay in reducing the invention to practice is per se lack of diligence.

(D) A, because the first to conceive of an invention to practice gets the rights, absent abandonment, suppression, or lack of diligence.

77. On the facts set forth in the last question above, how would the parties' rights be affected if A published an article fully disclosing the invention in March 2006 in a widely distributed scientific journal?

(A) The pre-AIA section 102 statutory bar would prevent both inventors from obtaining the patent.

(B) The pre-AIA section 102 statutory bar would prevent A from obtaining the patent, but would not affect other parties' ability to get the patent.

(C) The pre-AIA section 102 statutory bar would prevent B from obtaining the patent, but would not prevent A from getting the patent.

(D) The publication of an article in March 2006 would have no impact on anyone's rights and the owner of the invention (as found above) would still get all patent rights.

78. Two competing inventors, C and D, independently develop an invention. Here is the timeline for the inventors' activities:

Inv.	Conceives of Invention	Reduces to Practice	Files Patent Application
C	February 2013	October 2013	June 2014
D	October 2013	November 2013	March 2014

Who will own the patent rights under *current* U.S. law?

(A) C, because the first to reduce an invention to practice gets the rights, absent abandonment, suppression, or lack of diligence.

(B) D, because the first inventor to file a patent application gets the rights, as long as there has been no earlier disclosure or filing that destroys novelty.

(C) D, because D was the first to file and less than a year passed between C's reduction to practice and D's patent filing, which means the invention is still novel as of D's filing date.

(D) Neither, because D was the first to file but more than a year passed between conception of the invention by C and D's patent filing, which means the invention is not novel as of D's filing date.

79. On the facts set forth in the last question above, how would the two inventors' rights be affected if inventor C had published an article fully disclosing the invention in October 2013 in an electronically distributed scientific journal?

ANSWER:

80. Worldwide, what is the most common method for determining priority of patent ownership?

(A) the first to reduce an invention to practice gets the rights

(B) the first to file a patent gets the rights

(C) the first to conceive of an invention gets the rights

(D) competing inventors are treated as joint inventors and are required to share the rights

81. What is the "shop rights" doctrine?

ANSWER:

82. Joint inventors must:

(A) work in the same location

(B) make the same amount or type of contribution to the invention

(C) contribute something to every claim in the patent

(D) none of the above

83. What is the general term of protection for a *utility patent* under present law (not counting any extensions of the patent term allowed by law)?

(A) seventeen years from the date of patent filing

(B) twenty years from the date of patent filing

(C) seventeen years from the date of patent issuance

(D) fourteen years from the date of patent issuance

84. What is the general term of protection for a *design patent* under present law?

(A) seventeen years from the date of patent filing.

(B) twenty years from the date of patent filing.

(C) fourteen years from the date of patent issuance.

(D) twenty years from the date of patent issuance.

85. If Congress wished to grant a perpetual patent, which of the following is most accurate?

(A) The Intellectual Property Clause (Art. I, sec. 8, cl. 8) expressly precludes such a law.

(B) The Intellectual Property Clause (Art. I, sec. 8, cl. 8) expressly precludes such a law, but Congress could easily avoid the problem by relying upon the Commerce Clause.

(C) The Intellectual Property Clause (Art. I, sec. 8, cl. 8) expressly precludes such a law, and while the law is unclear, it is likely that the Commerce Clause would give Congress the power to circumvent the express limits of the Intellectual Property Clause.

(D) Congress has already granted perpetual patents in the utility patent field.

86. How long does trade secret protection last?

(A) indefinitely, as long as the requisite secrecy and competitive advantage exist

(B) perpetually, regardless of whether the information remains secret

(C) for 20 years from the date of first use

(D) for as long as it takes any one competitor to reverse engineer the subject matter of the trade secret

87.   What are reasonable secrecy measures and why are they relevant in trade secret law?

ANSWER:

88.   What is a breach of confidence and why is it relevant in trade secret law?

ANSWER:

89.   Patent infringement can be shown by proof of:

   (A)   a likelihood of confusion

   (B)   literal infringement or infringement under the doctrine of equivalents

   (C)   breach of confidence or use of improper means

   (D)   literal infringement but not the doctrine of equivalents

90.   Which of the following is not an example of an infringement of a patent?

   (A)   making a patented product

   (B)   selling an unpatented product that was manufactured using a patented process

   (C)   importation of a product covered by a patent

   (D)   practicing the invention for purely experimental purposes

91.   What is the prosecution history estoppel (or file wrapper estoppel) doctrine?

ANSWER:

92.   Which of the following most accurately describes appellate jurisdiction in patent cases under current law?

   (A)   Appeals go to the Federal Circuit, with certiorari review (discretionary) by the Supreme Court.

(B) Appeals go to the Federal Circuit, with no Supreme Court review possible (the Federal Circuit has the final say).

(C) Appeals go to the regional court of appeals (for example, the Fifth Circuit for cases filed in Louisiana), with certiorari review (discretionary) by the Supreme Court.

(D) Appeals go to the regional court of appeals (for example, the Fifth Circuit for cases filed in Louisiana), with en banc review (discretionary) by the Federal Circuit.

93. Plaintiff operates a take-out restaurant and carefully guards the recipe for what it calls its "secret sauce." A competitor purchases an order of plaintiff's product, takes it to a chemical laboratory, and has its composition analyzed. Based on this chemical analysis, defendant begins selling the same sauce. Plaintiff sues the competitor under trade secret law. What is the result?

(A) Plaintiff will probably lose because the defendant's action constitutes lawful reverse engineering.

(B) Plaintiff will probably lose because recipes for food items cannot be protected as trade secrets.

(C) Plaintiff will probably prevail, because the defendant obtained the trade secret through improper means.

(D) Plaintiff will probably prevail, because the defendant knew or should have known that the recipe was a trade secret and intended to be held in confidence.

94. Using a random password generator to identify an employee's confidential password in order to gain access to a competitor's computer system to obtain confidential information is likely to be actionable as:

(A) patent infringement

(B) trade secret misappropriation based on breach of confidence

(C) trade secret misappropriation based on improper means

(D) none of the above

95. What of the following would constitute "improper means" for purposes of proving misappropriation of a trade secret?

(A) eavesdropping with an amplifying microphone

(B) trespassing (breaking and entering)

(C) surveillance using overflights and high-powered zoom lenses

(D) all of the above

96. In patent cases, injunctive relief is:

    (A) available upon a showing of a four-factor equitable test

    (B) presumptively available to prevailing patent plaintiffs

    (C) automatically available to prevailing patent plaintiffs

    (D) only available in cases of bad faith on the part of the defendant (i.e., only in exceptional cases)

97.   What evidence must be shown in order to receive lost profits in a patent case?

ANSWER:

98.   What evidence must be shown in order to receive attorney's fees and costs in a patent case?

ANSWER:

99. What is reverse engineering, and is it a violation of trade secret law? What about use of the information learned as a result of the reverse engineering — could such use misappropriate a trade secret?

ANSWER:

100. Does reverse engineering a patented product violate patent law? What about use of the information learned as a result of the reverse engineering — could such use infringe patent rights?

ANSWER:

101. The following are, with the proper facts, valid defenses to a claim of patent infringement for making, using, or selling a patented device:

(A) invalidity of the patent

(B) lack of knowledge of the patent

(C) expiration of the statute of limitations

(D) all of the above

102. A medical practitioner makes use of a patented process in order to provide medical treatment. The physician is:

(A) liable for patent infringement

(B) liable for contributory infringement

(C) not liable because he or she did not make the patented invention

(D) not liable because of statutory immunity for medical providers

103. If a process for manufacturing gasoline for use in consumer automobiles is patented in 2014 based on an application filed in 2013 by Company A, but Company B began to use the same process in secret — but in good faith — in 2010 (including commercially selling the gasoline it produced), then Company B is likely:

    (A) liable for patent infringement for using the process and selling the gasoline

    (B) liable for inducing infringement by consumers who use its gasoline

    (C) not liable because of the innocent infringer doctrine

    (D) not liable because of statutory immunity for good faith prior users of business methods

104. Company A, the owner of a patent on a new type of fastener for quickly but securely attaching automobile body parts to the automobile frame, licenses the patent to B, a manufacturer of automobile parts. B sells parts that include fasteners embodying the patent to C, an automobile manufacturer, who in turn attaches those automobile parts to its automobile frames and sells the resulting cars — including the fasteners — to consumers. Company A wishes to sue C for patent infringement for using the patent (by attaching the parts to the frames) and selling products embodying the patent (by selling the cars), both without a license from A. What is the result?

    (A) Company A should succeed, because selling and using are both infringing activities, and only B has a license.

    (B) Company A should succeed, because C is actively inducing B to make and to sell the fasteners.

    (C) Company A should not succeed, because C is not making the fasteners, and C is also not inducing B to make them.

    (D) Company A should not succeed, because the license to B to make the fasteners exhausts A's right to control the later sale and use of B's fasteners.

105. What is the patent misuse doctrine?

ANSWER:

106. Trademark law is designed to further which of the following policies?

    (A)   promoting competition in the marketplace

    (B)   preventing consumer confusion or deception

    (C)   protection of the goodwill and reputation of sellers

    (D)   all of the above

107. What is the meaning and significance of a generic term in trademark law?

ANSWER:

108. The source of Congress's authority to enact the Lanham Act (trademark law) is:

    (A)   the Intellectual Property Clause

    (B)   the Commerce Clause

    (C)   the First Amendment

    (D)   the Impeachment Clause

109. Explain the meaning of an "arbitrary" trademark.

ANSWER:

110. Explain the meaning of a "fanciful" trademark.

ANSWER:

111. A trademark term that is a surname, such as "Dell" for computers (named for founder Michael Dell), is treated, for distinctiveness purposes, the same as a:

    (A)   descriptive mark

(B) suggestive mark

(C) arbitrary mark

(D) fanciful mark

112. The trademark term "Camel" for cigarettes is:

(A) descriptive

(B) suggestive

(C) arbitrary

(D) fanciful

113. The trademark term "Exxon" for petroleum products is:

(A) descriptive

(B) suggestive

(C) arbitrary

(D) fanciful

114. The trademark term "7-Eleven," for a chain of convenience stores that were originally open during the hours of 7a.m.–11p.m. is:

(A) descriptive

(B) suggestive

(C) arbitrary

(D) fanciful

115. The trademark term At-A-Glance for calendars is:

(A) descriptive

(B) suggestive

(C) arbitrary

(D) fanciful

116. Which of the following marks are precluded from federal registration on the Principal Register?

(A) immoral marks

(B) disparaging marks

(C) scandalous marks

(D) any of the above

117. Consider the ability to protect the color red for pills designed to treat blood conditions (that is, the pills themselves are red in color). This type of trademark application would likely be considered:

(A) unprotectable on grounds of functionality (i.e., aesthetically functional)

(B) suggestive, and protectable without a showing of secondary meaning

(C) arbitrary, and protectable without a showing of secondary meaning

(D) descriptive, and protectable only upon a showing of secondary meaning

118. Product packaging trade dress:

(A) is always inherently distinctive and is protectable regardless of secondary meaning or acquired distinctiveness

(B) is never inherently distinctive; it is treated as if it were descriptive, and it is therefore protectable only upon a showing of secondary meaning or acquired distinctiveness

(C) can be either treated as non-inherently distincitve (and therefore protectable only upon a showing of secondary meaning or acquired distinctiveness) or inherently distinctive (protectable regardless of secondary meaning or acquired distinctiveness), just like an ordinary word or design mark

(D) is protected only when it is famous because it is only protected under a dilution theory

119. A product configuration or product design trade dress:

(A) is always inherently distinctive and is protectable regardless of secondary meaning or acquired distinctiveness

(B) is never inherently distinctive; it is treated as if it were descriptive, and it is therefore protectable only upon a showing of secondary meaning or acquired distinctiveness

(C) can be either treated as non-inherently distinctive (and therefore protectable only upon a showing of secondary meaning or acquired distinctiveness) or inherently distinctive (protectable regardless of secondary meaning or acquired distinctiveness), just like an ordinary word or design mark

(D) is protected only when it is famous because it is only protected under a dilution theory

120. FedEx Corp. offers shipping services, but it also sells large numbers of caps, pens, and t-shirts bearing its logo (some are given away as well). Which of the following most accurately describes the situation?

  (A) FedEx can obtain trademarks for the goods it sells, as well as service marks for its shipping business.

  (B) FedEx can obtain collective marks for the goods it sells, as well as service marks for its shipping business.

  (C) FedEx must elect between trademarks and service marks.

  (D) FedEx cannot obtain trademarks for the goods because they are merely promotional.

121. The trademark term "UL Listed" (Underwriter's Labs) used to distinguish a product that meets the safety standards of Underwriter's Labs, a testing company, is a:

  (A) deceptive mark

  (B) certification mark

  (C) collective mark

  (D) service mark

122. What is a collective mark?

ANSWER:

123. What is the trademark incontestability doctrine and when does it apply?

ANSWER:

124. Under the common law, trademark rights are established through:

    (A) use in the marketplace

    (B) registration with the state trademark or secretary of state's office

    (C) successful suit for unfair competition against a competitor

    (D) all the above

125. Priority over others as to trademark ownership under the Lanham Act can be attained through:

    (A) use in commerce only

    (B) use in commerce or filing an application with a bona fide intent to use (regardless of whether actual use in commerce ever takes place)

    (C) use in commerce or filing an application with bona fide intent to use (upon following the proper procedures to establish actual use in commerce)

    (D) use in commerce or the filing of an international trademark statement

126. Company A develops a coined trademark on January 1, test markets it before a focus group on February 1, and begins to make use of the mark on its products in West Coast stores on June 1. Company B, coincidentally and in good faith, develops the same coined trademark on February 15, files a federal intent-to-use trademark application for it on February 20 and begins to make use of the mark on the same type of products in East Coast stores on June 15. B ultimately receives a notice of allowance to register the mark. Who owns the rights to the trademark? Assume all dates are in the year 2010, and that the two companies operate in the same product market.

    (A) Company A, because it was the first to come up with the trademark

    (B) Company A, because it was the first to use the trademark in commerce

    (C) Company B, because it filed the intent-to-use application before A used the mark and ultimately received the notice of allowance

    (D) Both companies, and a court will equitably divide the rights between the two parties based on their geographic market areas

127. Company A begins using a trademark in Oregon and California in 2007. Company B begins using the same trademark to sell the same product state-wide in Arkansas and Tennessee in 2009. Company A files to federally register its trademark in 2010 and receives its registration in 2011. Which of the following most accurately describes the situation?

   (A) Company A obtains all the rights to the trademark nationwide, by virtue of its federal registration.

   (B) Company A obtains all rights to the trademark nationwide, except that it must share or overlap with Company B state-wide in Arkansas and Tennessee.

   (C) Company A obtains all rights to the trademark nationwide, except that Company B has exclusive rights state-wide in Arkansas and Tennessee.

   (D) Company A obtains rights only in Oregon and California, and Company B has rights in Arkansas and Tennessee. Other states are open to the first to use the mark in the area.

128. Which of the following most accurately describes the term of protection for trademarks under the Lanham Act?

   (A) Trademarks are limited to 50-year terms.

   (B) Trademarks are perpetual once they are first used in commerce.

   (C) Trademarks can be perpetual as long as they have not been abandoned.

   (D) Trademarks can be perpetual as long as they have not been abandoned or become generic.

129. A trademark becomes inconstestable under the Lanham Act when:

   (A) it is continuously used in interstate commerce for five years and an affidavit of incontestability has been filed

   (B) it is continuously used in interstate commerce for 10 years and an affidavit of incontestability has been filed

   (C) it is registered under federal law and continuously for five years

   (D) it is registered under federal law and continuously used for five years and an affidavit of incontestability has been filed

130. What are the typical elements of the likelihood of confusion test?

ANSWER:

131. According to the various federal circuit courts, the analysis of likelihood of confusion is:

    (A) a question of fact

    (B) a question of law

    (C) a mixed question of law and fact

    (D) circuits are split with some courts adopting (A) and others adopting (C)

132. Which of the following best describes the role of proof of actual confusion in trademark cases?

    (A) Actual confusion must be proven in order for the trademark owner to recover.

    (B) Actual confusion is one of the less important factors in a likelihood of confusion analysis.

    (C) Actual confusion is not required, but if it is proven it is persuasive evidence of a likelihood of confusion.

    (D) Actual confusion is easily shown and is given the same weight as other factors.

133. How can a trademark plaintiff prove actual confusion?

ANSWER:

134. A trademark owner has not obtained federal registration for its trademark. Which of the following most accurately describes the trademark owner's situation?

    (A) The trademark owner has all the same rights as those who have registered a trademark.

(B) The trademark owner can bring suit under section 43(a) of the Lanham Act, but is limited to injunctive relief (i.e., cannot recover monetary relief).

(C) The trademark owner cannot bring suit under section 43(a) until it has registered the trademark, but can bring suit upon obtaining registration.

(D) The trademark owner can bring suit for all relief available under section 43(a), but does not have other statutory rights that a registered trademark holder would have.

135. Which of the following statements most accurately describes the approach taken by federal trademark law to questions of remedies?

(A) The presumptive form of relief is money damages, and injunctions are rarely available.

(B) The presumptive form of relief is injunctive relief, and money damages are rarely available.

(C) Injunctive relief is frequently granted, and money damages are available only upon a showing of bad faith.

(D) Injunctive relief is frequently granted, and money damages are available upon a showing of bad faith or actual harm.

136. What is corrective advertising, and what is its role in trademark law and litigation?

ANSWER:

137. In what circumstances can attorney's fees be obtained in trademark litigation?

ANSWER:

138. The strongest theory for infringement of a long-standing and widely known trademark such as "Nike" when used by someone in a totally unrelated field of enterprise, such as a taco stand, is:

(A) unfair competition under state law

(B) federal trademark infringement

(C) dilution by tarnishment

(D) dilution by blurring

139. What factors determine whether a trademark is famous for purposes of federal dilution law?

ANSWER:

140. What is the difference between a claim of trademark dilution by tarnishment and dilution by blurring?

ANSWER:

141. The validity of an incontestable registration can be challenged by an accused infringer on the ground that the mark is:

    (A) descriptive

    (B) generic

    (C) disparaging

    (D) both (B) and (C) above

142. Which of the following would be a basis for arguing that a trademark owner's mark is invalid because it has been abandoned?

    (A) naked licensing

    (B) nonuse with no intent to resume use

    (C) assignment in gross

    (D) all of the above

143. What are the elements of the statutory fair use defense to an infringement claim?

ANSWER:

144. Company A wishes to make reference to Company B's competing product in a television commercial. Which of the following would be the best advice to Company A?

    (A) Do not use Company B's name in the commercial as it will constitute trademark dilution.

    (B) Do not use Company B's name in the commercial as it will constitute trademark infringement.

    (C) Company B's name can be used in the commercial as comparative advertising, even if the advertisement is misleading, as long as no false statements of fact are made.

    (D) Company B's name can be used in the commercial as comparative advertising, but only if the advertisement is truthful and non-misleading.

145. Cochran Industries makes sunglass lenses. It purchases old sunglasses in which the lens has been broken or scratched, puts a new lens into them, and sells them in mass quantities under the original brand name on the sunglasses. Which of the following would be the best advice to Cochran Industries?

    (A) The sunglasses can be sold under the original brand name with no additional markings, as this is a lawful repair of the product.

    (B) The sunglasses can be sold under the original brand name as long as they are clearly marked as reconditioned and assuming that replacing the lens is not considered unlawful reconstruction.

    (C) The sunglasses cannot be sold under the original brand name, because there is no label or marking that could be added to avoid likely consumer confusion.

    (D) The sunglasses can be sold under the original brand name under the doctrine of reverse palming off.

146. Which of the following would *not* be actionable under the right of publicity, if it were commercially used without the individual's consent?

   (A) a sound-alike performance closely imitating an individual's voice

   (B) a look-alike performance closely imitating an individual's appearance

   (C) a signature of an individual, who is a private citizen

   (D) personal information in a book written by a famous individual

147. The right of publicity can be viewed as:

   (A) both a personal privacy right and a commercial right

   (B) a personal privacy right only

   (C) a commercial right only

   (D) both a personal privacy right and a federal constitutional right

148. Does the right of publicity survive the death of the person whose name or likeness was used for commercial purposes?

ANSWER:

149. An ordinary citizen (i.e., not a celebrity) is photographed while walking down a public street. The person's image is then used in a cellular phone advertisement without his or her consent. What is the best intellectual property claim to assert in this situation?

   (A) the right of publicity

   (B) trade secret

   (C) copyright

   (D) false endorsement

150. Which of the following legal theories could not be used to protect an idea?

   (A) quasi-contract or unjust enrichment

(B) express contract

(C) implied contract

(D) copyright law

151. Protection of intellectual property rights can be described as solving which type of economic problem?

    (A) moral hazard

    (B) public goods

    (C) monopoly

    (D) all of the above

152. The strongest form of intellectual property protection (i.e., offering the greatest exclusivity) is:

    (A) trademark

    (B) patent

    (C) copyright

    (D) trade secret (under the Uniform Trade Secret Act)

153. What form or forms of intellectual property protection are available for computer software?

    (A) patents

    (B) copyrights

    (C) trade secret

    (D) all of the above

154. Functional aspects of a product can be protected under:

    (A) utility patent law

    (B) copyright law

    (C) design patent law

    (D) both (A) and (C)

155. A short phrase or slogan can be protected under:

    (A) copyright law

    (B) trademark law

    (C) patent law

    (D) both (A) and (B)

156. Copying a competitor's unpatented product and selling a duplicate of it at a lower price is:

    (A) not actionable under intellectual property

    (B) unfair competition

    (C) trade secret infringement

    (D) a violation of the right of publicity

157. Under present U.S. copyright law, how long ago must a work have been published in order for it to be assuredly in the public domain?

ANSWER:

158. What are the four typical requirements for enforcement of an employee's covenant not to compete with his or her employer?

ANSWER:

159. The Berne Convention primarily addresses protection under which area of law?

    (A) copyright

    (B) patent

    (C) trade secret

    (D) trademark

160. The McDonald's "golden arches" can be protected under:

    (A) patent law

    (B) copyright law

    (C) trademark law

    (D) trade secret law

QUESTIONS & ANSWERS: INTELLECTUAL PROPERTY

161. What are the elements of a "hot news" claim of misappropriation under *INS v. AP* and its progeny?

ANSWER:

162. Which of the following receive *sui generis* protection under current federal law?

   (A) boat hull designs and semiconductor products (mask works)

   (B) databases and semiconductor products (mask works)

   (C) databases and boat hull designs

   (D) none of the above

163. What is cybersquatting and what remedies are available against this activity?

ANSWER:

164. Music file-sharing can be a violation of what aspect of copyright protection?

   (A) public performance rights

   (B) reproduction rights

   (C) distribution rights

   (D) either (B) or (C) or both depending on the circumstances

165. What is the best defense in a music file-sharing case?

   (A) copyright misuse

   (B) first sale

   (C) fair use

   (D) none of the above

166. What is the test for determining whether a mark is deceptive under the Lanham Act?

ANSWER:

167. How important is the presence of the defendant's commercial or profit-making purpose in analysis of fair use in copyright cases?

(A) A commercial or profit-making purpose weighs against fair use but is only one of the relevant factors.

(B) A commercial or profit-making purpose establishes a presumption against fair use.

(C) A commercial or profit-making purpose establishes a presumption of harm to the copyright owner, which weighs against fair use.

(D) A commercial or profit-making purpose is irrelevant to the fair use analysis.

168. Customer goes to a photography studio and has portraits made. The customer pays for 10 prints from the photographer. The customer scans a photograph onto a disk, uses photo editing software to remove the copyright notice placed on the photo, and makes 20 extra prints of the photo without the copyright notice. The extra prints are kept in the customer's home office drawer. In a copyright suit brought by the photographer, the court will likely find that:

(A) the customer violated the photographer's reproduction, distribution, and public display rights

(B) the customer violated the photographer's reproduction rights, as well as the Digital Millennium Copyright Act ("DMCA")

(C) the customer violated the photographer's reproduction rights but no other rights

(D) the customer did not violate the Copyright Act because the customer owns the photograph

169. Which of the following types of claims can only be brought in federal court (i.e., there is no concurrent state court jurisdiction)?

(A) patent claims

(B) federal copyright claims

(C) both (A) and (B)

(D) neither (A) nor (B)

170. A patent owner who imposes a tying arrangement on customers who purchase its patented product (requiring that they also purchase a second, unpatented product) is likely to:

(A) have waived its patent rights

(B) have committed patent misuse, if the patent owner has market power

(C) have committed patent misuse, regardless of whether the patent owner has market power

(D) be barred from recovery under the doctrine of prosecution history estoppel

171. If a computer manufacturer wished to obtain trademark protection for the color dark green (standing alone) for use on the outer surface of all of its laptop computers, this green trademark would most likely be found:

    (A) protected once secondary meaning is shown, because it is not inherently distinctive

    (B) protected even without a showing of secondary meaning, because it is inherently distinctive

    (C) unprotected on grounds of functionality

    (D) unprotected because a color standing alone does not qualify for trademark protection

172. Independent creation or development of the subject matter is a defense to the following causes of action:

    (A) patent infringement

    (B) trademark infringement

    (C) copyright infringement

    (D) none of the above

173. Paula Pilot concocted, during one of her long, trans-Pacific flights, a great idea for a movie. She created a fairly detailed, creative plot that utilized her knowledge of the inner workings of the airline industry. She did not disclose the movie plot to any of her co-pilots or friends. Pilot met Steven Screenwriter at a cocktail party in Los Angeles, and immediately after introducing herself, she pitched her idea to him while he waited for a bartender to mix his drink. As he walked away, Screenwriter said, taking Pilot's business card: "Nice meeting you. Sounds like a great movie. I'll see what I can do with it and will get you in touch with the right people." A movie whose plot was based on the intricate inner workings of the airline industry was, indeed, soon thereafter written and co-produced by Screenwriter, but he never contacted Pilot again. She might have a claim against him for:

    (A) copyright infringement

    (B) breach of implied contract

    (C) trade secret misappropriation

    (D) none of the above

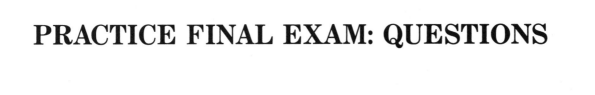

PRACTICE FINAL EXAM: QUESTIONS

PRACTICE FINAL EXAM

1. Discuss the status of the "first to file" method for determining ownership of patents under U.S. law.

ANSWER:

2. Aesthetic or non-functional aspects of a product can be protected under:

    (A) utility patent law

    (B) trade secret law

    (C) design patent law

    (D) both (B) and (C)

3. A lawfully purchased music CD can be resold based on which copyright law doctrine?

    (A) first sale

    (B) misuse

    (C) merger

    (D) fair use

4. Which of the following is *not* protected by copyright law?

    (A) an accounting system

    (B) computer software

    (C) sculptural works

    (D) architectural works

5. What is the minimum standard of originality for copyright protection, as announced in the Supreme Court's decision in *Feist Publications, Inc. v. Rural Telephone Service Co.*, 499 U.S. 340 (1991)?

ANSWER:

6.   The Visual Artists Rights Act of 1990 does not protect limited-edition or single-copies of:

   (A) films

   (B) paintings

   (C) prints

   (D) drawings

7.   What is a certification mark in federal trademark law?

ANSWER:

8.   Which of the following *cannot* be protected as a utility patent under the Patent Act:

   (A) a genetically modified animal, such as a faster growing, bigger chicken

   (B) a new mathematical algorithm

   (C) a process for producing a synthetic motor oil

   (D) an improved version of a mousetrap

9.   Which of the following is *not* an example of an infringement of a patent?

   (A) reselling a used product covered by a patent

   (B) selling a product manufactured using a patented process

   (C) importation of a product covered by a patent

   (D) offering to sell a patented product, if the product was not actually produced or sold by the defendant

10.   How long should injunctive relief in a trade secret case last?

   (A) indefinitely, as long as the requisite secrecy and competitive advantage exist.

   (B) perpetually, as a deterrent to future infringers

   (C) until the end of 20 years from the date of the plaintiff's first use of the trade secret

   (D) for as long as it takes to reverse engineer the subject matter of the trade secret

11.   What level of secrecy is required in order for information to be protected as a trade secret (in comparison with the patent law standard of novelty)?

ANSWER:

12. What is the best way to protect a general idea for a new motion picture?

   (A) There is no way to protect such an idea.

   (B) trademark law

   (C) copyright law

   (D) contracts and confidentiality agreements

13. Trade secret misappropriation can occur by:

   (A) breach of confidence

   (B) use of improper means

   (C) reverse engineering

   (D) either (A) or (B) above

14. The overall appearance and presentation of a restaurant can be protected as:

   (A) a utility patent

   (B) as trade dress

   (C) as a certification mark

   (D) as a trade secret

15. What is the merger doctrine in copyright law?
ANSWER:

16. Which of the following would *not* be patentable subject matter under current law?

   (A) a genetically modified plant

   (B) a business method, such as a method of using computer automation to solve a complex accounting problem

   (C) a newly discovered human gene sequence useful in testing for certain types of leukemia

   (D) an aesthetically pleasing design for an existing automobile battery

17. Which of the following statements most accurately describes the approach taken by federal patent law to questions of remedies?

(A) The presumptive form of relief is money damages, and injunctions are rarely available.

(B) The presumptive form of relief is injunctive relief, and money damages are rarely available.

(C) Injunctive relief is frequently granted, and money damages are available only upon a showing of bad faith or actual loss of profits.

(D) Injunctive relief is frequently granted, and money damages are generally available.

18. If Congress wished to grant a perpetual copyright, which of the following is most accurate?

(A) The Intellectual Property Clause (Art. I, sec. 8, cl. 8) would expressly permit such a law.

(B) The Intellectual Property Clause (Art. I, sec. 8, cl. 8) expressly precludes such a law, but Congress could easily avoid the problem by relying upon the Commerce Clause.

(C) The Intellectual Property Clause (Art. I, sec. 8, cl. 8) expressly precludes such a law, and the Commerce Clause probably would not give Congress the power to circumvent the express limits of the Intellectual Property Clause.

(D) Congress has already granted perpetual copyrights for foreign works.

19. Assume that someone writes a new novel under a pseudonym in the year 2010. What is the current term of copyright protection for this work not published in the author's own name?

(A) ninety-five years from the date of publication or 120 years from the date of creation, whichever comes first

(B) seventy-five years

(C) life of the author plus 50 years

(D) life of the author plus 70 years

20. Your client wishes to use a copyrighted song and sound recording in a movie. This would require what type of license?

(A) a public performance right from BMI, ASCAP, or SESAC

(B) a mechanical (reproduction) license from the Harry Fox Agency

(C) a distribution right from the copyright owners

(D) synchronization and master use licenses from the copyright owners

21. Assume that a professor at a private college copies a single news article from the local newspaper (to which he or she subscribes) and distributes these copies to her class the day following the initial publication. Does this action violate copyright law?

(A) Yes, this action probably violates the Copyright Act.

(B) No, it does not, because there is no respondeat superior or vicarious liability under the Copyright Act.

(C) No, it does not, because the fair use defense (and related educational copying guidelines) should eliminate copyright liability in these circumstances.

(D) No, the copying did not violate the Copyright Act, because no profit was made by either the professor or the college.

22. A company hires a freelance professional website designer to create and design its website. What are the relative rights of the parties?

(A) The website designer most likely owns the copyright to the work, absent an agreement to the contrary.

(B) The hiring party (the company) most likely owns the copyright to the work, absent an agreement to the contrary.

(C) Copyright law does not address ownership in this circumstance, which is governed solely by contract law.

(D) The website designer and the hiring party (the company) are most likely joint authors of the work.

23. What is the general term of protection for a plant patent under the Plant Patent Act?

(A) seventeen years from the date of patent filing

(B) twenty years from the date of patent filing

(C) seventeen years from the date of patent issuance

(D) twenty years from the date of patent issuance

24. Which of the following most accurately describes the current importance of a copyright notice for a work first written and published in 2014?

(A) Copyright notices are required and works published without the copyright notice fall into the public domain under the Copyright Act of 1976.

(B) Copyright notices are required and works published without the copyright notice fall into the public domain unless "cured" under the Copyright Act of 1976.

(C) Copyright notice is no longer required in light of the Berne Convention Implementation Act.

(D) Copyright notice is no longer required under the Sonny Bono Copyright Term Extension Act.

25. A law student prepares a written outline of a course based on the casebook readings and classroom discussion. Which of the following is most accurate?

(A) The law student has a valid copyright on the outline because it is minimally creative and involves some judgment.

(B) The law student has a valid copyright, as there is no minimum level of creativity required and courts do not assess the artistic merit of works.

(C) The law student does not have a valid copyright, because the notes are based solely on the casebook and classroom discussion (i.e., are purely derivative).

(D) The law student does not have a valid copyright, because purely factual works are not protected by copyright law.

26. The source of Congress's authority to protect semiconductors (i.e., computer chips or mask works) is:

(A) the Intellectual Property Clause (Art. I, sec. 8, cl. 8)

(B) the Commerce Clause

(C) the First Amendment

(D) the Impeachment Clause

27. Which of the following best describes the role of proof of greater sophistication of purchasers in trademark cases?

(A) Purchaser sophistication is irrelevant to a finding of likelihood of confusion analysis.

(B) A high level of purchaser sophistication weighs against a finding of likelihood of confusion analysis.

(C) A high level of purchaser sophistication weighs in favor of a finding of likelihood of confusion analysis.

(D) A high level of purchaser sophistication must be proven in order for the trademark owner to recover.

28. The market for in-line skates is highly competitive, and "Rollerblade" is the leading brand (and the mark has been registered for many years). A new competitor wishes to make use of the name "Rychlak Rollerblades" and does not wish to use the more cumbersome term "in-line skates." Which of the following most accurately describes the situation?

(A) Rychlak can use the name "Rychlak Rollerblades" under the doctrine of trademark fair use.

(B) Rychlak can use the name "Rychlak Rollerblades" if he can prove that "Rollerblades" is or has become generic.

(C) Rychlak cannot use the term "Rychlak Rollerblades" even if he can prove that it is or has become generic, because the mark is incontestable.

(D) Rychlak cannot use the term "Rychlak Rollerblades" because "in-line skates" is a reasonable alternative to "Rollerblades."

29. The trademark term "Sun" for a bank is:

(A) descriptive

(B) suggestive

(C) arbitrary

(D) fanciful

30. The trademark term "Good Housekeeping Seal of Approval," used to denote approval of third parties' goods, is a:

(A) deceptive mark

(B) certification mark

(C) collective mark

(D) service mark

31. The trademark term "Roquefort" used for any cheese originating in Roquefort, France, that meets the production standard for that community's cured sheep's milk cheeses, is best characterized as a:

(A) primarily geographically descriptive mark

(B) certification mark

(C) collective mark

(D) service mark

32. The trademark term "Dallas Steak Company" for a steak restaurant in Dallas, Texas is:

(A) generic

(B) descriptive

(C) suggestive

(D) a certification mark

33. A candy maker produces a new candy product that is made with artificial chocolate flavoring and which it would like to call "Chocolaty Chompers." This mark is likely to be:

    (A) generic

    (B) descriptive

    (C) suggestive

    (D) deceptive

34. An automobile parts manufacturer develops a revolutionary new engine. The process of manufacturing the engine and the engine itself both involve significant improvements over existing automobile technology. Which of the following would be the best legal advice in this situation?

    (A) The manufacturer should seek only patent protection for the engine itself and weigh its options on whether trade secret or patent law offers the best form of protection for its new manufacturing process.

    (B) The manufacturer should seek only patent protection for both the engine itself and for its new manufacturing process because it cannot maintain the process as a trade secret once it obtains patent protection for or begins to sell the engine.

    (C) The manufacturer should seek only trade secret protection for both the engine itself and for its new manufacturing process because trade secret law offers longer potential exclusivity than patent law.

    (D) The manufacturer should seek only patent protection for its new manufacturing process and weigh its options on whether trade secret or patent law offers the best form of protection for the engine itself.

35. What is the significance of a transformative use in analysis of copyright infringement cases?

ANSWER:

36. The best form of intellectual property protection for a certain clothing design feature or fabric design is likely to be:

    (A) a design patent

    (B) a trademark

    (C) a copyright

    (D) none of the above

37. The trademark term "Xerox" for photocopy machines and other office equipment is:

    (A) descriptive

(B) suggestive

(C) arbitrary

(D) fanciful

38. What is the minimum amount of damages recoverable under the language of the Patent Act?

(A) a reasonable royalty

(B) lost profits

(C) harm to reputation

(D) statutory damages

39. Nonobviousness can be best described as a showing that:

(A) the invention was not publicly used or sold prior to the date the patent applicant files a patent application

(B) the invention was not known by any other person prior to the date the patent applicant invents the device

(C) the invention involves an inventive step, i.e., a departure from the prior art that would not be apparent to a person having ordinary skill in the art (PHOSITA)

(D) the invention involves an inventive step, i.e., a departure from the prior art that would not be apparent to a reasonable inventor similar to the applicant

40. The changes to sections 102 and 103 of the Patent Act enacted as part of the America Invents Act (AIA) took effect on March 16, 2013, and they:

(A) affect the validity of all patents containing claims with an effective filing date on or after March 16, 2013

(B) affect the validity of all patents containing claims that are subject to a reexamination proceeding with an effective filing date on or after March 16, 2013

(C) affect the validity of all patents litigated in a patent infringement case with an effective filing date on or after March 16, 2013

(D) all of the above

41. A work is published in the U.S. without proper copyright notice in 1970. Under present law, what is the likely legal status of this work?

(A) Copyright notices were required under the 1909 Act and works published without the copyright notice fell into the public domain. Later amendments did not change this result.

(B) Copyright notices are required and works published without the copyright notice fall into the public domain unless "cured" under the Copyright Act of 1976.

(C) Copyright notice is no longer required in light of the Berne Convention.

(D) Copyright notice is no longer required under the Sonny Bono Copyright Term Extension Act.

42. In most states, misappropriation of a trade secret includes:

(A) obtaining the trade secret

(B) using the trade secret

(C) disclosing the trade secret to others

(D) all of the above

43. An ordinary citizen (who is not a famous celebrity) has her clearly visible and recognizable image used to in a billboard advertisement for a restaurant without her consent. Her best claim is:

(A) common law copyright

(B) right of publicity under applicable state law

(C) the federal right of publicity

(D) none of the above, because the right of publicity protects only celebrity names and images

44. What is the minimum amount of damages recoverable for infringement of an unpublished novel under the language of the Copyright Act?

(A) lost profits

(B) harm to reputation

(C) statutory damages

(D) none of the above

45. Which of the following remedies are included in the plaintiff patent owner's monetary award in a typical patent infringement case where the infringement was unintentional?

(A) the defendant's profits

(B) the plaintiff's attorney's fees

(C) the plaintiff's lost profits

(D) all of the above

46. Imagine that you represent the owner of a trademark that has been used from 2006 up to present in North and South Carolina but never registered anywhere. You are advising that client in which courts in the United States — state or federal — you could file a civil suit for infringement without additional filings or registrations. Without diversity between the client and the infringer, you could file in:

(A) state court

(B) federal court

(C) either state or federal court

(D) neither state nor federal court

47. Imagine that you represent the owner of a trademark that has been used from 2006 up to present in North and South Carolina and was registered in 2014 with the U.S. Patent & Trademark Office. You are advising that client in which courts in the United States — state or federal — you could file a civil suit for infringement without additional filings or registrations. Without diversity between the client and the infringer, you could file in:

(A) state court

(B) federal court

(C) either state or federal court

(D) neither state nor federal court

48. Inventor A conceives of an invention and reduces it to practice in the year 2001, but does not proceed to seek patent protection. Inventor B independently conceives of the same invention in December 2009. She reduces it to practice in March 2010. Learning of B's efforts, A applies for a patent in May 2010. B applies for a patent in June 2010. Who gets the patent rights?

(A) Inventor A is entitled to the patent, because he acted diligently in reducing the invention to practice.

(B) Inventor A is entitled to the patent, because he was the first to conceive of the invention.

(C) Inventor B is entitled to the patent, because Inventor A did not act diligently and was "spurred" by the actions of Inventor B to seek patent protection.

(D) Inventors A and B are joint inventors, and both share the patent rights.

49. What form of protection is available for an ornamental feature of a useful device?

(A) a copyright only

(B) a design patent only

(C) both a copyright and a design patent

(D) neither a copyright nor a design patent

50. A consumer buys a copyrighted print and scans it to create a digital file and then posts a full-size image of the print on her personal blog. The consumer has:

(A) violated the right of reproduction only

(B) violated the right of public display only

(C) violated both the right of reproduction and the right of public display

(D) not violated any protected right, because of the first sale doctrine and the exception for private copies

51. A teenage computer hacker develops software code to enable anyone receiving streaming video, such as a movie watched via the Internet from Netflix, to be able to download a permanent copy onto a computer despite a streaming technology that disables such copying and storage. The hacker posts the code onto the Internet, with the announcement — "I am king of the world. Anyone can download movies for free now. Have at it, people!" The hacker most likely has:

(A) directly violated reproduction and distribution rights of affected movie copyright owners

(B) violated the Digital Millennium Copyright Act ("DMCA")

(C) committed secondary copyright infringement by contributory infringement or inducement

(D) violated rights under both (B) and (C)

52. What factors are considered under the common law agency standard for defining a "work made for hire" by an employee under copyright law?

ANSWER:

53. Record Co. sells its copyrighted songs worldwide. It licenses a British company to make and sell CDs in the United Kingdom but not to import them into the United States. The British company makes CDs in a factory in England. One of its wholesale distributors sells them to a U.S. distributor, which sells them to buyers in the U.S., resulting in a copyright suit by Record Co. against the U.S. distributor. What is the result when Record Co. brings suit?

(A) Record Co. will lose because of the first sale doctrine.

(B) Record Co. will prevail because the first sale doctrine does not apply to musical recordings.

(C) Record Co. will prevail because the first sale doctrine does not apply to works made abroad and imported into the United States.

(D) Record Co. will lose because of the fair use doctrine.

54. Which of the following types of patentable subject matter has the shortest term (14 years)?

(A) utility patents

(B) plant patents

(C) design patents

(D) both (B) and (C)

55. Which of the following most accurately describes the current importance of a copyright notice for a work first published in 1982?

(A) Copyright notices are required and works published without the copyright notice fall into the public domain under the Copyright Act of 1976.

(B) Copyright notices are required and works published without the copyright notice fall into the public domain unless "cured" under the Copyright Act of 1976.

(C) Copyright notice is no longer required in light of the Berne Convention.

(D) Copyright notice is no longer required under the Sonny Bono Copyright Term Extension Act.

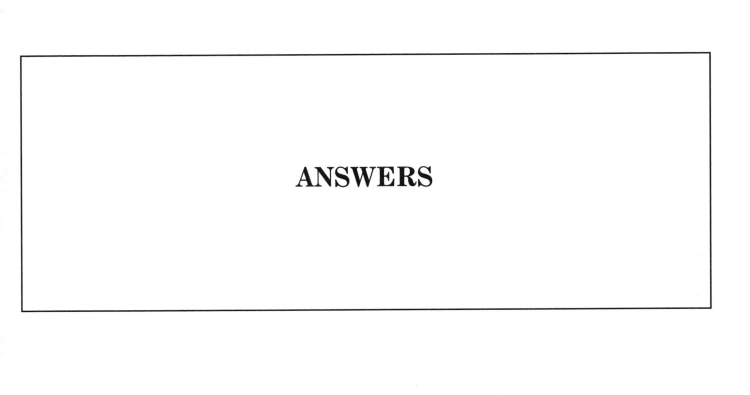

ANSWERS

TOPIC 1:   **ANSWERS**

COPYRIGHTS — SUBJECT MATTER & VALIDITY

1.   **Answer (C) is correct.** Section 102(b) of the Copyright Act expressly precludes copyright protection for ideas, stating: "In no case does copyright protection for an original work of authorship extend to any idea, procedure, process, system, method of operation, concept, principle, or discovery, regardless of the form in which it is described, explained, illustrated, or embodied in such work." 17 U.S.C. § 102(b).

Answer (A) is incorrect. Section 102(a) of the Copyright Act provides a general statement of copyrightable subject matter and then identifies specific types of subject matter that are eligible for copyright protection, including literary works. It states:

> Copyright protection subsists, in accordance with this title, in original works of authorship fixed in any tangible medium of expression, now known or later developed, from which they can be perceived, reproduced, or otherwise communicated, either directly or with the aid of a machine or device. Works of authorship include the following categories:
>
> (1) literary works;
>
> (2) musical works, including any accompanying words;
>
> (3) dramatic works, including any accompanying music;
>
> (4) pantomimes and choreographic works;
>
> (5) pictorial, graphic, and sculptural works;
>
> (6) motion pictures and other audiovisual works;
>
> (7) sound recordings; and
>
> (8) architectural works.

17 U.S.C. § 102(a).

Answer (B) is incorrect. Section 102(a) of the Copyright Act provides a general statement of copyrightable subject matter and then identifies specific types of subject matter that are eligible for copyright protection. As quoted above, musical works are included in this list.

Answer (D) is incorrect. Section 102(a) of the Copyright Act provides a general statement of copyrightable subject matter and then identifies specific types of subject matter that are eligible for copyright protection. As quoted above, architectural works are included in this list.

2.   **Answer (A) is correct.** Section 101 of the Copyright Act states that a work is "fixed in a tangible medium of expression" for copyright law purposes when "its embodiment in a copy or phonorecord, by or under the authority of the author, is sufficiently permanent or stable to permit it to be perceived, reproduced, or otherwise communicated for a period of more than transitory duration. A work consisting of sounds, images, or both, that are being

transmitted, is 'fixed' for purposes of this title if a fixation of the work is being made simultaneously with its transmission." 17 U.S.C. § 101. Materials that are handwritten on paper, recorded on film, stored on a hard drive, or even stored in a computer's random access memory (RAM — i.e., memory that would be lost if the computer lost power) all satisfy this requirement. The first three of these examples are rather straightforward, and the last was addressed in the case of *MAI Systems Corp. v. Peak Computer, Inc.*, 991 F.2d 511, 518–19 (9th Cir. 1993) (storage in RAM sufficient for purposes of fixation requirement).

Answer (B) is incorrect. This answer is "second best," as it correctly recognizes that the first three situations would clearly satisfy the "fixation" requirement of the Copyright Act. As discussed above, however, material stored on a computer's RAM has been found to be sufficiently permanent to satisfy the statutory (fixation) and constitutional (writing) standard.

Answer (C) is incorrect. A work that is merely handwritten on paper still satisfies the requirements of copyright law — indeed, many early works were handwritten, and some folks still use this form of technology even today.

Answer (D) is incorrect. As discussed above, all four of these methods of recording a work in a tangible form are sufficient to satisfy the requirements of copyright law.

3.   **Answer (C) is correct.** The directory is not copyrightable, but the guide is copyrightable. Applying the minimum standard of creativity for copyright protection as set forth in *Feist*, a directory listing (in alphabetical order) the names, addresses, and telephone numbers of all lawyers who are members of the Louisiana Bar is not copyrightable. Such a directory is very similar to the white pages telephone directory found to be uncopyrightable in *Feist*. As the Court stated in that case:

> The selection, coordination, and arrangement of Rural's white pages do not satisfy the minimum constitutional standards for copyright protection. As mentioned at the outset, Rural's white pages are entirely typical. . . . In preparing its white pages, Rural simply takes the data provided by its subscribers and lists it alphabetically by surname. The end product is a garden-variety white pages directory, devoid of even the slightest trace of creativity.

Id. at 362. The guide, however, is copyrightable under the Feist standard, as it satisfies the requirement of an original selection and arrangement of factual information — creative judgment is involved in selecting the best lawyers in a state, and no facts here indicate that Myers copied the selection or arrangement from another source. Moreover, the full explanations by Myers would very likely constitute additional copyrightable expression, even beyond the selection and judgment involved in identifying the 50 best lawyers in the state.

Answer (A) is incorrect. As discussed above, the guide is copyrightable under the *Feist* standard, but the directory is not.

Answer (B) is incorrect. As discussed above, the guide is copyrightable under the *Feist* standard, but the directory is not.

Answer (D) is incorrect. It is true that the guide will be copyrightable, as discussed above, but the directory is not copyrightable, even if it is maintained and updated. The guide satisfies the *Feist* requirement of an original selection and arrangement of factual information — creative, intellectual judgment is involved in selecting the best lawyers in a state, and no facts here indicate that Myers copied the selection or arrangement from another source. As to the directory, however, as set forth in *Feist* itself, no amount of effort, labor, "sweat of the brow," or other non-creative or non-intellectual output can confer the requisite minimum level of originality required for copyright protection. See the answer to Question 7 in this Topic regarding "sweat of the brow."

4. **Answer (A) is correct.** The law student has a valid copyright on the images captured by the camera, assuming they are minimally creative or involve some judgment. For example in *Mannion v. Coors Brewing Co.*, 377 F. Supp. 2d 444 (S.D.N.Y. 2005), the court identified three aspects of creativity in photographs: rendition, composition, and timing. Rendition involves photographic skill, composition involves setting the scene, and timing involves when to press the shutter, which may have an element of luck. The photographs in question involve at least some selection of scene, angle, and timing.

    Answer (B) is incorrect. This answer reaches the right result but for the wrong reasons. The law student does indeed have a valid copyright, but there a minimum level of creativity required, as set forth in the discussion above. Although it is true that courts do not assess the artistic merit of works, a purely mechanical reproduction does not satisfy the copyright standard for originality. *See Bridgeman Art Library, Ltd. v. Corel Corp.*, 36 F. Supp. 2d 191, 197 (S.D.N.Y. 1999) (exact photographic duplication of public domain art works not copyrightable).

    Answer (C) is incorrect. Section 102(a) of the Copyright Act expressly lists photographs among the types of copyrightable subject matter.

    Answer (D) is incorrect. It is incorrect to state that only artistic and creative works of recognized stature are protected by copyright law. As Justice Holmes wrote in *Bleistein v. Donaldson Lithographing*, 188 U.S. 239, 251–52 (1903), "[i]t would be a dangerous undertaking for persons trained only to the law to constitute themselves final judges of the worth of pictorial illustrations, outside of the narrowest and most obvious limits." There is consideration of the public recognition of a work only in the context of moral rights protections under the Visual Artists Rights Act, which is discussed in Topic 3 below.

5. **Answer (A) is correct.** This scenario presents a rare example of material that might arguably be protected under state copyright law. A famous celebrity meets a friend for a casual lunch. Unbeknownst to the celebrity, the "friend" has surreptitiously audio-taped the conversation (the celebrity did most of the talking). *See Estate of Hemingway v. Random House, Inc.*, 244 N.E.2d 250, 254 (N.Y. 1968) (state law claim involving similar facts). The key to the lack of federal protection here is understanding who the "author" is — the celebrity, for the celebrity's comments — and how that affects the definition of "fixed" and the extent of federal protection under section 102(a). "A work is "fixed in a tangible medium of expression when its embodiment in a copy or phonorecord, *by or under the authority of the author*, is sufficiently permanent or stable to permit it to be perceived, reproduced, or otherwise communicated for a period of more than transitory duration." 17 U.S.C. § 101 (emphasis added). Copyright preemption under section 301 of the Copyright Act does not preclude the state copyright law claim, as that claim does not involve "fixed" material:

    > On and after January 1, 1978, all legal or equitable rights that are equivalent to any of the exclusive rights within the general scope of copyright as specified by section 106 in works of authorship that are fixed in a tangible medium of expression and come within the subject matter of copyright as specified by sections 102 and 103, whether

created before or after that date and whether published or unpublished, are governed exclusively by this title. Thereafter, no person is entitled to any such right or equivalent right in any such work under the common law or statutes of any State.

17 U.S.C. § 301(a) (emphasis added). The legislative history of the 1976 Act recognizes the possibility of a state law copyright in the case of unfixed works: "section 301(b) explicitly preserves common law copyright protection for one important class of works: works that have not been 'fixed in any tangible medium of expression.' . . . [Unfixed works] would continue to be subject to protection under State statute or common law until fixed in tangible form." H.R. Rep. No. 94 1476, at 131 (1976), *reprinted in* 1976 U.S.C.C.A.N. 5659, 5747.

Answer (B) is incorrect. Section 101 of the Copyright Act specifically requires that a work be fixed in tangible form by authority of the author in order for federal copyright protection to attach. *See above.*

Answer (C) is incorrect. It is true that state law might offer protection. As noted above, however, section 101 of the Copyright Act specifically states that a work be fixed in tangible form by authority of the author in order for copyright protection to attach.

Answer (D) is incorrect. As discussed above, state copyright law might offer protection in this situation. Copyright preemption under section 301 of the Copyright Act does not preclude the state copyright law claim, as it does not involve copyrightable subject matter under federal law (material fixed in a tangible form of expression).

6.   **Answer (C) is correct.** The 1790 Copyright protected only three types of works, stating: "Be it enacted . . . That from and after the passing of this act, the author and authors of any map, chart, book or books . . . shall have the sole right and liberty of printing, reprinting, publishing and vending such map, chart, book or books, for the term of fourteen years from the recording the title thereof in the clerk's office, as is herein after directed. . . ." Copyright Act of 1790, Section 1, 1 Statutes at Large 124.

      Answer (A) is incorrect. Books are expressly protected under the 1790 Copyright Act.

      Answer (B) is incorrect. Charts are expressly protected under the 1790 Copyright Act.

      Answer (D) is incorrect. Maps are expressly protected under the 1790 Copyright Act.

7.   The "sweat of the brow" theory for copyright protection suggests that copyright is a reward for the hard work or industrious collection involved in compiling facts. The Supreme Court has unanimously rejected this doctrine: " 'The sweat of the brow' doctrine had numerous flaws, the most glaring being that it extended copyright protection in a compilation beyond selection and arrangement — the compiler's original contributions — to the facts themselves. Under the doctrine, the only defense to infringement was independent creation. A subsequent compiler was 'not entitled to take one word of information previously published,' but rather had to 'independently wor[k] out the matter for himself, so as to arrive at the same result from the same common sources of information.' . . . 'Sweat of the brow' courts thereby eschewed the most fundamental axiom of copyright law — that no one may copyright facts or ideas." *Feist Publications, Inc. v. Rural Telephone Service Co.*, 499 U.S. 340, 345 (1991).

8.   **Answer (C) is correct.** Copyright registration for United States authors is required as a

condition precedent to filing suit. Section 411 of the Copyright Act states:

> Except for an action brought for a violation of the rights of the author under section 106A(a), and subject to the provisions of subsection (b), no action for infringement of the copyright in any United States work shall be instituted until preregistration or registration of the copyright claim has been made in accordance with this title. In any case, however, where the deposit, application, and fee required for registration have been delivered to the Copyright Office in proper form and registration has been refused, the applicant is entitled to institute an action for infringement if notice thereof, with a copy of the complaint, is served on the Register of Copyrights. The Register may, at his or her option, become a party to the action with respect to the issue of registrability of the copyright claim by entering an appearance within sixty days after such service, but the Register's failure to become a party shall not deprive the court of jurisdiction to determine that issue.

17 U.S.C. § 411(a). It should be noted that registration is a condition precedent only for a "United States work" — i.e., by its express terms, the requirement does not apply to foreign works. Copyright protection attaches to a work when it is fixed in a tangible medium of expression, and a copyright owner can recover compensatory and injunctive relief for infringements occurring at any time thereafter. However, a copyright plaintiff cannot recover statutory damages and attorney's fees when the infringement precedes copyright registration (except when infringement and registration take place within three months after publication). *See* 17 U.S.C. § 412.

Answer (A) is incorrect. Registration is not required in order to recover compensatory damages for copyright infringement. Compensatory damages for infringement are recoverable whether they occur before or after registration. The availability of statutory damages can be affected by the timing of registration, as noted above.

Answer (B) is incorrect. Registration is not required in order to obtain injunctive relief, even if the infringement began before registration.

Answer (D) is incorrect. As noted above, copyright registration for United States authors is required as a condition precedent to filing suit. Moreover, registration can have an impact on the ability to recover attorney's fees and statutory damages for all works, whether domestic or foreign.

9.   **Answer (B) is correct.** The current importance of a copyright notice for a work first written and *published in 1980* can best be stated as follows: copyright notices are required and works published without the copyright notice fall into the public domain unless "cured" under the Copyright Act of 1976. The Copyright Act of 1976 provisions in effect in 1980 essentially still apply to this work because it was published in that year. The 1976 Act ameliorated the harsh effect of the copyright notice requirement under the 1909 Copyright Act, under which a work published without notice fell into the public domain. The 1976 Act continued to require copyright notice, but it allowed for a cure of, or excuse for the omission of, the notice in some circumstances. The cure provision continues to be relevant even though current law no longer requires copyright notice. Section 405(a) of the Copyright Act, which would govern the work in question, states:

> (a) Effect of Omission on Copyright. — With respect to copies and phonorecords publicly distributed by authority of the copyright owner before the effective date of the Berne Convention Implementation Act of 1988, the omission of the copyright

notice described in sections 401 through 403 from copies or phonorecords publicly distributed by authority of the copyright owner does not invalidate the copyright in a work if—

(1) the notice has been omitted from no more than a relatively small number of copies or phonorecords distributed to the public; or

(2) registration for the work has been made before or is made within five years after the publication without notice, and a reasonable effort is made to add notice to all copies or phonorecords that are distributed to the public in the United States after the omission has been discovered; or

(3) the notice has been omitted in violation of an express requirement in writing that, as a condition of the copyright owner's authorization of the public distribution of copies or phonorecords, they bear the prescribed notice.

17 U.S.C. § 405(a). *See generally Hasbro Bradley, Inc. v. Sparkle Toys, Inc.*, 780 F.2d 189 (2d Cir. 1985) (applying 1976 Act notice requirement and cure provisions).

Answer (A) is incorrect. As discussed above, a strict notice requirement applied prior to the effective date of the Copyright Act of 1976, but was modified by that statute.

Answer (C) is incorrect. This rule only applies to works published after March 1, 1989, when the Berne Convention Implementation Act of 1988 ("BCIA") took effect. If the 1980 work were *re*-published after March 1, 1989, the new copies of the work would not need copyright notices, but the copyright status of the work would still be affected by any uncured omissions in the 1980 publication.

The BCIA was enacted to bring the United States into compliance with the Berne Convention, thereby eliminating the notice requirement for works published after its effective date. Article 5(2) of the Berne Convention states: "The enjoyment and the exercise of these rights shall not be subject to any formality; such enjoyment and such exercise shall be independent of the existence of protection in the country of origin of the work. Consequently, apart from the provisions of this Convention, the extent of protection, as well as the means of redress afforded to the author to protect his rights, shall be governed exclusively by the laws of the country where protection is claimed."

Answer (D) is incorrect. As noted above, the BCIA eliminated the notice requirement for works published after March 1, 1989. The Sonny Bono Copyright Term Extension Act made a number of modifications to copyright law, but it did not address the notice requirement.

10.   The copyright notice requirement was mandatory under the 1909 Copyright Act. Works published without the copyright notice fell into the public domain and thus could be freely used without permissions or payment. Later amendments have not retroactively changed this result, meaning that a work published without notice before the effective date of the 1976 Copyright Act (the effective date was January 1, 1978) is still deemed to be in the public domain.

11.   The copyright notice is no longer mandatory under present law. The BCIA eliminated the mandatory notice requirement and applies to works published after March 1, 1989, the BCIA's effective date. Section 401(a) of the Copyright Act states:

> Whenever a work protected under this title is published in the United States or elsewhere by authority of the copyright owner, a notice of copyright as provided by this section *may be placed* on publicly distributed copies from which the work can be visually perceived, either directly or with the aid of a machine or device.

17 U.S.C. § 401(a) (emphasis added). Copyright notice still serves important informational purposes, including identification of the copyright owner and practical notice of the claim of copyright. Thus, although the notice is entirely optional, it is a simple way to assert ownership of a copyrighted work. It can also eliminate mitigation of damages based on a defense of innocent infringement, as provided in section 401(d):

> If a notice of copyright in the form and position specified by this section appears on the published copy or copies to which a defendant in a copyright infringement suit had access, then no weight shall be given to such a defendant's interposition of a defense based on innocent infringement in mitigation of actual or statutory damages, except as provided in the last sentence of section 504(C)(2).

17 U.S.C. § 401(d).

12. The so-called *poor man's copyright* is a layperson's term for the practice of placing a copy of a work in a sealed envelope and then mailing it to himself or herself. This action has no direct legal significance under the Copyright Act, but is based on the notion that the mailed copy can serve as a record of the work's authorship or provenance. Although the mailed copy might be introduced into evidence in a dispute over authorship, the poor man's copyright has no formal recognition in copyright law. An author's postage money would be better spent on a proper copyright registration with the Copyright Office.

13. **Answer (C) is correct.** The Visual Artists Rights Act of 1990 ("VARA") does not protect limited-edition or single copies of architectural plans. VARA provides protections for a "work of visual art," a term of art defined in the Copyright Act as follows:

> (1) a painting, drawing, print, or sculpture, existing in a single copy, in a limited edition of 200 copies or fewer that are signed and consecutively numbered by the author, or, in the case of a sculpture, in multiple cast, carved, or fabricated sculptures of 200 or fewer that are consecutively numbered by the author and bear the signature or other identifying mark of the author; or

> (2) a still photographic image produced for exhibition purposes only, existing in a single copy that is signed by the author, or in a limited edition of 200 copies or fewer that are signed and consecutively numbered by the author.

17 U.S.C. § 101. Thus, sculptures, prints, and photographs are eligible for protection under VARA, but architectural plans are not.

Answer (A) is incorrect. As noted above, VARA expressly protects sculptures as works of visual art as long as they are signed and numbered limited-editions or single copies.

Answer (B) is incorrect. As noted above, VARA expressly protects prints as works of visual art as long as they are signed and numbered limited-editions or single copies.

Answer (D) is incorrect. As noted above, VARA expressly protects photographs as works of visual art as long as they are signed and numbered limited-editions or single copies.

14. **Answer (B) is correct.** An original design for a trash can is protectable if the original,

aesthetic features are either physically or conceptually separable from the utilitarian aspects of the trash can. The trash can be viewed as a "useful article" under the Copyright Act. *See* 17 U.S.C. § 101 ("A 'useful article' is an article having an intrinsic utilitarian function that is not merely to portray the appearance of the article or to convey information."). A useful article can gain copyright protection as a "pictorial, graphic, or sculptural work" if, "and only to the extent that, [the design of the useful article] incorporates pictorial, graphic, or sculptural features that can be identified separately from, and are capable of existing independently of, the utilitarian aspects of the article." 17 U.S.C. § 101 (definition of "pictorial, graphic, and sculptural works"). Case law has interpreted the "identified separately from" and "capable of existing independently of" requirements to mean that the original, creative aspects of the work must be either conceptually or physically separable (or both) from the underlying function of the article. *See, e.g., Brandir Int'l., Inc. v. Cascade Pacific Lumber Co.*, 834 F.2d 1142 (2d Cir. 1987) (affirming copyright protection via either physical or conceptual separability, and stating that: "[I]f design elements reflect a merger of aesthetic and functional considerations, the artistic aspects of a work cannot be said to be conceptually separable from the utilitarian elements. Conversely, where design elements can be identified as reflecting the designer's artistic judgment exercised independently of functional influences, conceptual separability exists."); *Kieselstein-Cord v. Accessories by Pearl, Inc.*, 632 F.2d 989, 993 (2d Cir. 1980).

Answer (A) is incorrect. It is true that the design would be protectable if the original, aesthetic features were physically separable from the utilitarian aspects of the trash can, but this is not the best answer because conceptual separability can also lead to protection, as explained above.

Answer (C) is incorrect. Although the original, aesthetic features must show a modicum of creativity in order to meet the minimum standard for copyright protection as a work of authorship, *see Feist Publications, Inc. v. Rural Telephone Service Co.*, 499 U.S. 340 (1991), the relative artistic or aesthetic merits of those features are not assessed in determining whether a work will be protected. *See Bleistein v. Donaldson Lithographing*, 188 U.S. 239, 251–52 (1903).

Answer (D) is incorrect. Copyright law does not protect functional *features* of an article, *see, e.g.*, 17 U.S.C. § 102(b) (excluding ideas, procedures, processes, concepts, etc. from copyright protection of a work "regardless of the form in which" they are "embodied in such work"), but the Copyright Act does expressly provide for protection of the non-utilitarian, non-functional features of a useful article if the original pictorial, graphic, or sculptural features of that article are separable from the utilitarian or functional aspects of the article, as explained above.

15.   The copyright doctrine of "scenes a faire" recognizes that certain inevitable background scenes may be necessary in order to depict the setting of a particular type of work at issue. Two movies about the Civil War, for example, might both include characters depicting Presidents Lincoln and Davis, Union and Confederate flags and regalia, Southern plantations, and generals such as Grant and Lee. These inevitable similarities would not be a basis for a claim of copyright infringement. *See Hoehling v. Universal Studios*, 618 F.2d 972 (2d Cir. 1980) (noting that movie depicting pre-World War II Germany would include beer hall scenes, Nazi uniforms and greetings, and other stock background items).

16.   The idea/expression distinction as it relates to copyright law provides that ideas are not

copyrightable but the expression of those ideas is protected. In other words, an idea or concept cannot be protected under the Copyright Act, but the particular manner of expressing it can be — the word choices, phrasing, and other particular ways in which an author might express a point. The idea/expression distinction is expressly stated in the Copyright Act: "In no case does copyright protection for an original work of authorship extend to any idea, procedure, process, system, method of operation, concept, principle, or discovery, regardless of the form in which it is described, explained, illustrated, or embodied in such work." 17 U.S.C. § 102. *See generally Hoehling v. Universal Studios*, 618 F.2d 972 (2d Cir. 1980) (theory of how Hindenberg disaster occurred constitutes an uncopyrightable idea).

17. **Answer (B) is correct.** The United States government can own rights to works assigned to it by non-governmental authors. Section 105 of the Copyright Act expressly precludes copyright protection for works of United States government employees acting in the scope of their duties, but allows the government to receive copyrights from others: "Copyright protection under this title is not available for any work of the United States Government, but the United States Government is not precluded from receiving and holding copyrights transferred to it by assignment, bequest, or otherwise." 17 U.S.C. § 105. A "work of the United States Government" is defined as "a work prepared by an officer or employee of the United States Government as part of that person's official duties." 17 U.S.C. § 101.

Answer (A) is incorrect. As discussed above, these works are in the public domain.

Answer (C) is incorrect. Factual databases are generally not copyrightable subject matter, absent creativity in their selection or arrangement.

Answer (D) is incorrect. As discussed above, only (B) is correct.

18. **Answer (C) is correct.** A student is hired to do research for a professor and provides 10 pages of material, which the professor copies largely verbatim into a 30-page article. The professor is most likely the sole author of the work under the Copyright Act, given that there was no intent to form a joint work. Section 101 of the Copyright Act defines a joint work as "a work prepared by two or more authors with the intention that their contributions be merged into inseparable or interdependent parts of a unitary whole." 17 U.S.C. § 101. As discussed in *Childress v. Taylor*, 945 F.2d 500 (2d Cir. 1991), two elements must be proven to form a joint work — (1) each author must make independently copyrightable contributions to the work and (2) there must be mutual intention that the contributions be combined into a unitary whole as a joint work. Although the student assistant did contribute copyrightable material, it is unlikely that there was a mutual intention to form a joint work. *See, e.g., Thomson v. Larson*, 147 F.3d 195 (2d Cir. 1998); *Clogston v. American Academy of Orthopaedic Surgeons*, 930 F. Supp. 1156 (W.D. Tex. 1996).

Answer (A) is incorrect. As discussed above, even though the student assistant did contribute copyrightable material, it is unlikely that there was a mutual intention to form a joint work.

Answer (B) is incorrect. It is likely that the professor or institution either paid the assistant or gave academic credit for the work, and the work performed is unlikely to have been taken without express or implied authorization.

Answer (D) is incorrect. There is no specific quantitative requirement for joint authorship, as long as the requirements discussed above are met.

19. If two coauthors specifically wish to have joint authorship of the copyright in their work, courts typically require that they meet the two-part test enunciated in *Childress v. Taylor*,

945 F.2d 500 (2d Cir. 1991) — (1) each author must make independently copyrightable contributions to the work and (2) there must be mutual intention that the contributions be combined into a unitary whole as a joint work. Thus, for example, there are many famous songwriting teams — such as John Lennon/Paul McCartney, Elton John/Bernie Taupin, Mick Jagger/Keith Richards, Alan Jay Lerner/Frederick Lowe, and George and Ira Gershwin. When these songwriters create joint works, they both contribute copyrightable material (whether one writes music or song lyrics or both), and they both intend to combine their efforts into a song.

20. If (for whatever reason) one person is sole author of a work, but desires to allow a second person to have an equal ownership interest in that work, this result can be accomplished by an assignment of a one-half interest in the copyright to the second person. The assignment should be in writing and signed by the author. Like many default rules in copyright law, the initial ownership of a work by one person can be altered by contract. For purposes such as the term of copyright, however, the copyright continues to be measured by the life of the original author, regardless of whether that author has assigned or licensed all or part of the copyright to others.

21. **Answer (D) is correct.** A famous author writes a new novel in the year 2010. The novel is written in his or her own name (i.e., not anonymously or under a pseudonym) and is not a work made for hire. The current term of copyright protection for this work is the life of the author plus 70 years. Section 302(a) of the Copyright Act states: "Copyright in a work created on or after January 1, 1978, subsists from its creation and, except as provided by the following subsections, endures for a term consisting of the life of the author and 70 years after the author's death." 17 U.S.C. § 302(a).

Answer (A) is incorrect. This is the term for a work made for hire or a work not in an author's actual name.

Answer (B) is incorrect. This is not a copyright term under present law.

Answer (C) is incorrect. This was the original term of protection under the Copyright Act of 1976, but the Sonny Bono Copyright Term Extension Act of 1988 added 20 years to the term of all existing copyrights. The Supreme Court upheld the constitutionality of this term extension in *Eldred v. Ashcroft*, 537 U.S. 186 (2003).

22. **Answer (D) is correct.** The copyright duration for a joint work is the life of the last surviving author plus 70 years. *See* 17 U.S.C. § 302(b) ("In the case of a joint work prepared by two or more authors who did not work for hire, the copyright endures for a term consisting of the life of the last surviving author and 70 years after such last surviving author's death.").

Answer (A) is incorrect. This is the term for a work made for hire or a work not in an author's actual name.

Answer (B) is incorrect. This is not a copyright term under present law.

Answer (C) is incorrect. This was the original term of protection under the Copyright Act of 1976, but the Sonny Bono Copyright Term Extension Act of 1988 added 20 years to the term of all existing copyrights.

23. **Answer (C) is correct.** A movie is produced in the year 2003. The movie is a "work made for

hire," which is true of nearly all movies released commercially. The current term of copyright protection for this work is 95 years from date of publication, or 120 years from date of creation, whichever term is shorter. *See* 17 U.S.C. § 302(c) ("In the case of an anonymous work, a pseudonymous work, or a work made for hire, the copyright endures for a term of 95 years from the year of its first publication, or a term of 120 years from the year of its creation, whichever expires first.").

Answer (A) is incorrect. This was the original term of protection under the Copyright Act of 1976, but the Sonny Bono Copyright Term Extension Act of 1988 added 20 years to the term of all existing copyrights.

Answer (B) is incorrect. This is not a copyright term under present law.

Answer (D) is incorrect. This is the current term for a work by a single identified author.

24.   **Answer (B) is correct.** You can freely use the 1915 Latin version, as the copyright has necessarily expired and the poem is in the public domain, but the 1935 English version may still be protected by copyright. Copyrighted works published before 1923 are in the public domain because their copyrights have necessarily expired. A work first published in 1935, on the other hand, can still be under copyright protection. And if the poem had been written but not published before 1923, then the 1915 poem would still be protected by copyright, assuming the publication contained proper notice and a renewal was timely filed. Section 304 of the Copyright Act sets forth the rather complex and specific rules governing copyrighted works that were already published when the 1976 Act took effect on January 1, 1978. *See* 17 U.S.C. § 304. Moreover, the fact that the 1935 work is a translation does not preclude protection under copyright law, as a translation can be protectable as a derivative work. *See* 17 U.S.C. § 101 (derivative work is "a work based upon one or more preexisting works, such as a translation, musical arrangement, dramatization, fictionalization, motion picture version, sound recording, art reproduction, abridgment, condensation, or any other form in which a work may be recast, transformed, or adapted. A work consisting of editorial revisions, annotations, elaborations, or other modifications which, as a whole, represent an original work of authorship, is a 'derivative work.' ").

Answer (A) is incorrect. As noted above, the copyright in the published 1915 Latin version has necessarily expired and the poem is in the public domain, but the 1935 English version may still be protected by copyright.

Answer (C) is incorrect. As noted above, the copyright in the published 1915 Latin version has necessarily expired and the poem is in the public domain, but the 1935 English version may still be protected by copyright.

Answer (D) is incorrect. Quoting the work in its entirety is unlikely to satisfy the fair use defense, absent unusual circumstances. Thus, this blanket statement is incorrect. Certainly the expiration of the copyright is a much stronger defense than the fact-specific fair use defense.

25.   A *work made for hire* under copyright law is defined as follows:

> (1) a work prepared by an employee within the scope of his or her employment; or

> (2) a work specially ordered or commissioned for use as a contribution to a collective work, as a part of a motion picture or other audiovisual work, as a translation, as a supplementary work, as a compilation, as an instructional text, as a test, as answer

material for a test, or as an atlas, if the parties expressly agree in a written instrument signed by them that the work shall be considered a work made for hire. For the purpose of the foregoing sentence, a "supplementary work" is a work prepared for publication as a secondary adjunct to a work by another author for the purpose of introducing, concluding, illustrating, explaining, revising, commenting upon, or assisting in the use of the other work, such as forewords, afterwords, pictorial illustrations, maps, charts, tables, editorial notes, musical arrangements, answer material for tests, bibliographies, appendixes, and indexes, and an "instructional text" is a literary, pictorial, or graphic work prepared for publication and with the purpose of use in systematic instructional activities.

17 U.S.C. § 101. When a work is a "work made for hire," the hiring party is considered the author of the work under U.S. law. *See* 17 U.S.C. § 201(b). Work-for-hire status affects not only initial ownership, *see* § 201(b), but also the term of the copyright, *see* § 302(c), and termination of transfers, *see* § 203 (transfers and licenses of works made for hire are not subject to termination).

26.   **Answer (C) is correct.** The Supreme Court has adopted the common law agency test for defining a "work made for hire" by an employee under copyright law. *See Community for Creative Non-Violence v. Reid*, 490 U.S. 730 (1989). The case involved a homeless advocacy group, which hired a well-known sculptor to create a work depicting the homeless. The Court ultimately held that the sculptor owned the copyright to the work, even though the advocacy group owned physical sculpture itself. To determine whether a work is created by an independent contractor or whether it is a "work made for hire" (in which case the hiring party would own the copyright), the Court considered all four of the tests listed in this question, but adopted the common law agency standard. This test involves analysis of the following factors:

> In determining whether a hired party is an employee under the general common law of agency, we consider the hiring party's right to control the manner and means by which the product is accomplished. Among the other factors relevant to this inquiry are the skill required; the source of the instrumentalities and tools; the location of the work; the duration of the relationship between the parties; whether the hiring party has the right to assign additional projects to the hired party; the extent of the hired party's discretion over when and how long to work; the method of payment; the hired party's role in hiring and paying assistants; whether the work is part of the regular business of the hiring party; whether the hiring party is in business; the provision of employee benefits; and the tax treatment of the hired party.

Id.

Answer (A) is incorrect. As discussed above, the Court considered all four of the tests listed in this question, but adopted the common law agency standard.

Answer (B) is incorrect. As discussed above, the Court considered all four of the tests listed in this question, but adopted the common law agency standard.

Answer (D) is incorrect. As discussed above, the Court considered all four of the tests listed in this question, but adopted the common law agency standard.

27.   **Answer (D) is correct.** Both an assignment and an exclusive license are required to be in writing under the Copyright Act. Section 204 states:

(a) A transfer of copyright ownership, other than by operation of law, is not valid unless an instrument of conveyance, or a note or memorandum of the transfer, is in writing and signed by the owner of the rights conveyed or such owner's duly authorized agent.

(b) A certificate of acknowledgment is not required for the validity of a transfer, but is prima facie evidence of the execution of the transfer if—

(1) in the case of a transfer executed in the United States, the certificate is issued by a person authorized to administer oaths within the United States; or

(2) in the case of a transfer executed in a foreign country, the certificate is issued by a diplomatic or consular officer of the United States, or by a person authorized to administer oaths whose authority is proved by a certificate of such an officer.

17 U.S.C. § 204. For purposes of section 204, an exclusive license is deemed a transfer, but a nonexclusive license is not (and thus need not be meet the writing requirement). *See* 17 U.S.C. § 101 (defining a transfer of copyright ownership as "an assignment, mortgage, exclusive license, or any other conveyance, alienation, or hypothecation of a copyright or of any of the exclusive rights comprised in a copyright, whether or not it is limited in time or place of effect, but not including a nonexclusive license").

Answer (A) is incorrect. As discussed above, both an assignment and an exclusive license are required to be in writing under the Copyright Act.

Answer (B) is incorrect. As discussed above, a non-exclusive license is not required to be in writing under the Copyright Act.

Answer (C) is incorrect. As discussed above, both an assignment and an exclusive license are required to be in writing under the Copyright Act.

28. The termination of transfers provision of the Copyright Act allows the author of a work who has assigned or licensed it to others essentially to cancel that transfer during a 5-year time frame from 35 to 40 years after the transfer. This provision gives an author (or the author's heirs) a non-waivable "second chance" to negotiate a better deal. Section 203(a) sets forth the conditions in which terminations can occur:

Conditions for Termination.— In the case of any work other than a work made for hire, the exclusive or nonexclusive grant of a transfer or license of copyright or of any right under a copyright, executed by the author on or after January 1, 1978, otherwise than by will, is subject to termination under the following conditions:

(1) In the case of a grant executed by one author, termination of the grant may be effected by that author or, if the author is dead, by the person or persons who, under clause (2) of this subsection, own and are entitled to exercise a total of more than one half of that author's termination interest. In the case of a grant executed by two or more authors of a joint work, termination of the grant may be effected by a majority of the authors who executed it; if any of such authors is dead, the termination interest of any such author may be exercised as a unit by the person or persons who, under clause (2) of this subsection, own and are entitled to exercise a total of more than one half of that author's interest.

(2) [Setting forth procedure when the author is deceased] . . .

(3) Termination of the grant may be effected at any time during a period of five years beginning at the end of thirty five years from the date of execution of the grant; or, if the grant covers the right of publication of the work, the period begins at the end of thirty five years from the date of publication of the work under the grant or at the end of forty years from the date of execution of the grant, whichever term ends earlier.

(4) [Setting forth notice requirements.] . . .

(5) Termination of the grant may be effected notwithstanding any agreement to the contrary, including an agreement to make a will or to make any future grant.

17 U.S.C. § 203(a). The termination provision serves a similar to the renewal term under copyright law prior to the enactment of the 1976 Copyright Act.

29.   **Answer (A) is correct.** The duration for rights under VARA for post-VARA works is the life of the author. *See* 17 U.S.C. § 106A(d)(1) ("With respect to works of visual art created on or after the effective date set forth in section 610(a) of the Visual Artists Rights Act of 1990, the rights conferred by subsection (a) shall endure for a term consisting of the life of the author."). Thus, the VARA moral rights of post-VARA authors are not given the same term as the economic rights under section 106 — life plus 70 years. Interestingly, and likely unintentionally, the VARA moral rights for a pre-VARA work sold by an author after June 1, 1991 extend for the entire copyright term of the work.

Answer (B) is incorrect. As noted above, the duration for rights under VARA is the life of the author.

Answer (C) is incorrect. As noted above, the duration for rights under VARA is the life of the author.

Answer (D) is incorrect. As noted above, the duration for rights under VARA is the life of the author.

30. **Answer (B) is correct.** Your client wishes to record and make 1000 copies of a cover version of a copyrighted song (like Lenny Kravitz's cover version of the Guess Who's "American Woman"). The easiest way to do this is to obtain a mechanical (reproduction) license from the Harry Fox Agency. Section 115 of the Copyright Act provides for compulsory mechanical licenses for new sound recordings based on musical works that have been previously recorded and released (i.e., cover versions of songs). *See* 17 U.S.C. § 115. The Harry Fox Agency is the easiest way to obtain and pay the statutory royalty for such a license. *See* http://www.harryfox.com/index.jsp. This type of license to reproduce musical works is not available for other types of copyrightable works.

Answer (A) is incorrect. Public performance rights from BMI, ASCAP, or SESAC do not include the right to make new CDs or digital downloads.

Answer (C) is incorrect. The client is seeking to reproduce the work, not just distribute it. The mechanical license discussed above includes a right to distribute the resulting sound recordings.

Answer (D) is incorrect. The public display right is not relevant to this fact pattern.

31. **Answer (D) is correct.** Sally's Hair Salon wants to hook up a CD player to its telephone system so that people placed on hold can hear music being played on the CD player in the store. The most accurate conclusion is that Sally has violated the Copyright Act by publicly performing copyrighted works. The section 106 public performance right is implicated when a work is (1) performed in some way and (2) that performance is deemed to be public. Each of these two terms is defined in the Copyright Act. To perform a work, as defined in section 101, "means to recite, render, play, dance, or act it, either directly or by means of any device or process or, in the case of a motion picture or other audiovisual work, to show its images in any sequence or to make the sounds accompanying it audible." Playing songs on a CD player and telephone line would clearly perform the musical works in question. The second prong is more complicated:

To perform or display a work "publicly" means—

(1) to perform or display it at a place open to the public or at any place where a substantial number of persons outside of a normal circle of a family and its social acquaintances is gathered; or

(2) to transmit or otherwise communicate a performance or display of the work to a place specified by clause (1) or to the public, by means of any device or process, whether the members of the public capable of receiving the performance or display receive it in the same place or in separate places and at the same time or at different times.

17 U.S.C. § 101. Thus, a work can be publicly performed if any one of the following three

events has taken place: (1) the work is performed in a public place ("a place open to the public"); (2) the work is performed in a semipublic place ("any place where a substantial number of persons outside of a normal circle of a family and its social acquaintances is gathered"); or (3) the work is transmitted or otherwise communicated to the public or to a public place, which includes radio and television broadcasts, as well as cable and satellite transmissions. On the present facts, the songs on the CD are essentially being "transmitted" to the public via the telephone line. This constitutes a public performance of the work.

Answer (A) is incorrect. There is a "safe harbor" provision for small businesses, but it does not apply to further transmissions of the work or to the playing of a CD, both of which are taking place in this fact scenario. *See* 17 U.S.C. § 110(5).

Answer (B) is incorrect. The "first sale" defense does not apply to violations of the public performance right. *See* 17 U.S.C. § 109.

Answer (C) is incorrect. As discussed above, playing a CD over a telephone line in the manner described here is a public performance.

32. **Answer (D) is correct.** If Bob were to turn a published and copyrighted novel into a movie without authorization and then sell DVDs of the movie, he would likely violate three rights of the author of the novel — derivative works, reproduction, and distribution. The movie version would be a derivative work based on the novel. *See* 17 U.S.C. § 101 (derivative work is "a work based upon one or more preexisting works, such as a translation, musical arrangement, dramatization, fictionalization, motion picture version, sound recording, art reproduction, abridgment, condensation, or any other form in which a work may be recast, transformed, or adapted"). It would also very likely reproduce significant amounts of copyrightable expression from the novel (such as scenes, dialogue, detailed plot development, and characters). Finally, the sale of the DVD copies would constitute distribution of the copied portions of the work.

Answer (A) is incorrect. As discussed above, all three rights are violated.

Answer (B) is incorrect. As discussed above, all three rights are violated.

Answer (C) is incorrect. As discussed above, all three rights are violated.

33. **Answer (C) is correct.** If Sally sells or rents a bootleg DVD (which Sally purchased from an anonymous seller who had the bootleg DVDs in the back of his van) she likely violates the distribution right of the copyright owner of the movie/DVD. Section 106 grants to copyright owners the right "to distribute copies or phonorecords of the copyrighted work to the public by sale or other transfer of ownership, or by rental, lease, or lending." This provision would be violated on the facts above.

Answer (A) is incorrect. No derivative work has been created on these facts.

Answer (B) is incorrect. The sale or rental of the bootleg DVD violates the distribution right, but the act of copying or reproducing the DVD was committed by someone else.

Answer (D) is incorrect. As noted above, only an unauthorized distribution has taken place on these facts.

34. **Answer (D) is correct.** A public performance takes place when a copyrighted work is performed by any of the following: (a) being played on CD in a semipublic place, (b) being played live in a place open to the public, or (c) being transmitted beyond the place it is

located by electronic means. As discussed earlier, a work can be publicly performed if any one of the following three events has taken place: (1) the work is performed in a public place ("a place open to the public") — here, the live performance; (2) the work is performed in a semipublic place ("any place where a substantial number of persons outside of a normal circle of a family and its social acquaintances is gathered") — here, the playing of the CD; or (3) the work is transmitted or otherwise communicated to the public or to a public place, which includes radio and television broadcasts, as well as cable and satellite transmissions — here, the transmission by electronic means.

Answer (A) is incorrect. As noted above, all three actions are public performances.

Answer (B) is incorrect. As noted above, all three actions are public performances.

Answer (C) is incorrect. As noted above, all three actions are public performances.

35.   **Answer (B) is correct.** Under present law, the owner of a copyright in a sound recording possesses the following rights — reproduction, distribution, and public performance by digital transmission, but not general public performance or public display. It is important to recognize that there are two copyrights on any song that has been recorded — the copyright in the musical work and the copyright in the sound recording. Authors of sound recordings do not have the full range of rights, whereas songwriters receive the full bundle of sticks. Section 106 grants the following rights:

> (1) to reproduce the copyrighted work in copies or phonorecords; (2) to prepare derivative works based upon the copyrighted work; (3) to distribute copies or phonorecords of the copyrighted work to the public by sale or other transfer of ownership, or by rental, lease, or lending; (4) in the case of literary, musical, dramatic, and choreographic works, pantomimes, and motion pictures and other audiovisual works, to perform the copyrighted work publicly; (5) in the case of literary, musical, dramatic, and choreographic works, pantomimes, and pictorial, graphic, or sculptural works, including the individual images of a motion picture or other audiovisual work, to display the copyrighted work publicly; and (6) in the case of sound recordings, to perform the copyrighted work publicly by means of a digital audio transmission.

17 U.S.C. § 106 (emphasis added). As a careful review of the language indicates, sound recordings do not have general public performance rights under section 106(4) or public display rights under section 106(5), but there are limited public performance rights for digital audio transmissions — such as satellite or internet music — under section 106(6). Musical works, in contrast, have full rights under sections 106(4) and 106(5). There have been bills put forward to provide broader public performance rights in sound recordings, but none have been enacted thus far. *See generally* Gary Myers & George Howard, *The Future of Music: Reconfiguring Public Performance Rights*, 17 J. INTELL. PROP. L. 207 (2010).

Answer (A) is incorrect. As discussed above, there are limited public performance rights for digital audio transmissions — such as satellite or internet music — under section 106(6).

Answer (C) is incorrect. As discussed above, there are no full public performance rights under section 106(4).

Answer (D) is incorrect. As discussed above, there are no full public performance or display rights under section 106(4)–(5).

36.   **Answer (D) is correct.** Two types of moral rights are protected under the Visual Artists

Rights Act of 1990 ("VARA") — attribution and integrity. Section 106A(a) states as follows:

Rights of attribution and integrity.

Subject to section 107 and independent of the exclusive rights provided in section 106, the author of a work of visual art—

(1) shall have the right—

(A) to claim authorship of that work, and

(B) to prevent the use of his or her name as the author of any work of visual art which he or she did not create;

(2) shall have the right to prevent the use of his or her name as the author of the work of visual art in the event of a distortion, mutilation, or other modification of the work which would be prejudicial to his or her honor or reputation; and

(3) subject to the limitations set forth in section 113(d), shall have the right—

(A) to prevent any intentional distortion, mutilation, or other modification of that work which would be prejudicial to his or her honor or reputation, and any intentional distortion, mutilation, or modification of that work is a violation of that right, and

(B) to prevent any destruction of a work of recognized stature, and any intentional or grossly negligent destruction of that work is a violation of that right.

17 U.S.C. § 106A(a). Attribution is protected under subsections 106A(a)(1) and (a)(2) and integrity is protection under subsection 106A(a)(3).

Answer (A) is incorrect. As noted above, both attribution and integrity are protected moral rights under VARA.

Answer (B) is incorrect. As noted above, both attribution and integrity are protected moral rights under VARA.

Answer (C) is incorrect. VARA does not provide a right as to divulgation or disclosure of the work. The much broader conception of moral rights in France includes this right. *See* GARY MYERS, PRINCIPLES OF INTELLECTUAL PROPERTY LAW 115 (2d ed. 2013) ("France recognizes four type[s] of moral rights: (1) droit de divulgation, or the right of disclosure; (2) droit de repentir ou de retrait, or the right to withdraw or correct works previously disclosed to the public; (3) droit de paternite, or the right of attribution, which includes rights to publish anonymously or pseudonymously, and (4) droit au respect de l'oeuvre, the right of integrity ('the right to respect of the work')").

37.   **Answer (D) is correct.** The Digital Millennium Copyright Act (DMCA) provides copyright owners with rights regarding both anticircumvention and anti-trafficking. First, under its anticircumvention provision, the DMCA prohibits a person from circumventing a technological measure that effectively controls access to a copyrighted work. This provision states: "No person shall circumvent a technological measure that effectively controls access to a work protected under this title." 17 U.S.C. § 1201(a)(1)(A). To circumvent a technological measure means: "to descramble a scrambled work, to decrypt an encrypted work, or otherwise to avoid, bypass, remove, deactivate, or impair a technological measure, without the authority of the copyright owner." 17 U.S.C. § 1201(a)(3)(A). A technological measure "effectively controls access to a work" when the measure "in the ordinary course of its operation, requires the application of information, or a process or a treatment, with the

authority of the copyright owner, to gain access to the work." 17 U.S.C. § 1201(a)(3)(B). Second, the DMCA also prohibits trafficking in anti-circumvention devices. *See* 17 U.S.C. § 1201(a)(2) ("No person shall manufacture, import, offer to the public, provide, or otherwise traffic in any technology, product, service, device, component, or part thereof, that — (A) is primarily designed or produced for the purpose of circumventing a technological measure that effectively controls access to a work protected under this title; (B) has only limited commercially significant purpose or use other than to circumvent a technological measure that effectively controls access to a work protected under this title; or (C) is marketed by that person or another acting in concert with that person with that person's knowledge for use in circumventing a technological measure that effectively controls access to a work protected under this title."); *Universal City Studios, Inc. v. Reimerdes*, 111 F. Supp. 2d 294 (S.D.N.Y. 2000), *aff'd sub nom. Universal City Studios, Inc. v. Corley*, 273 F.3d 429 (2d Cir. 2001).

Answer (A) is incorrect. As discussed above, the DMCA provides copyright owners with rights regarding both anticircumvention and anti-trafficking.

Answer (B) is incorrect. As discussed above, the DMCA provides copyright owners with rights regarding both anticircumvention and anti-trafficking.

Answer (C) is incorrect. The DMCA does not address moral rights.

38. **Answer (D) is correct.** The Copyright Act preempts state law when all three of the following are shown regarding a state law — the state law (1) is equivalent to rights under copyright law, (2) is within the general scope of copyrightable subject matter, and (3) involves works of authorship fixed in a tangible medium of expression. Section 301 of the Copyright Act states:

> On and after January 1, 1978, all legal or equitable rights that are *equivalent to any of the exclusive rights* within the general scope of copyright as specified by section 106 in works of authorship that are *fixed in a tangible medium* of expression and come *within the subject matter of copyright* as specified by sections 102 and 103, whether created before or after that date and whether published or unpublished, are governed exclusively by this title. Thereafter, no person is entitled to any such right or equivalent right in any such work under the common law or statutes of any State.

17 U.S.C. § 301(a) (emphasis added).

Answer (A) is incorrect. As discussed above, all three points must be proven to establish preemption of state law under section 301.

Answer (B) is incorrect. As discussed above, all three points must be proven to establish preemption of state law under section 301.

Answer (C) is incorrect. As discussed above, all three points must be proven to establish preemption of state law under section 301.

39. **Answer (D) is correct.** The following statement most accurately describes the approach taken by federal copyright law to questions of remedies — injunctive relief is frequently granted, and actual monetary damages and profit are available upon a showing of bad faith or actual harm. Section 502(a) of the Copyright Act authorizes courts to provide injunctive relief, albeit not presumptively: "Any court having jurisdiction of a civil action arising under this title may, subject to the provisions of section 1498 of title 28, grant temporary and final

injunctions on such terms as it may deem reasonable to prevent or restrain infringement of a copyright." Section 504 of the Copyright Act permits the award of either compensatory or statutory damages, at the election of the plaintiff. Compensatory damages are provided as follows:

> The copyright owner is entitled to recover the actual damages suffered by him or her as a result of the infringement, and any profits of the infringer that are attributable to the infringement and are not taken into account in computing the actual damages. In establishing the infringer's profits, the copyright owner is required to present proof only of the infringer's gross revenue, and the infringer is required to prove his or her deductible expenses and the elements of profit attributable to factors other than the copyrighted work.

17 U.S.C. § 504(b). The alternative monetary remedy of statutory damages is discussed more fully below and may be recovered regardless of proof of bad faith or actual harm.

Answer (A) is incorrect. As discussed above, both injunctions and actual monetary damages and profits can be obtained on proper proof.

Answer (B) is incorrect. As discussed above, both injunctions and actual monetary damages and profits can be obtained on proper proof. There are no presumptions for or against a remedy, as implied in this statement.

Answer (C) is incorrect. As discussed above, both injunctions and actual monetary damages and profits can be obtained on proper proof.

40.   **Answer (C) is correct.** Section 504(a) of the Copyright Act states: "Except as otherwise provided by this title, an infringer of copyright is liable for *either* — (1) the copyright owner's actual damages and any additional profits of the infringer, as provided by subsection (b); *or* (2) statutory damages, as provided by subsection (c)." (Emphasis added.) In other words, a copyright plaintiff can elect to receive either statutory or actual damages, but not both.

Answer (A) is incorrect. As noted above, a copyright plaintiff can elect to receive either statutory or actual damages.

Answer (B) is incorrect. As noted above, a copyright plaintiff can elect to receive either statutory or actual damages.

Answer (D) is incorrect. As noted above, a copyright plaintiff can elect to receive either statutory or actual damages, but not both.

41.   **Answer (A) is correct.** Statutory damages can be increased or decreased based on the bad faith or good faith of the defendant. In cases of bad faith, the award can be increased to as much as $150,000; in cases of good faith, it can be reduced to as little as $200. *See* 17 U.S.C. 504(c)(2) ("In a case where the copyright owner sustains the burden of proving, and the court finds, that infringement was committed willfully, the court in its discretion may increase the award of statutory damages to a sum of not more than $150,000. In a case where the infringer sustains the burden of proving, and the court finds, that such infringer was not aware and had no reason to believe that his or her acts constituted an infringement of copyright, the court in its discretion may reduce the award of statutory damages to a sum of not less than $200.") Proper notice will eliminate mitigation for an innocent infringement defense, as noted in the answer to Question 11 in Topic 1.

Answer (B) is incorrect. As discussed above, the award can either be increased or decreased based on the defendant's conduct and state of mind.

Answer (C) is incorrect. As discussed above, the award can either be increased or decreased based on the defendant's conduct and state of mind.

Answer (D) is incorrect. As discussed above, the award can either be increased or decreased based on the defendant's conduct and state of mind.

42.   **Answer (C) is correct.** Innocent copying is not a defense to a copyright infringement action. Independent creation is a crucial defense because copyright only prevents the copying from the plaintiff's work, not independent creation of a similar work. As expressed by Judge Hand: "Borrowed the work must indeed not be, for a plagiarist is not himself pro tanto an 'author'; but if by some magic a man who had never known it were to compose anew Keats's Ode on a Grecian Urn, he would be an 'author,' and, if he copyrighted it, others might not copy that poem, though they might of course copy Keats's." *Sheldon v. Metro Goldwyn Pictures Corp.*, 81 F.2d 49, 54 (2d Cir. 1936). Common source is a second important defense, involving a showing that two works are similar because they are based on a common source — either a public domain work or a work by a third party. For example, two adaptations of a Shakespeare play are likely to have similarities resulting from their common source in the work of the Bard. Finally, consent or license involves conduct or an agreement, express or implied, by the copyright owner that would reasonably provide that the use of the copyrighted work was authorized.

       Answer (A) is incorrect. As discussed above, independent creation is a defense.

       Answer (B) is incorrect. As discussed above, common source is a defense.

       Answer (D) is incorrect. As discussed above, consent or license is a defense.

43.   **Answer (A) is correct.** Public performances of an audiovisual work in a classroom are permitted so long as the copy of the work being performed is lawfully made. *See* 17 U.S.C. § 110(1) (exempting "performance or display of a work by instructors or pupils in the course of face-to-face teaching activities of a nonprofit educational institution, in a classroom or similar place devoted to instruction, unless, in the case of a motion picture or other audiovisual work, the performance, or the display of individual images, is given by means of a copy that was not lawfully made under this title, and that the person responsible for the performance knew or had reason to believe was not lawfully made").

       Answer (B) is incorrect. Section 110(1) does not require notice to the copyright owner.

       Answer (C) is incorrect. Section 110(1) does not require that the educational institution register with the copyright office.

       Answer (D) is incorrect. As noted above, section 110(1) does not require notice to the copyright owner.

44.   **Answer (D) is correct.** The traditional "homestyle" exemption for public performances requires: (1) receipt of a radio or television broadcast (or the equivalent cable/satellite), (2) compliance with requirements regarding the number and type of receiving apparatus, and (3) no direct charge for admission. *See* 17 U.S.C. § 110(5)(a) (exempting "communication of a transmission embodying a performance or display of a work by the public reception of the transmission on a single receiving apparatus of a kind commonly used in private homes,

unless — (i) a direct charge is made to see or hear the transmission; or (ii) the transmission thus received is further transmitted to the public"). The Fairness in Music Licensing Act of 1988 expanded the scope of this exemption, particularly as to the size of exempt venues (particularly bars and restaurants up to specified square footage) and the number and types of receiving apparatus that would qualify, the basic elements of the exemption continue to remain in effect. *See* 17 U.S.C. § 110(5)(b) (exempting some larger venues with somewhat more complex sound systems).

Answer (A) is incorrect. As discussed above, all three requirements must be met.

Answer (B) is incorrect. As discussed above, all three requirements must be met.

Answer (C) is incorrect. As discussed above, all three requirements must be met.

45.   **Answer (D) is correct.** Internet service providers ("ISPs") are immune from copyright liability for user-generated material they store for their customers unless they either (1) have actual knowledge of the infringement, (2) fail to take down infringing material after sufficient notice and opportunity, or (3) have control of and receive substantial financial benefit from the infringement. In other words, failure to satisfy any of these three elements extinguishes the immunity. *See* 17 U.S.C. § 512(c). Several prior cases had addressed ISP liability, applying common law rules focusing on whether the ISP was a mere conduit for infringing material or whether it was liable because it had knowledge or control over the information. In the Digital Millennium Copyright Act, codified at 17 U.S.C. § 512, Congress established various detailed safe harbors for ISPs, including the one in § 512(c) related to material stored by the ISP at the direction of a user.

Answer (A) is incorrect. As discussed above, all three requirements must be met to establish immunity.

Answer (B) is incorrect. As discussed above, all three requirements must be met to establish immunity.

Answer (C) is incorrect. As discussed above, all three requirements must be met to establish immunity.

46.   **Answer (D) is correct.** An undergraduate student buys one copy of a commercial outline. The student sells the book (in its original form) to another student the next semester, and that student sells it the semester after that. The first student has not violated any copyright, because of the first sale doctrine. This scenario provides the classic illustration of the first sale defense, which limits the copyright owner's right of distribution in cases involving lawful copies of the work. 17 U.S.C. § 109(a) ("Notwithstanding the provisions of section 106(3), the owner of a particular copy or phonorecord lawfully made under this title, or any person authorized by such owner, is entitled, without the authority of the copyright owner, to sell or otherwise dispose of the possession of that copy or phonorecord.").

Answer (A) is incorrect. As discussed above, the first sale defense limits the copyright owner's right of distribution in cases involving lawful copies of the work.

Answer (B) is incorrect. On this set of facts, no derivative work was created.

Answer (C) is incorrect. On this set of facts, the work was not reproduced.

47.   **Answer (A) is correct.** A professor at a state college copies an entire textbook and distributes the copies to the professor's class of 30 students. The professor charges the

students only for the actual cost of making the copies. The college's best defense in a suit brought by the publisher of the textbook is the argument that sovereign immunity under the Eleventh Amendment bars suits against the state college. Although this area of the law is somewhat unsettled, there is a strong argument that the Eleventh Amendment generally bars various types of claims against state institutions in federal court, including claims under intellectual property law, unless the state has waived its sovereign immunity for the relevant type of claim. *See Chavez v. Arte Publico Press*, 204 F.3d 601 (5th Cir. 2000) (dismissing copyright and Lanham Act suit against state university on grounds of Eleventh Amendment immunity). *See generally College Savings Bank v. Florida Prepaid Postsecondary Educ. Expense Bd.*, 527 U.S. 666 (1999) (Lanham Act); *Florida Prepaid Postsecondary Educ. Expense Bd. v. College Savings Bank*, 527 U.S. 627 (1999) (Patent Act). No other defense would be particularly strong on this set of facts, given the circumstances, number of copies, and blatant copying involved.

Answer (B) is incorrect. Secondary liability can be imposed in copyright cases.

Answer (C) is incorrect. Applying the various factors in the fair use analysis, it is unlikely that fair use would be found in this case, given the wholesale copying of the book, which would displace sales that would normally be made by the copyright owner. Limited copying of excerpts might result in a different outcome.

Answer (D) is incorrect. Contrary to popular belief, a copyright violation can occur even if no profit was obtained. The professor in this case reproduced entire copies of works, displacing sales that the copyright owner was likely to make.

48. **Answer (A) is correct.** The following statement most accurately describes the fair use defense under federal copyright law — the scope of fair use is broader for factual works (i.e., fair use is more likely to be found when the taking is from a fact work), and the commercial purpose of the defendant's taking is but one factor in the analysis. This is the first in a series of questions addressing the fair use defense. Section 107 of the Copyright Act sets forth a series of factors to be balanced in analyzing every fair use case:

> Notwithstanding the provisions of sections 106 and 106A, the fair use of a copyrighted work, including such use by reproduction in copies or phonorecords or by any other means specified by that section, for purposes such as criticism, comment, news reporting, teaching (including multiple copies for classroom use), scholarship, or research, is not an infringement of copyright. In determining whether the use made of a work in any particular case is a fair use the factors to be considered shall include—
>
> (1) the purpose and character of the use, including whether such use is of a commercial nature or is for nonprofit educational purposes;
>
> (2) the nature of the copyrighted work;
>
> (3) the amount and substantiality of the portion used in relation to the copyrighted work as a whole; and
>
> (4) the effect of the use upon the potential market for or value of the copyrighted work.
>
> The fact that a work is unpublished shall not itself bar a finding of fair use if such

finding is made upon consideration of all the above factors.

17 U.S.C. § 107. Whether a work is factual or fictional is relevant to the second prong of the fair use analysis, "the nature of the copyrighted work." Because facts are not copyrightable, the scope of fair use is broader as to factual works than as to works of fiction. *See generally Feist Publications, Inc. v. Rural Telephone Service Co.*, 499 U.S. 340 (1991) (facts alone are not copyrightable). In *Campbell v. Acuff-Rose Music Inc.*, 510 U.S. 569 (1994), the Supreme Court held that a commercial purpose (such as selling CDs for profit) did not give rise to a presumption against fair use and was only one factor in the overall balancing test, which must be done on a case-by-case basis.

Answer (B) is incorrect. As noted above, the Supreme Court has rejected the presumption against commercial uses for purposes of fair use.

Answer (C) is incorrect. As noted above, the scope of fair use is broader in the case of factual works, not fictional works.

Answer (D) is incorrect. As noted above, the scope of fair use is broader in the case of factual works, not fictional works, and the Supreme Court has rejected the presumption against commercial uses for purposes of fair use.

49.   **Answer (A) is correct.** The following statement most accurately describes the fair use defense under federal copyright law — the qualitative and quantitative amount taken in relation to the plaintiff's copyrighted work is relevant, and good faith (or bad faith) is taken into account. The third prong of the fair use analysis specifically focuses on the quantitative and qualitative amount of the taking: "the amount and substantiality of the portion used in relation to the copyrighted work as a whole." In *Harper & Row v. Nation Enterprises*, 471 U.S. 539 (1985), the well-known fair use case involving President Gerald Ford's memoir, "A Time to Heal," the Supreme Court found that excerpts quoted by the Nation magazine did not involve a large number of words quantitatively (three to four hundred words were taken from the lengthy Ford memoir). The Court nonetheless held that the quoted excerpts were the *heart of the work*, the most important and significant aspects of the copyrighted book in a qualitative sense:

> In absolute terms, the words actually quoted were an insubstantial portion of "A Time to Heal." The District Court, however, found that "[T]he Nation took what was essentially the heart of the book." We believe the Court of Appeals erred in overruling the District Judge's evaluation of the qualitative nature of the taking. A Time editor described the chapters on the pardon as "the most interesting and moving parts of the entire manuscript." The portions actually quoted were selected by Mr. Navasky as among the most powerful passages in those chapters.

Id. at 565 (citing *Roy Export Co. Establishment v. Columbia Broadcasting System, Inc.*, 503 F. Supp. 1137, 1145 (S.D.N.Y. 1980) (taking of 55 seconds out of 1.5 hour film deemed qualitatively substantial). The first prong of the fair use analysis takes into consideration the good faith or bad faith of the defendant: "the purpose and character of the use." Once again, the Court's analysis in *Harper & Row v. Nation Enterprises*, is relevant — the Court took into account the defendant's bad faith in having made use of a stolen manuscript in order to write its story. The Court's overall conclusion was that the Nation failed to prove the fair use defense despite its news reporting purpose and factual and historical nature of the Ford memoir.

Answer (B) is incorrect. The third prong of the fair use test focuses on the amount in relation to the copyrighted work, not as to the defendant's alleged infringing work.

Answer (C) is incorrect. As discussed above, good faith or bad faith is relevant to the first prong of the fair use test (the character of the use).

Answer (D) is incorrect. As discussed above, the third prong of the fair use test focuses on the amount in relation to the copyrighted work, not as to the defendant's alleged infringing work. Moreover, good faith or bad faith is relevant to the first prong of the fair use test (the character of the use).

50. **Answer (C) is correct.** The following statement most accurately describes the fair use defense under federal copyright law — a legitimate parody is taken into account in analyzing the fair use factors on a case-by-case basis. In *Campbell v. Acuff-Rose Music Inc.*, 510 U.S. 569 (1994), which involved a Two Live Crew rap parody version of the copyrighted song "Oh Pretty Woman," the Court specifically addressed parodies. Analyzing whether the parody was a fair use under the Copyright Act, the Court emphasized the need to analyze each fair use situation on a case-by-case, fact-specific basis. The Court viewed the parody as a favored purpose in fair use analysis, to be weighed in the overall balancing:

> The fact that *parody can claim legitimacy for some appropriation* does not, of course, tell either parodist or judge much about where to draw the line. Like a book review quoting the copyrighted material criticized, parody may or may not be fair use, and petitioners' suggestion that any parodic use is presumptively fair has no more justification in law or fact than the equally hopeful claim that any use for news reporting should be presumed fair, see *Harper & Row*. The Act has no hint of an evidentiary preference for parodists over their victims, and no workable presumption for parody could take account of the fact that parody often shades into satire when society is lampooned through its creative artifacts, or that a work may contain both parodic and nonparodic elements. Accordingly, parody, like any other use, has to work its way through the relevant factors, and be *judged case by case, in light of the ends of the copyright law.*

Id. at 581. (emphasis added)

Answer (A) is incorrect. As discussed above, the Court rejected any assertion that parody is automatically fair use.

Answer (B) is incorrect. As discussed above, the Court rejected the presumption that parody is fair use.

Answer (D) is incorrect. As discussed above, the Court weighed parody as a favorable factor in the fair use analysis.

51. **Answer (C) is correct.** The following statement most accurately describes the fair use defense under federal copyright law — whether a work is published or unpublished is a factor in a fair use analysis, and fair use is more likely to be found if a work is published rather than unpublished. Whether a work is published is relevant to the second prong of the fair use analysis — the nature of the copyrighted work. In *Harper & Row v. Nation Enterprises*, 471 U.S. 539 (1985), the Court weighed the fact that the Ford memoir had not yet been published as a factor against finding fair use. The Court found that the Nation magazine had usurped book publisher Harper & Row's right of first publication. In other

words, the defendant interfered with the copyright owner's right to decide when and how the book is first published. After this ruling, some lower courts interpreted the *Harper & Row v. Nation Enterprises* decision as imposing a presumption against finding fair use when the copyrighted work was unpublished. In response, Congress added the last sentence to the section 107 standard: "The fact that a work is unpublished shall not itself bar a finding of fair use if such finding is made upon consideration of all the above factors." 17 U.S.C. § 107.

Answer (A) is incorrect. The Copyright Act protects works as soon as they are fixed in a tangible medium of expression. Thus, unpublished works are protected under federal copyright law.

Answer (B) is incorrect. As discussed above, whether a work is published or unpublished is a factor in a fair use analysis, although it is not determinative by itself.

Answer (D) is incorrect. As discussed above, fair use is more likely to be found if a work is published, not unpublished.

52.   **Answer (D) is correct.** The following copyrighted works are not eligible for commercial rental under the first sale doctrine — both computer programs and sound recordings of musical works. Although the first sale doctrine under section 109 of the Copyright Act generally permits the rental or other disposition of lawful copies of works, there is a specific exception in section 109(b) for the commercial rental of computer software and sound recordings in any form:

> Notwithstanding the provisions of subsection (a), unless authorized by the owners of copyright in the sound recording or the owner of copyright in a computer program (including any tape, disk, or other medium embodying such program), and in the case of a sound recording in the musical works embodied therein, neither the owner of a particular phonorecord nor any person in possession of a particular copy of a computer program (including any tape, disk, or other medium embodying such program), may, for the purposes of direct or indirect commercial advantage, dispose of, or authorize the disposal of, the possession of that phonorecord or computer program (including any tape, disk, or other medium embodying such program) by rental, lease, or lending, or by any other act or practice in the nature of rental, lease, or lending. Nothing in the preceding sentence shall apply to the rental, lease, or lending of a phonorecord for nonprofit purposes by a nonprofit library or nonprofit educational institution. The transfer of possession of a lawfully made copy of a computer program by a nonprofit educational institution to another nonprofit educational institution or to faculty, staff, and students does not constitute rental, lease, or lending for direct or indirect commercial purposes under this subsection.

17 U.S.C. § 109(b).

Answer (A) is incorrect. A DVD can be rented commercially under the general provisions of the first sale doctrine.

Answer (B) is incorrect. As discussed above, both computer software and music CDs cannot be offered for commercial rental under the first sale provision.

Answer (C) is incorrect. As discussed above, both computer software and music CDs cannot be offered for commercial rental under the first sale provision.

53.   **Answer (C) is correct.** The three fundamental requirements for a utility patent are novelty, nonobviousness, and usefulness. Section 101 of the Patent Act requires novelty and usefulness: "Whoever invents or discovers any new and *useful* process, machine, manufacture, or composition of matter, or any new and *useful* improvement thereof, may obtain a patent therefor, subject to the conditions and requirements of this title." *See* 35 U.S.C. § 101. Section 102 sets out the content of the novelty requirement, which examines whether the invention — in full — was available to the public ("the claimed invention was patented, described in a printed publication, or in public use, on sale, or otherwise available to the public") or described in a prior-filed patent application before the filing date of the application containing the claimed invention. *See* 35 U.S.C. § 102(a). Certain exceptions to the general novelty rule are set forth in section 102(b). Section 103 of the Patent Act requires nonobviousness by barring a patent:

> if the differences between the claimed invention and the prior art are such that the claimed invention as a whole would have been obvious before the effective filing date of the claimed invention to a person having ordinary skill in the art to which the claimed invention pertains. Patentability shall not be negated by the manner in which the invention was made.

35 U.S.C. § 103.

Answer (A) is incorrect. These are the requirements for a design patent — novelty, nonobviousness, and ornamentality.

Answer (B) is incorrect. These are the requirements for a plant patent — novelty, nonobviousness, and distinctness.

Answer (D) is incorrect. This list omits the crucial requirement of nonobviousness under section 103(a) of the Patent Act, substituting a requirement of "concreteness," which is not found in the language of the Patent Act.

54.   *Prior art* is a term of art in patent law. It refers to the level of existing information and innovations relevant to a particular invention. Prior art is relevant to determinations of novelty and nonobviousness, as the claimed invention must not be part of the prior art defined in section 102 (novelty) and must involve an inventive step beyond that prior art in order to establish nonobviousness under section 103. The critical date for defining the scope of the prior art changed in the AIA — from the date of invention to the effective filing date (with some exceptions to provide a grace period for filing).

55.   A *PHOSITA* is a Person Having Ordinary Skill in the Art (often abbreviated as "PHOSITA"). It is a person possessing the technical knowledge of a typical person with skills in the relevant field — for example, an understanding of basic and applied

biochemistry concepts. In determining whether an invention satisfies the nonobviousness requirement of section 103 of the Patent Act, the basic question is whether the invention would or would not be obvious to a PHOSITA.

56.   A *constructive reduction to practice* is a description of an invention that is sufficiently detailed to allow a person having ordinary skill in the art (PHOSITA) to make the invention, but the invention need not have been actually reduced to practice. It is closely related to the term enablement — a patent disclosure is said to be enabling if it is sufficiently detailed to allow a person having ordinary skill in the art to make the invention. The filing of a complete, enabling patent application provides a constructive reduction to practice.

57.   **Answer (D) is correct.** Under the pre-AIA law of novelty, lack of novelty precludes patentability of an invention when the device is known or used in the United States, or is patented or described in a printed publication anywhere in the world, prior to date the patent applicant invents the device. This standard for novelty is set forth in pre-AIA section 102(a) of the Patent Act, which states: "A person shall be entitled to a patent unless . . . the invention was known or used by others in this country, or patented or described in a printed publication in this or a foreign country, before the invention thereof by the applicant for patent. . . ." In pre-AIA section 102, Congress expressly drew a distinction between knowledge or use of an invention in the United States — which would preclude patentability — and knowledge or use abroad, which would not. On the other hand, Congress deemed information published or patented anywhere in the world to be sufficiently available to preclude a U.S. patent.

    Answer (A) is incorrect. To state that the pre-AIA novelty standard is not met "when the device is either known or used, or patented or described in a printed publication, in the United States prior to date the patent applicant invents the device" ignored the relevance of foreign publications and foreign patents, both of which also preclude a pre-AIA finding of novelty.

    Answer (B) is incorrect. This statement ignores knowledge or use in the United States, as well as foreign patents or publications, any of which would preclude a pre-AIA finding of novelty.

    Answer (C) is incorrect. If an invention is known or used elsewhere prior to date the patent applicant invents the device, but is not known or used in the United States, it is still eligible for patent protection under pre-AIA law (i.e., it can still be found to be novel).

58.   **Answer (C) is correct.** Under the post-AIA law of novelty, lack of novelty precludes patentability of an invention when the device is publicly used or sold, or is patented or described in a printed publication anywhere in the world, before the date the patent applicant files the patent application. This standard for novelty is set forth in post-AIA section 102(a) of the Patent Act, which states: "A person shall be entitled to a patent unless — (1) the claimed invention was patented, described in a printed publication, or in public use, on sale, or otherwise available to the public before the effective filing date of the claimed invention." 35 U.S.C. § 102 (a). The AIA novelty provision also implements a first-to-file rule, in part, by adding a novelty bar when the claimed invention was described in another inventor's patent application "effectively filed before the effective filing date of the claimed invention." *Id*. Section 102(b) provides the applicant with a one-year grace period by excluding from the prior art the inventor's own disclosures within the year before filing. *See*

35 U.S.C. § 102 (b). It also excludes third party disclosures within the year before filing, but only if the third party disclosure was preceded by a public disclosure by the inventor. *See id.*

Answer (A) is incorrect. To state that the post-AIA novelty standard is not met when certain events occur in the United States ignored the relevance of foreign prior art which will also preclude a post-AIA finding of novelty.

Answer (B) is incorrect. This statement ignores sales or use, which would preclude a post-AIA finding of novelty.

Answer (D) is incorrect. Although under pre-AIA law Congress expressly drew a distinction between sales or use of an invention in the United States — which would preclude patentability — and sales or use abroad, which would not, the AIA eliminates geographic distinctions in prior art.

59. **Answer (D) is correct.** Under current law, a business method, such as a method of matching bidders and sellers in an online reverse auction, is potentiall patentable under a utility patent. In *Bilski v. Kappos*, 130 S. Ct. 3218 (2010), the Supreme Court rejected a categorical exclusion of business methods from statutory subject matter as a "process," despite a four-justice concurrence that would have done exactly that. The invention at issue, which the Court characterized as "a procedure for instructing buyers and sellers how to protect against the risk of price fluctuation in a discrete section of the economy" was nevertheless ruled to be unpatentable subject matter by virtue of being an "abstract idea": "allowing petitioners to patent risk hedging would preempt use of this approach in all fields, and would effectively grant a monopoly over an abstract idea."

Answer (A) is incorrect. As noted above, the Supreme Court has rejected the "business methods" exception.

Answer (B) is incorrect. A business method would not meet the requirements of design patent law as it would involve functional material and not ornamental features.

Answer (C) is incorrect. Once again, these are the requirements for protection under design patent law. A business method would involve functional material and not ornamental features.

60. **Answer (A) is correct.** Utility patent protection is available for functional features of a product. Section 101 of the Patent Act states: "Whoever invents or discovers any new and useful process, machine, manufacture, or composition of matter, or any new and useful improvement thereof, may obtain a patent therefor, subject to the conditions and requirements of this title." This provision grants utility patent protection to three types of inventions: (1) products (i.e., a machine, manufacture, or composition of matter), (2) processes (such as a new chemical manufacturing process), and (3) improvements on existing products or processes. Historical examples of utility patents include the Wright Brothers' airplane, Alexander Graham Bell's telephone, and Thomas Edison's light bulb. Examples of more modern inventions include new pharmaceutical products such as the nasal allergy spray Nasonex, biotechnological inventions (such as Monsanto's genetically modified soybeans or Harvard's "oncomouse," a laboratory mouse for cancer research), and certain functional features of the Apple iPod music player.

Answer (B) is incorrect. Design patents do not have a utility requirement, given that functional features of a product cannot be the subject of a design patent. Instead, the plain language of the statute dictates that the design must be ornamental in nature. Section 171 of the Patent Act states: "Whoever invents any new, original, and ornamental design for an article of manufacture may obtain a patent therefor, subject to the conditions and requirements of this title." Examples of design patent subject matter include the appearance or ornamental features of athletic shoe uppers or of a beverage container.

Answer (C) is incorrect. The same features of a product cannot be protected under both a design patent and a utility patent. It is possible for the functional features of a product to be covered by a utility patent while distinctly different ornamental aspects of the same product are protected by a design patent.

Answer (D) is incorrect. As noted above, utility patent protection is available for functional features of a product.

61.   **Answer (D) is correct.** A utility patent can protect a product, process, or an improvement on an existing product or process. Section 101 of the Patent Act states: "Whoever invents or discovers any new and useful process, machine, manufacture, or composition of matter, or any new and useful improvement thereof, may obtain a patent therefor, subject to the conditions and requirements of this title." This provision grants utility patent protection to three types of inventions: (1) products (i.e., a machine, manufacture, or composition of matter), (2) processes (such as a new chemical manufacturing process), and (3) improvements on existing products or processes.

Answer (A) is incorrect. As noted above, any of the examples in this question qualify as patentable subject matter.

Answer (B) is incorrect. As noted above, any of the examples in this question qualify as patentable subject matter.

Answer (C) is incorrect. As noted above, any of the examples in this question qualify as patentable subject matter.

62.   **Answer (D) is correct.** Abstract ideas, mathematical algorithms, and printed matter are all ineligible for patent protection. Despite the broad scope of patentable subject matter law, there are some types of information that are ineligible for patent protection. As the Court noted in *Diamond v. Chakrabarty*:

> This is not to suggest that § 101 has no limits or that it embraces every discovery. The laws of nature, physical phenomena, and abstract ideas have been held not patentable. Thus, a new mineral discovered in the earth or a new plant found in the wild is not patentable subject matter. Likewise, Einstein could not patent his celebrated law that $E=mc^2$; nor could Newton have patented the law of gravity.

447 U.S. 303 (1980). In *Diamond v. Diehr*, 450 U.S. 175 (1981), the Supreme Court found mathematical algorithms to be unpatentable, such as one used to convert binary code decimal numbers to equivalent pure binary numbers.

> The sole practical application of the algorithm was in connection with the programming of a general-purpose digital computer. We defined 'algorithm' as a 'procedure for solving a given type of mathematical problem,' and we concluded that such an algorithm, or mathematical formula, is like a law of nature, which cannot be the subject of a patent. Mathematical algorithms so defined are thus not patentable subject matter to the extent that they are merely abstract ideas. To be patented, the

algorithm must be used for some type of practical application — a useful, concrete and tangible result. Unpatentable mathematical algorithms are merely abstract ideas constituting disembodied concepts or truths that are not useful in a way cognizable under patent law.

Another category of material said to be beyond the subject matter of patent law is "printed matter." The Manual of Patent Examining Procedure ("MPEP") states that "a mere arrangement of printed matter, though seemingly a 'manufacture,' is rejected as not being within the statutory classes." MPEP § 2112.01. The central issue, according to the Federal Circuit "is whether there exists any new and unobvious functional relationship between the printed matter and the substrate." *In re Lowry*, 32 F.3d 1579, 1582 (Fed. Cir. 1994). The printed matter doctrine prevents patenting of mere arrangements of printed lines, characters, or other material, but it does not preclude patents on inventions that have functional applications, that are connected to physical features of a product, or that require a machine to process the information. Thus, as long as the printed material relates to a physical object or function of some sort, it can be patented. Cases where printed material with a related physical structure was found to be patentable have involved such things as detachable travel coupons and tear-off menu coupons.

Answer (A) is incorrect. As noted above, abstract ideas, mathematical algorithms, and printed matter are all ineligible for patent protection.

Answer (B) is incorrect. As noted above, abstract ideas, mathematical algorithms, and printed matter are all ineligible for patent protection.

Answer (C) is incorrect. As noted above, abstract ideas, mathematical algorithms, and printed matter are all ineligible for patent protection.

63. **Answer (D) is correct.** A genetically modified asexually reproduced plant is eligible for protection under the Plant Patent Act or as a traditional utility patent. This result may seem counterintuitive, but the Supreme Court expressly resolved this question in *J.E.M. Ag Supply, Inc. v. Pioneer Hi-Bred International, Inc.*, 534 U.S. 124 (2001), which held that plants can qualify as patentable subject matter under section 101 of the Patent Act, if they meet the ordinary requirements of novelty, non-obviousness, and usefulness. This holding confirmed the Patent Office's practice of granting utility patents on plants that satisfy the ordinary utility patent standard. In other words, utility patent protection is only available if the plant characteristic is the product of human ingenuity. This requires that the plant characteristic be the result of genetic engineering or other similar methods of plant modification, as opposed to conventional plant breeding techniques. The concept of utility patent protection for genetically modified plants logically follows from the Supreme Court's biotechnology ruling in *Diamond v. Chakrabarty*. Just as a genetically modified bacterium can receive utility patent protection, so too might a genetically modified strain of corn or soybeans. Plant patents protect distinct plant varieties that are asexually reproduced. These plant varieties receive protection under the Plant Patent Act of 1930 ("PPA"). Sexually reproduced plants, in contrast, are eligible for protection under the Plant Variety Protection Act of 1970 ("PVPA"). The distinction between these two forms of protection hinges upon the method by which the new plant variety was developed. Asexual reproduction includes methods such as cutting, budding, and grafting. Sexual reproduction, on the other hand, involves traditional cross-breeding of plant varieties and is covered by the PVPA. The rights of plant breeders in sexually reproduced plants are protected with certificates issued under

the PVPA. The PVPA is not part of the patent system, but offers patent-like protection. To be eligible, the plant must be new, distinct, uniform, and stable (i.e., it must "breed true"). The Plant Patent Act did not cover plant breeding because it was believed that new varieties could not be reproduced true to type through seedlings. By 1970, however, true-to-type reproduction was possible and the PVPA was enacted to protect such efforts. The PVPA has two important exceptions — plants may be used by other breeders to perform research, and farmers are permitted to save and replant seeds. Utility patent protection is valuable as it provides broader protection for plants than either the PPA or the PVPA. For example, there are no independent development defenses as in the Plant Patent Act or farmer seed-saving exemptions as under the PVPA. Congress enacted specific protections for plants for two main reasons. First, it was thought at the time that plants, even when artificially bred, were products of nature for purposes of the patent law. The second obstacle was the fact that plants were thought not amenable to the "written description" requirement of the patent law. In essence, identifying a plant in a patent would not necessarily enable one skilled in the art to replicate it. When it enacted the Plant Patent Act, Congress addressed both of these concerns. First it stated that efforts of a plant breeder in aid of nature constituted a patentable invention. Second, section 162 provides that the written description requirement was satisfied by a reasonably complete description: "No plant patent shall be declared invalid for noncompliance with section 112 of this title if the description is as complete as is reasonably possible. The claim in the specification shall be in formal terms to the plant shown and described." With regard to plant patents, section 161 of the Plant Patent Act does not contain a utility requirement, instead requiring distinctness — that the plant be a distinct new variety: "Whoever invents or discovers and asexually reproduces any distinct and new variety of plant, including cultivated sports, mutants, hybrids, and newly found seedlings, other than a tuber propagated plant or a plant found in an uncultivated state, may obtain a patent therefor, subject to the conditions and requirements of this title."

Answer (A) is incorrect. As noted above, a genetically modified plant could be protected under either the Plant Patent Act or as a traditional utility patent.

Answer (B) is incorrect. As noted above, a genetically modified plant could be protected under either the Plant Patent Act or as a traditional utility patent.

Answer (C) is incorrect. As noted above, a genetically modified plant could be protected under either the Plant Patent Act or as a traditional utility patent.

64.   **Answer (B) is correct.** In early 2009, Bob Builder, an inventor working out of his garage, develops an innovative new machine that inexpensively makes pure fresh water out of salt water. In April 2009, Builder begins selling his machine on the Internet. In July 2010, Builder files a patent application on his machine. Builder will be precluded from patenting his machine because of the prior sale in April 2009, which triggers the on-sale bar in pre-AIA Section 102(b). That section sets forth ways in which there can be a loss of rights to an otherwise valid patent, including an on-sale bar and a public use bar:

> A person shall be entitled to a patent unless — the invention was patented or described in a printed publication in this or a foreign country or in public use or on sale in this country, more than one year prior to the date of the application for patent in the United States.

See pre-AIA § 102(b). This rule essentially placed a one-year time limit for filing a patent application once there had been a public use of the invention or the invention had been sold or offered for sale in the United States. The inventor in this case failed to file the patent application within the one-year period. Although this rule may seem harsh, it encouraged the prompt filing of patents and was more lenient than the patent law rule in many foreign countries, which do not provide the one-year grace period.

Answer (A) is incorrect. As noted above, Builder would be precluded from patenting his machine because of the prior sale.

Answer (C) is incorrect. As noted above, Builder would be precluded from patenting his machine because of the prior sale. A statute of limitations places a time limit on when a plaintiff can bring suit once a cause of action has accrued. *Cf.* 35 U.S.C. § 286 (not providing a statute of limitations but limiting damage recovery in patent suits to infringement occurring within six years of filing of suit).

Answer (D) is incorrect. The 15-month delay in filing the patent application does trigger the on-sale bar, but it is highly unlikely to have been long enough to constitute suppression of the invention, even if there were a competing inventor vying for the rights in an interference (*see* pre-AIA § 102(g)).

65.   **Answer (B) is correct.** In early 2013, Bob Builder, an inventor working out of his garage, develops an innovative new machine that inexpensively makes pure fresh water out of salt water. In April 2013, Builder begins selling his machine on the Internet. In July 2014, Builder files a patent application on his machine. Builder will be precluded from patenting his machine because of the prior sale in April 2013. Post-AIA rules of novelty and priority still allow an inventor a one-year grace period, but only as to his or her own disclosures, by excluding from the prior art the inventor's own disclosures occurring within the year before filing. This rule is thought to encourage the prompt filing of patents and, although it is more restrictive than the pre-AIA section 102(b) grace period, which covered third-party disclosures as well, the U.S. rule remains more lenient than the patent law rule in many foreign countries, which do not provide a one-year grace period.

Answer (A) is incorrect. As noted above, Builder will be precluded from patenting his machine because of the prior sale.

Answer (C) is incorrect. As noted above, Builder will be precluded from patenting his machine because of the prior sale. A statute of limitations places a time limit on when a plaintiff can bring suit once a cause of action has accrued. *Cf.* 35 U.S.C. § 286 (not providing a statute of limitations but limiting damage recovery in patent suits to infringement occurring within six years of filing of suit).

Answer (D) is incorrect. Suppression of an invention is not relevant in post-AIA novelty or priority determinations.

66.   Experimental uses do not destroy the novelty required for patent protection. The experimental use exception, which excludes experimental uses from prior art "in public use" under section 102, recognizes the common-sense idea that an inventor often seeks to test the invention to assure that it works properly. This type of experimentation is entirely proper and should not lead to forfeiture of rights to the invention. The scope of the experimental use exception requires a careful analysis. In *Baxter International, Inc. v. Cobe Laboratories, Inc.*, 88 F.3d 1054, 1060 (Fed. Cir. 1996), the Federal Circuit identified a series of factors for assessing whether a use is experimental:

An analysis of experimental use, which is also a question of law, requires consideration of the totality of the circumstances and the policies underlying the public use bar. Evidentiary factors in determining if a use is experimental include the length of the test period, whether the inventor received payment for the testing, any agreement by the user to maintain the use confidential, any records of testing, whether persons other than the inventor performed the testing, the number of tests, and the length of the test period in relation to tests of similar devices.

On the facts of the case, the court found that the use in question was not experimental. Tests were conducted on the inventor's device (a blood-processing centrifuge) by a third party to determine if the centrifuge would have additional uses, and the court concluded that these tests would not fall within the experimental use exception. The court focused on the fact that the additional applications for the centrifuge were not recited in the patent application and that the inventor did not have any direction or control over the third-party testing:

> The experimental use doctrine operates in the inventor's favor to allow the inventor to refine his invention or to assess its value relative to the time and expense of prosecuting a patent application. If it is not the inventor or someone under his control or 'surveillance' who does these things, there appears to us no reason why he should be entitled to rely upon them to avoid the statute.

Id. The court therefore held that the public testing by the third party for its own purposes was an invalidating public use, not an experimental use. All of the case law regarding the experimental use exception is under pre-AIA section 102, but there is no reason to think that "in public use," a type of prior art reference carried forward in the AIA with the same language, would differ under post-AIA section 102.

67.   The non-obviousness standard involves a qualitative judgment regarding the differences between the prior art and the claimed invention. The invention must involve a significant creative or inventive step beyond what was already known. Section 103 of the Patent Act sets forth the general non-obviousness requirement:

> A patent for a claimed invention may not be obtained, notwithstanding that the claimed invention is not identically disclosed as set forth in section 102, if the differences between the claimed invention and the prior art are such that the claimed invention as a whole would have been obvious before the effective filing date of the claimed invention to a person having ordinary skill in the art to which the claimed invention pertains. Patentability shall not be negated by the manner in which the invention was made.

The landmark case addressing non-obviousness is *Graham v. John Deere Co.*, 383 U.S. 1, 17–18 (1966). The Court set forth the following framework for assessing whether section 103 is satisfied:

> Under § 103, the scope and content of the prior art are to be determined; differences between the prior art and the claims at issue are to be ascertained; and the level of ordinary skill in the pertinent art resolved. Against this background the obviousness or nonobviousness of the subject matter is determined.

68.   "Secondary considerations" are relevant to the determination of nonobviousness, a fundamental requirement for patent validity. In *Graham v. John Deere Co.*, 383 U.S. 1, 17–18 (1966), the Supreme Court set forth the standard for nonobviousness, as discussed above.

The Court then stated: "Such secondary considerations as commercial success, long felt but unsolved needs, failure of others, etc., might be utilized to give light to the circumstances surrounding the origin of the subject matter sought to be patented." In other words, these considerations can help shed light on whether or not the invention satisfies the nonobviousness standard. In 2007, the Supreme Court again addressed the subject of nonobviousness in *KSR International Co. v. Teleflex Inc.*, 550 U.S. 398, 415 (2007):

> Throughout this Court's engagement with the question of obviousness, our cases have set forth an expansive and flexible approach. . . . To be sure, *Graham* recognized the need for 'uniformity and definiteness.' Yet the principles laid down in *Graham* reaffirmed the 'functional approach' of *Hotchkiss*. To this end, *Graham* set forth a broad inquiry and invited courts, where appropriate, to look at any secondary considerations that would prove instructive.

69. The written description requirement is found in Section 112 of the Patent Act, which states in relevant part:

> The specification shall contain a written description of the invention, and of the manner and process of making and using it, in such full, clear, concise, and exact terms as to enable any person skilled in the art to which it pertains, or with which it is most nearly connected, to make and use the same. . . .

This provision requires specific disclosures in a patent application — a complete and enabling written description of the invention. The enablement requirement focuses upon the completeness and clarity of the specification from a skilled person's point of view. Because it is written for an audience composed of persons skilled in the relevant art, the "patent need not disclose what is well known in the art." *In re Wands*, 858 F.2d 731, 735 (Fed. Cir. 1988). The skilled person should merely be able to make and use the invention without "undue experimentation." Whether a disclosure would require undue experimentation includes:

> (1) the quantity of experimentation necessary, (2) the amount of direction or guidance presented, (3) the presence or absence of working examples, (4) the nature of the invention, (5) the state of the prior art, (6) the relative skill of those in the art, (7) the predictability or unpredictability of the art, and (8) the breadth of the claims.

Id. at 737. In *Ariad Pharmaceuticals, Inc. v. Eli Lilly & Co.*, 598 F.3d 1336 (Fed. Cir. 2010), the Federal Circuit emphasized that the specification must also, in addition to enabling a skilled person to make and use the invention, include sufficient information to demonstrate that, as of the filing date, the "inventor had possession of the claimed subject matter . . . . [T]he specification must describe an invention understandable to [a person of ordinary skill in the art] and show that the inventor actually invented the invention claimed." *Id.* at 1351. According to the Federal Circuit, how much information and detail section 112 requires will vary from patent to patent, depending on the type of the invention, the scope of the claims, the existing prior art, and how complex or predictable the relevant field of technology may be.

70. **Answer (A) is correct.** Green Co. probably has a legal remedy against both the employee and the competitor, because the bid is protected as a trade secret under the Uniform Trade Secrets Act ("UTSA") as providing an actual or potential advantage. The employee is liable for divulging the trade secret (which is at least implicitly confidential) and the competitor is liable because it knew or should have known that it was receiving trade secret information. Even though the bid is a one-time piece of information, it is protected under the UTSA as

long as it provides a business advantage.

Answer (B) is incorrect. As noted above, under the UTSA the competitor is liable because it knew or should have known that it was receiving trade secret information.

Answer (C) is incorrect. As noted above, the UTSA covers a wide array of information. Even though the bid is a one-time piece of information, it is protected under the UTSA as long as it provides a business advantage. Thus, if the information is secret and sufficient secrecy measures have been taken, trade secret protection can encompass almost any kind of information. The law in most states does not require that information be continuously used in a business (i.e., of long-term value) to be protectable as a trade secret, although a few states still follow the prior Restatement rule (which only protected information that is regularly used in a business). For example, in *Inflight Newspapers, Inc. v. Magazines In-Flight, LLC*, 990 F. Supp. 119 (E.D.N.Y. 1997), the court held that an airline magazine distributor's secret bids were protectable trade secrets because information would permit underbidding. Similarly, in *Martin Marietta Corp. v. Dalton*, 974 F. Supp. 37 (D.D.C. 1997), a government contractor's Navy bid was trade secret because it contained confidential cost, pricing, and strategy information and thus bids could not be revealed under the trade secret exemption to the Freedom of Information Act.

Answer (D) is incorrect. Trade secret law can protect formulas, but it also covers almost any kind of proprietary information that has value to a firm, that is maintained making use of reasonable secrecy measures, and that is not common knowledge. In other words, the subject matter of trade secrets is extremely broad. Thus, a trade secret can involve any type of information, such as technical or non technical data, a formula, a pattern, a compilation (a collection of data or information), a computer program, a device or product, a method or technique, a drawing, a process (such as a manufacturing or fabrication process), financial data, or a list of actual or potential customers, prospects, or suppliers.

71.   Yes, a customer list, consisting of names, addresses, telephone numbers, and the name and title of the primary sales contact, can be protected as a trade secret, but it will depend on additional facts and circumstances. In particular, the party claiming ownership of the list as a trade secret needs to show that the information is not readily ascertainable by proper means, such as by observing the front door of the business or by simply researching all of the relevant businesses in the area who need the goods or services offered by that party. For some businesses, a customer list might well not be readily ascertainable or generally known, particularly where it also includes — as it does here — the name of the primary sales contact for each customer. Knowing the person at the customer entity who makes purchasing decisions would also enhance the economic value of the list compared to other information known by or readily available to a competitor. The person claiming that the list is a trade secret must also be able to demonstrate that it uses efforts reasonable under the circumstances to maintain the list's secrecy. *See* Uniform Trade Secrets Act § 1(4) (defining a trade secret).

72. Section 100 (f) of the Patent Act defines an *inventor* as "the individual or, if a joint invention, the individuals collectively who invented or discovered the subject matter of the invention." Section 101 clearly designates inventorship as the fundamental requirement for obtaining a valid patent: "Whoever invents or discovers [patentable subject matter] may obtain a patent therefor.. . ." And as stated by the Federal Circuit (and other courts) many times, "conception is the touchstone of inventorship," which means that an inventor is the person or persons who conceive of the invention, not any other person or persons who might assist in reducing the invention to practice without contributing to the intellectual or mental part of invention. *See, e.g., Burroughs Wellcome Co. v. Barr Laboratories, Inc.*, 40 F.3d 1223 (Fed. Cir. 1994). Section 115 of the Patent Act requires each patent application to include an oath or declaration from each named inventor stating the he or she "believes himself or herself to be the original inventor or an original joint inventor of a claimed invention in the application." 35 U.S.C. § 115 (a)–(b). The pre-AIA required oath included a belief that the inventor was "the original *and first* inventor" (emphasis added). Section 111 of the Patent Act provides that "[a]n application for patent shall be made, or authorized to be made, by the inventor except as otherwise provided in this title," while post-AIA section 118 states, "A person to whom the inventor has assigned or is under an obligation to assign the invention may make an application for patent." Pre-AIA section 102(f) further emphasized the inventorship requirement by making derivation part of the novelty and statutory bars to patentability "A person shall be entitled to a patent unless . . . (f) he did not himself invent the subject matter sought to be patented."

73. **Answer (B) is correct.** When an employee in a research and development department creates an invention during the normal course of employment, the rights to the invention belong to the employer. There are three types of employment relationships, each with different implications for ownership of the invention. A research and development employee is hired specifically to perform research functions within the scope of his or her duties, and it is well understood that the fruits of these efforts should inure to the benefit of the employer. Thus, the inventions developed by research and development employees within the scope of their duties are generally assigned to their employers and are then wholly owned by the employer. At the other end of the spectrum, an employee whose duties do not involve research and development and who develops an invention on the employee's own time and using the employee's own materials is entitled to full ownership of any resulting inventions. The third situation is known as the "shop right." This scenario involves an employee whose duties do not involve research and development, but who develops an invention on company time, using the employer's materials, or both. In this case, the employee retains ownership of the invention, but the employer is entitled to a non-exclusive license to use the invention for its own business operations (this right is known as a "shop right").

Answer (A) is incorrect. As noted above, a research and development employee would not retain ownership rights in the invention on the facts presented here.

Answer (C) is incorrect. As noted above, this case does not involve a "shop rights" fact pattern.

Answer (D) is incorrect. It is true that contracts can always govern ownership, but in many employment settings the ownership issue is not addressed by contract (and no contract is mentioned in the fact pattern). The question is seeking the default rule, which is discussed above.

74.   As discussed above, a patent must name as inventor(s) the particular individual employee(s) who created the invention. In the case of inventions developed by a research and development employee within the scope of the employee's duties, the employer will ultimately own the rights to that patent by assignment from the employee/inventor.

75.   **Answer (A) is correct.** Pre-AIA United States patent law gave priority to the "first to conceive" an invention, as long as that inventor does not suppress, conceal, or act with a lack of diligence. Thus, even though Inventor B was the first to develop a prototype (or to develop detailed drawings from which a prototype could be made, i.e., constructive reduction to practice), Inventor A conceived of the invention in January 2011 and would still have priority under then-current law. The first inventor could lose his or her priority if that inventor failed to exercise reasonable diligence in reducing the invention to practice or if he or she abandoned, suppressed, or concealed the invention.

Answer (B) is incorrect. As discussed above, one situation in which the first inventor could lose his or her priority under pre-AIA law occurred when that inventor failed to exercise reasonable diligence in reducing the invention to practice.

Answer (C) is incorrect. Pre-AIA Patent law gave priority to the first to conceive of an invention, not the first to reduce it to practice.

Answer (D) is incorrect. Joint inventors are required to work together. Section 116 of the Patent Act states in relevant part:

> When an invention is made by two or more persons jointly, they shall apply for patent jointly and each make the required oath, except as otherwise provided in this title. Inventors may apply for a patent jointly even though (1) they did not physically work together or at the same time, (2) each did not make the same type or amount of contribution, or (3) each did not make a contribution to the subject matter of every claim of the patent.

Although this statutory language allows for a wide range of collaborative settings, joint inventorship requires at least some degree of collaboration or connection between the inventors. *See Kimberly-Clark Corp. v. Procter & Gamble Distributing Co.*, 973 F.2d 911 (Fed. Cir. 1992). The AIA modified section 116 slightly, but not in any way that affected the substantive law of joint inventorship.

76.   **Answer (D) is correct.** This question involves facts similar to those in the previous question, except that filing dates are included. Once again, however, the first to conceive the invention was given priority under pre-AIA law, absent abandonment or suppression or lack of diligence. Thus, even though Inventor A was second in reducing the invention to practice and second in filing, his or her priority continues to control.

Answer (A) is incorrect. As discussed above, pre-AIA priority was generally given to the first to conceive an invention, not the first to reduce it to practice.

Answer (B) is incorrect. As discussed above, pre-AIA priority was generally given to the first to conceive an invention, not the first to file a patent application.

Answer (C) is incorrect. The delay on these facts is not sufficiently long to constitute a lack of diligence.

77. **Answer (D) is correct.** This printed publication appeared less than one year before the patent filing date, which does not result in a statutory bar to patenting this invention. Pre-AIA section 102(b) sets forth various statutory bars under federal patent law:

> A person shall be entitled to a patent unless . . . (b) the invention was patented or described in a printed publication in this or a foreign country or in public use or on sale in this country, more than one year prior to the date of the application for patent in the United States.

These rules essentially require the inventor to proceed diligently (within a year or less) in filing a patent application after initiating any of the enumerated activities but they do not require absolute novelty at the time of filing. The Federal Circuit in *Baxter Int'l, Inc. v. COBE Laboratories, Inc.*, 88 F.3d 1054 (Fed. Cir. 1996), identified four policies underlying the rule:

> (1) discouraging the removal, from the public domain, of inventions that the public reasonably has come to believe are freely available; (2) favoring the prompt and widespread disclosure of inventions; (3) allowing the inventor a reasonable amount of time following sales activity to determine the potential economic value of a patent; and (4) prohibiting the inventor from commercially exploiting the invention for a period greater than the statutorily prescribed time.

Id. at 1058.

Answer (A) is incorrect. Although this printed publication disclosed the invention to the public, it occurred less than one year before the relevant filing date.

Answer (B) is incorrect. By the express terms of pre-AIA section 102(b), this statutory bar can be invoked against either party. The issue under pre-AIA law is not who made a public use, obtained a patent, or caused a printed publication to issue, but whether more than a year has passed since the public disclosure.

Answer (C) is incorrect. As noted above, by the express terms of pre-AIA section 102(b), this statutory bar can be invoked against either party.

78. **Answer (B) is correct.** Under current U.S. law — namely, the changes to novelty and priority instituted by the AIA, the dominant means of determining priority will be the order of the applicants' effective filing dates, *see* 35 U.S.C. § 102(a)(2), although an earlier public disclosure or patent filing by a third party could immediately destroy the novelty of the claimed invention. *See* 35 U.S.C. § 102(a)–(b) (barring a patent either if a third party has earlier disclosed the claimed invention as set forth in section 102(a)(1) (or described the invention in a filing as set forth in section 102(a)(2)) or if the applicant's own filing is made after the section 102(b)(1) grace period (further discussed below with respect to answer (C)) has passed).

Answer (A) is incorrect. Under current U.S. law — namely, the changes to novelty and priority instituted by the AIA, an inventor's date of reduction to practice (regardless of abandonment, suppression, or lack of diligence) will not be determinative of either the novelty of the invention or priority of rights as between two competing inventors (unless there is an issue of derivation by one inventor from the other, which is not present in these bare facts). See above and below for more on the determination of novelty and priority under current law.

Answer (C) is incorrect. Novelty is determined by reference to the types of disclosures or patent filings listed in section 102(a), not by reference to the passage of time after a private reduction to practice. If another inventor's reduction to practice were not maintained in confidence, it could potentially qualify as a public use or "otherwise available to the public" under section 102(a)(1) — but in that case, the claimed invention would *immediately* be rendered not novel for all other inventors, including the first inventor to file, as there is no longer a one-year grace period in which another inventor's application may be filed after a third-party public disclosure. Current law only gives an inventor a one-year grace period in which to file an application after his or her *own* disclosure of the invention, and that grace period protects the inventor from third-party patent filings, or third-party disclosures made during the one-year grace period, if the inventor's own disclosure is a "public disclosure" and was made before any third party disclosure (or patent filing) of the same invention. *Compare* 35 U.S.C. § 102(b)(1)(A) (eliminating from the prior art the inventor's own 102(a)(1)-type disclosures within the year before the effective filing date) *with* 102(b)(1)(B) (eliminating from the prior art a third party's section 102(a)(1)-type disclosure within the year before the effective filing date only if it was preceded by the applicant's own "public" disclosure) *and* (b)(2)(B) (eliminating from the prior art a third party's patent filing only if it was preceded by the applicant's own "public" disclosure).

Answer (D) is incorrect. Novelty is determined by reference to the types of disclosures or patent filings listed in section 102(a), and whether they occurred before the applicant's effective filing date (and whether they may be excluded from the prior art under section 102(b)), not by reference to the passage of time after another inventor's conception of the invention.

79.   On the facts set forth in question 78, but with the additional fact that inventor C had published an article fully disclosing the invention in October 2013 in an electronically distributed scientific journal — Inventor C would have priority in the invention, even though C filed his or her application after inventor D filed. Section 102(b)(1)(A) eliminates from the prior art an inventor's own section 102(a)(1)-type disclosures made within the year before the inventor's filing date (thus preserving the invention's novelty for inventor C as of the June 2014 filing date despite the October 2013 journal publication, which would either be considered a "printed publication" under pre-AIA case law or would be "otherwise available to the public"). Section 102(b)(2)(B) eliminates from the prior art disclosures in prior filed patent applications if they are preceded by a "public" disclosure (thus eliminating D's patent application from the prior art to inventor C's application). Inventor D's claimed invention, although it is claimed in the first application to be filed, would be rendered not novel by C's October 2013 journal publication. Inventor D cannot exclude that publication from the prior art under these facts.

80.   **Answer (B) is correct.** The most common method for determining priority of patent

ownership worldwide is that the first to file a patent application is entitled to ownership of the rights.

Answer (A) is incorrect. This rule is not generally followed in the United States or abroad.

Answer (C) is incorrect. This rule was followed in the U.S. until March 2013, but it is not the general rule in most foreign nations and is not the rule in the U.S. for new applications filed on or after the AIA's March 16, 2013 effective date.

Answer (D) is incorrect. This rule is not generally followed in the United States or abroad. Consider the transaction costs that would arise if independent inventors were forced to share rights to an invention. Although this rule may sound evenhanded or fair in an abstract way, it would create serious problems in the managing the patent rights.

81.   The *shop right* involves an employee whose duties do not involve research and development, but who develops an invention on company time, using the employer's materials, or both. In *United States v. Dubilier Condenser Corp.*, 289 U.S. 178 (1933), the Supreme Court defined the employer's shop right with regard to ideas and inventions developed by employees who are not specifically hired to perform research and development:

> Recognition of the nature of the act of invention also defines the limits of the so-called shop right, which, shortly stated, is that, where a servant, during his hours of employment, working with his master's materials and appliances, conceives and perfects an invention for which he obtains a patent, he must accord his master a nonexclusive right to practice the invention. This is an application of equitable principles. Since the servant uses his master's time, facilities, and materials to attain a concrete result, the latter is in equity entitled to use that which embodies his own property and to duplicate it as often as he may find occasion to employ similar appliances in his business. But the employer in such a case has no equity to demand a conveyance of the invention, which is the original conception of the employee alone, in which the employer had no part. This remains the property of him who conceived it, together with the right conferred by the patent, to exclude all others than the employer from the accruing benefits.

Id. at 188–189.

The shop right doctrine effectively confers upon employers a free and nonexclusive license to use the employee's innovation. As Judge Wisdom observed in *Hobbs v. United States*, 376 F.2d 488, 495 (5th Cir. 1967), "[t]he classic shop rights doctrine ordains that when an employee makes and reduces to practice an invention on his employer's time, using his employer's tools and the services of other employees, the employer is the recipient of an implied, nonexclusive, royalty-free license." The shop right doctrine rests upon several policy rationales:

> First, it seems only fair that when an employee has used his employer's time and equipment to make an invention, the employer should be able to use the device without paying a royalty. Second, under the doctrine of estoppel, if an employee encourages his employer to use an invention, and then stands by and allows him to construct and operate the new device without making any claim for compensation or royalties, it would not be equitable to allow the employee later to assert a claim for royalties or other compensation.

Id. at 495. Another justification for the shop rights doctrine is the concept of implied consent. The employee has implicitly consented to allow the employer limited use of the invention based on the employee's acceptance of assistance or resources from the employer while developing the invention. *See Solomons v. United States*, 137 U.S. 342 (1890).

82.   **Answer (D) is correct.** Even though joint inventors are required to work together in some way (i.e., to be collaborative), section 116 of the Patent Act states in relevant part:

> When an invention is made by two or more persons jointly, they shall apply for patent jointly and each make the required oath, except as otherwise provided in this title. Inventors may apply for a patent jointly even though (1) they did not physically work together or at the same time, (2) each did not make the same type or amount of contribution, or (3) each did not make a contribution to the subject matter of every claim of the patent.

The statute expressly disavows any requirement that joint inventors work in the same location, make the same amount or type of contribution to the invention, or contribute something as to every claim in the patent. This statutory language allows for a wide range of collaborative settings, as long as there is at least some degree of collaboration or connection between the inventors. *See Kimberly-Clark Corp. v. Procter & Gamble Distributing Co.*, 973 F.2d 911 (Fed. Cir. 1992).

Answer (A) is incorrect. As noted above, section 116 expressly disavows any requirement that joint inventors work in the same location.

Answer (B) is incorrect. As noted above, section 116 expressly disavows any requirement that joint inventors make the same amount or type of contribution to the invention.

Answer (C) is incorrect. As noted above, section 116 expressly disavows any requirement that joint inventors contribute something as to every claim in the patent.

83.   **Answer (B) is correct.** Section 154(a)(2) of the Patent Act provides that the general term of protection for a *utility patent* (or a plant patent) under present law is *20 years from the date of patent filing* (not counting any extensions of the patent term allowed by law). The statute provides:

> Subject to the payment of fees under this title, such grant shall be for a term beginning on the date on which the patent issues and ending 20 years from the date on which the application for the patent was filed in the United States or, if the application contains a specific reference to an earlier filed application or applications under section 120, 121, or 365(c) of this title, from the date on which the earliest such application was filed.

The Uruguay Round Agreements Act of 1994 ("URAA") established the present term for patents sought after June 8, 1995. Prior to the URAA, the standard patent term was 17 years from the date of patent issuance. Note that a patent cannot be enforced until it has been issued by the PTO. Thus, the delay that occurs while a patent application is being examined reduces the effective term of the patent, usually by a period of several years. Thus, the actual term of enforceable patent rights may or may not be longer than under prior law, depending on the extent of the delay in gaining patent issuance. In recent years, delays in the Patent Office have increased because of the growth in the number of patent applications.

Answer (A) is incorrect. As discussed above, the term is 20 years from the filing date.

Answer (C) is incorrect. As discussed above, before the enactment of the URAA, the standard patent term was 17 years from the date of patent issuance. Thus, this is the governing term for utility patents issued prior to June 8, 1995, but is not the current law. As a transitional measure, section 154 (c) provides that: "the term of a patent that is in force on or that results from an application filed before [June 8, 1995] shall be the greater of the 20-year term as provided in subsection (a), or 17 years from grant."

Answer (D) is incorrect. As discussed above, the term is 20 years from the filing date.

84. **Answer (C) is correct.** The term for *design patents* is only *14 years from the date of issuance.* Section 173 of the Patent Act states: "Patents for designs shall be granted for the term of fourteen years from the date of grant." In contrast to utility and plant patents discussed above, the design patent term was not addressed by the URAA, and is thus still governed by the prior law regarding the patent term. The design patent term is therefore keyed to the issuance date of the patent, rather than to the application date.

   Answer (A) is incorrect. As discussed above, the term is 14 years from the date of issuance.

   Answer (B) is incorrect. This is the current term of protection for utility and plant patents, but not for design patents.

   Answer (D) is incorrect. As discussed above, the term is 14 years from the date of issuance.

85. **Answer (A) is correct.** If Congress attempted to grant a perpetual patent, this action would be directly contrary to the clearly expressed "limited times" language of the Intellectual Property Clause (Art. I, sec. 8, cl. 8) of the Constitution, which states: "The Congress shall have Power . . . To promote the Progress of Science and useful Arts, by securing for limited Times to Authors and Inventors the exclusive Right to their respective Writings and Discoveries."

   Answer (B) is incorrect. Because the Intellectual Property Clause does expressly include a "limited times" requirement, it is highly likely that Congress *could not* avoid the problem by relying upon the Commerce Clause as an end run around this express limitation on its power.

   Answer (C) is incorrect. This is the second best answer, as it might be argued that Congress could rely on the Commerce Clause. It is likely, however, that such a law would be struck down by the Supreme Court, because it contravenes a clear, express limitation of power under the Intellectual Property Clause.

   Answer (D) is incorrect. Congress has not granted perpetual patents in any field.

86. **Answer (A) is correct.** Trade secret protection can extend indefinitely, as long as the requisite secrecy and competitive advantage exist. A classic example of a trade secret that has been maintained for many years is the formula for Coca-Cola.

   Answer (B) is incorrect. If the information no longer remains sufficiently secret so as to offer a competitive advantage, then the trade secret ceases to satisfy the requirements of any state's trade secret law.

   Answer (C) is incorrect. There is no express term for trade secrets, unlike the term for patents.

   Answer (D) is incorrect. Even if one competitor were to reverse engineer a trade secret, the original trade secret owner might still have a competitive advantage over other competitors.

87. Reasonable secrecy measures are essential for purposes of maintaining information as a trade secret. *See* UTSA § 1 (4) (defining a trade secret, in part, as information that is "the subject of efforts that are reasonable under the circumstances to maintain its secrecy"). A company seeking to protect its trade secrets should consider a variety of secrecy measures. The UTSA requires only reasonable secrecy measures, which recognizes that secrecy measures will involve some cost or inconvenience, and thus a balancing of the benefits of a particular measure against its cost is necessary. *See, e.g., E.I. du Pont de Nemours & Co. v. Christopher*, 431 F.2d 1012 (5th Cir. 1970). A firm might consider adoption of some or all of the following measures: (1) external physical security measures to protect the plant from intrusion; (2) internal physical security measures to prevent employees and visitors from gaining access to areas in which proprietary information is kept; (3) confidentiality agreements or clauses for all employees, customers, suppliers, and other third parties who have access to any trade secret information; (4) prohibiting persons who are not bound by these agreement from gaining access to trade secret information; (5) requiring employees with access to proprietary information to sign reasonable covenants not to compete; (6) keeping trade secret information "under lock and key," including securing all documents and insuring that computers have password protection; (7) identifying and labeling all confidential information; and (8) maintaining a policy of informing all incoming and departing employees of the firm's trade secret policies and of the particular types of information considered to be trade secrets (and to which the employee has had or will have access). Whether adequate action has been taken to protect a trade secret is ordinarily a fact question.

88. A breach of confidence for purposes of trade secret law is one of two methods for establishing that the trade secret information has been improperly acquired. (The other method is by showing improper means were used to obtain the trade secret.) Section 41 of the RESTATEMENT (THIRD) OF UNFAIR COMPETITION describes the typical situations in which a duty of confidence can be found:

> A person to whom a trade secret has been disclosed owes a duty of confidence to the owner of the trade secret for purposes of the rule stated in § 40 if:
>
> (a) the person made an express promise of confidentiality prior to the disclosure of the trade secret; or
>
> (b) the trade secret was disclosed to the person under circumstances in which the relationship between the parties to the disclosure or the other facts surrounding the disclosure justify the conclusions that, at the time of the disclosure,
>
> (1) the person knew or had reason to know that the disclosure was intended to be in confidence, and
>
> (2) the other party to the disclosure was reasonable in inferring that the person

consented to an obligation of confidentiality

For a general overview of the different ways in which trade secret infringement can be shown, consider this summary from the RESTATEMENT (THIRD) OF UNFAIR COMPETITION, section 38:

> One is subject to liability for the appropriation of another's trade secret if:
>
> (a) the actor acquires by means that are improper under the rule stated in § 43 information that the actor knows or has reason to know is the other's trade secret; or
>
> (b) the actor uses or discloses the other's trade secret without the other's consent and, at the time of the use or disclosure,
>
> (1) the actor knows or has reason to know that the information is a trade secret that the actor acquired under circumstances creating a duty of confidence owed by the actor to the other under the rule stated in § 41; or
>
> (2) the actor knows or has reason to know that the information is a trade secret that the actor acquired by means that are improper under the rule stated in § 43; or
>
> (3) the actor knows or has reason to know that the information is a trade secret that the actor acquired from or through a person who acquired it by means that are improper under the rule stated in § 43 or whose disclosure of the trade secret constituted a breach of a duty of confidence owed to the other under the rule stated in § 41; or
>
> (4) the actor knows or has reason to know that the information is a trade secret that the actor acquired through an accident or mistake, unless the acquisition was the result of the other's failure to take reasonable precautions to maintain the secrecy of the information.

89.   **Answer (B) is correct.** Patent infringement can be shown by proof of literal infringement or infringement under the doctrine of equivalents. Literal infringement, as the term implies, involves a showing that the accused device (i.e., the defendant's product) reads on every element of the claimed invention — it is a duplication of the claimed invention. The Supreme Court described the doctrine of equivalents in *Graver Tank & Mfg. Co. v. Linde Air Products Co.*, 339 U.S. 605, 609 (1950):

> What constitutes equivalency must be determined against the context of the patent, the prior art, and the particular circumstances of the case. Equivalence, in the patent law, is not the prisoner of a formula and is not an absolute to be considered in a vacuum. It does not require complete identity for every purpose and in every respect. In determining equivalents, things equal to the same thing may not be equal to each other and, by the same token, things for most purposes different may sometimes be equivalents. Consideration must be given to the purpose for which an ingredient is used in a patent, the qualities it has when combined with the other ingredients, and the function which it is intended to perform. An important factor is whether persons reasonably skilled in the art would have known of the interchangeability of an ingredient not contained in the patent with one that was.

More recently, the Court has declined to determine the precise definition of the doctrine of equivalents. One version of the test focused on whether the accused device performs substantially the same function in substantially the same way to achieve substantially the same result, while another formulation focused on whether there were insubstantial differences between the accused device and the claimed invention.

> Both the parties and the Federal Circuit spend considerable time arguing whether the so called "triple identity" test focusing on the function served by a particular claim element, the way that element serves that function, and the result thus obtained by that element is a suitable method for determining equivalence, or whether an "insubstantial differences" approach is better. There seems to be substantial agreement that, while the triple identity test may be suitable for analyzing mechanical devices, it often provides a poor framework for analyzing other products or processes. On the other hand, the insubstantial differences test offers little additional guidance as to what might render any given difference "insubstantial."

> In our view, the particular linguistic framework used is less important than whether the test is probative of the essential inquiry: Does the accused product or process contain elements identical or equivalent to each claimed element of the patented invention? Different linguistic frameworks may be more suitable to different cases, depending on their particular facts. A focus on individual elements and a special vigilance against allowing the concept of equivalence to eliminate completely any such elements should reduce considerably the imprecision of whatever language is used. An analysis of the role played by each element in the context of the specific patent claim will thus inform the inquiry as to whether a substitute element matches the function, way, and result of the claimed element, or whether the substitute element plays a role substantially different from the claimed element.

Warner Jenkinson Co., Inc. v. Hilton Davis Chemical Co., 520 U.S. 17, 39–40 (1997).

Answer (A) is incorrect. The likelihood of consumer confusion standard is relevant to trademark law, not patent law.

Answer (C) is incorrect. A showing of breach of confidence or use of improper means is relevant to trade secret law, not patent law.

Answer (D) is incorrect. As discussed above, patent infringement can be shown by proof of either literal infringement or infringement under the doctrine of equivalents.

90. **Answer (D) is correct.** Practicing an invention for purely experimental purposes does not impinge on any of the exclusive rights of the patent holder. This is a very narrow exception, however, under Federal Circuit case law. *See, e.g., Madey v. Duke University*, 307 F.3d 1351 (Fed. Cir. 2002) ("[T]he defense [i]s limited to actions performed 'for amusement, to satisfy idle curiosity, or for strictly philosophical inquiry.' . . . [U]se is disqualified if it has the 'slightest commercial implication.' Moreover, use in keeping with the legitimate business of the alleged infringer does not qualify for the experimental use defense.").

Answer (A) is incorrect. Making a patented invention would infringe on one of the exclusive rights provided in section 271(a). Section 271(a) of the Patent Act states: "Except as otherwise provided in this title, whoever without authority makes, uses, offers to sell, or sells any patented invention, within the United States, or imports into the United States any patented invention during the term of the patent therefor, infringes the patent." Thus, patent infringement occurs when a party makes, uses, sells, offers to sell, or imports the patented invention into the United States.

Answer (B) is incorrect. Selling a product manufactured using a patented process would infringe on the exclusive right provided in section 271(g). Of course, the use of the patented process to manufacture the product would infringe under section 271(a).

Answer (C) is incorrect. As noted above, importation of a product covered by a patent would infringe on one of the exclusive rights provided in section 271(a).

91. The prosecution history estoppel (or file wrapper estoppel) doctrine places a limit on the extent to which the doctrine of equivalents can expand the scope of claims under the patent. The court explained the role of the prosecution history or file wrapper in *Autogiro Co. of America v. United States*, 384 F.2d 391, 398–99 (Ct. Cl. 1967):

> The file wrapper contains the entire record of the proceedings in the Patent Office from the first application papers to the issued patent. Since all express representations of the patent applicant made to induce a patent grant are in the file wrapper, this material provides an accurate charting of the patent's pre-issuance history. One use of the file wrapper is file wrapper estoppel, which is the application of familiar estoppel principles to Patent Office prosecution and patent infringement litigation.

Prosecution history estoppel thus comes into play when the patent applicant has made amendments to its application to avoid prior art or to address other objections (such as obviousness) that might render the claimed subject matter unpatentable. Applying estoppel principles, the patent holder cannot then use the doctrine of equivalents to reassert claims or claim in breadth given up during the patent application process. For instance, in *Keystone Driller Co. v. Northwest Engineering Corp.*, 294 U.S. 42, 48 (1935), the allegedly infringing equivalent element was part of the prior art that formed the basis for the rejection of the some patent claims. The revised claims did not include this element, and the Court applied the prosecution history estoppel doctrine to prevent use of the doctrine of equivalents to encompass the element in later patent litigation. In *Warner Jenkinson Co., Inc. v. Hilton Davis Chemical Co.*, 520 U.S. 17, 39–40 (1997), the Court stated:

> Prosecution history estoppel continues to be available as a defense to infringement, but if the patent holder demonstrates that an amendment required during prosecution had a purpose unrelated to patentability, a court must consider that purpose in order to decide whether an estoppel is precluded. Where the patent holder is unable to establish such a purpose, a court should presume that the purpose behind the required amendment is such that prosecution history estoppel would apply.

More recently, in *Festo Corp. v. Shoketsu Kinzoku Kogyo Kabushiki Co., Ltd.*, 535 U.S. 722 (2002), the Court held that prosecution history estoppel applies to any amendment made to satisfy the requisites of patent law, but that the amendment is not an absolute bar to a claim of infringement under doctrine of equivalents. Instead, the patent holder has the burden of proving that the particular amendment did not surrender the equivalent material at issue.

92. **Answer (A) is correct.** Appellate jurisdiction in patent cases is within the exclusive purview of the United States Court of Appeals for the Federal Circuit, with certiorari review (discretionary) by the Supreme Court. This unusual feature of patent law is set forth in 28 U.S.C. § 1295:

> The United States Court of Appeals for the Federal Circuit shall have exclusive jurisdiction—

(1) of an appeal from a final decision of a district court of the United States, the District Court of Guam, the District Court of the Virgin Islands, or the District Court of the Northern Mariana Islands, in any civil action arising under, or in any civil action in which a party has asserted a compulsory counterclaim arising under, any Act of Congress relating to patents or plant variety protection.

Thus, appeals from any district court's patent infringement rulings must be filed in the Federal Circuit, rather than the regional court of appeals in which the parties are located or in which the case was litigated. By virtue of its exclusive appellate jurisdiction, decisions of the Federal Circuit on patent law issues are effectively controlling throughout the United States, unless they are overruled by the Supreme Court (or by the Federal Circuit itself sitting en banc). Decisions by the Court of Customs and Patent Appeals (a predecessor of the Federal Circuit) are also considered as governing precedent. Neither federal copyright nor federal trademark law vests appellate jurisdiction in this manner — appeals generally go the regional circuit, just as with any ordinary federal case. The Federal Circuit's exclusive jurisdiction serves to increase the national uniformity of patent law, although that court's patent law decisions have been overruled by the Supreme Court on a number of occasions in the last decade.

Answer (B) is incorrect. As discussed above, the Federal Circuit does have exclusive appellate jurisdiction, but the Supreme Court has the final say by virtue of its certiorari review.

Answer (C) is incorrect. As discussed above, the Federal Circuit has exclusive appellate jurisdiction over patent appeals.

Answer (D) is incorrect. As discussed above, the Federal Circuit has exclusive appellate jurisdiction over patent appeals.

93.   **Answer (A) is correct.** A fundamental rule in trade secret law is that reverse engineering is a lawful means of competition. Thus, a competitor is free to purchase a sample of a product and attempt to determine its composition, structure, and chemical makeup. Similarly, independent development is a lawful method of competition. In either case, the owner of the original trade secret has no cognizable claim under trade secret law. In contrast, patent law does not include exceptions for reverse engineering or independent development.

Answer (B) is incorrect. This answer could be second-best, because many recipes for food items are in fact too well known to be protected as trade secrets. There are, however, many exceptions to this rule. The formula for Coca-Cola (arguably a food item) is a long-time trade secret; so too is the recipe for Kentucky Fried Chicken, although a recent book suggests it has uncovered the recipe by reverse engineering.

Answer (C) is incorrect. As discussed above, reverse engineering is a lawful means of competition and does not constitute improper means.

Answer (D) is incorrect. A defendant's knowledge that information was a trade secret and intended to be held in confidence is only relevant if knowledge of the information (the secret) was obtained by accident or mistake. Reverse engineering is lawful and not within "accident" or "mistake."

94.   **Answer (C) is correct.** Hacking into a competitor's computer system to obtain confidential information — in this case by using a random password generator to identify an employee's

confidential password — is likely to be actionable as trade secret misappropriation based on improper means. Under section 43 of the RESTATEMENT (THIRD) OF UNFAIR COMPETITION,

> [i]mproper means of acquiring another's trade secret . . . include theft, fraud, unauthorized interception of communications, inducement of or knowing participation in a breach of confidence, and other means either wrongful in themselves or wrongful under the circumstances of the case. Independent discovery and analysis of publicly available products or information are not improper means of acquisition.

Some methods are clearly improper because they violate existing laws, such as discovery of information through fraud, trespass, eavesdropping, or wiretapping. Hacking a computer might fall into this category. But even if a competitor uses methods having ambiguous legitimacy, courts will focus on whether the means used fall below the generally accepted standards of commercial morality and reasonable conduct. This standard dovetails with the extent of reasonable secrecy measures that a firm can be expected to take. If the defendant engages in a method of discovering information that would breach the wall of reasonable secrecy measures, it is more likely that the means used will be deemed improper.

Answer (A) is incorrect. There is no indication that a patent is in effect on these facts.

Answer (B) is incorrect. Absent unusual circumstances, there is no reason to assume that one competitor would have an obligation of confidentiality toward another.

Answer (D) is incorrect. As discussed above, computer hacking is likely to be an improper means of discovering trade secret information, and thus a violation is likely to have occurred.

95. **Answer (D) is correct.** Each of the following would likely constitute improper means for purposes of proving misappropriation of a trade secret: eavesdropping, trespassing (breaking and entering), and surveillance using overflights and high-powered zoom lenses. The first two types of conduct are independently unlawful and thus clearly improper, as discussed in the previous question above. The use of surveillance by overflights aided by high-powered zoom lenses was found to be improper in the landmark case of *E.I. du Pont de Nemours & Co. v. Christopher*, 431 F.2d 1012 (5th Cir. 1970). In that case, a competitor of du Pont, the chemical manufacturer, hired the defendants to fly a plane over a du Pont plant while it was under construction. The plane used a highly sophisticated telephoto camera to take pictures of the plant design, arguably revealing trade secrets to the competitor. The court held that despite the lack of violation of any laws, the fly-over constituted an improper means of obtaining a trade secret.

Answer (A) is incorrect. As discussed above, all three examples constitute improper means under trade secret law.

Answer (B) is incorrect. As discussed above, all three examples constitute improper means under trade secret law.

Answer (C) is incorrect. As discussed above, all three examples constitute improper means under trade secret law.

96. **Answer (A) is correct.** In patent cases, injunctive relief is available upon a showing of a four-factor equitable test. This conclusion reflects recent Supreme Court guidance on the issue. In *eBay, Inc. v. MercExchange, L.L.C.*, 547 U.S. 388, 393–94 (2006), the Supreme Court held that a patent holder must make a four-part showing in order to receive injunctive relief:

(1) that it has suffered an irreparable injury; (2) that remedies available at law, such as monetary damages, are inadequate to compensate for that injury; (3) that, considering the balance of hardships between the plaintiff and defendant, a remedy in equity is warranted; and (4) that the public interest would not be disserved by a permanent injunction.

The Court rejected the Federal Circuit's presumption that injunctions should be granted except in unusual cases. Injunctive relief is a very important remedy because it permits the patent holder to maintain its exclusivity in the marketplace, which is the essence of the patent reward. Section 283 of the Patent Act states: "The several courts having jurisdiction of cases under this title may grant injunctions in accordance with the principles of equity to prevent the violation of any right secured by patent, on such terms as the court deems reasonable."

Answer (B) is incorrect. As discussed above, the Supreme Court in *eBay, Inc. v. MercExchange, L.L.C.*, rejected the Federal Circuit's presumption that injunctions should be granted except in unusual cases.

Answer (C) is incorrect. There is no authority for automatic grants of injunctive relief in patent cases.

Answer (D) is incorrect. As discussed above, the Supreme Court in *eBay, Inc. v. MercExchange, L.L.C.*, required a four-part showing in order to grant injunctive relief. Although the defendant's bad faith could be a consideration, it is not required in order for equitable relief to be granted. The statutory language regarding equitable relief does not make reference to "exceptional cases."

97. Section 284 of the Patent Act sets forth the types of damages recoveries available to patent holders: "Upon finding for the claimant the court shall award the claimant damages adequate to compensate for the infringement but in no event less than a reasonable royalty for the use made of the invention by the infringer, together with interest and costs as fixed by the court." This provision expressly contemplates the use of expert testimony to determine either damages or a reasonable royalty, the minimum recovery to which patent holders are entitled: "The court may receive expert testimony as an aid to the determination of damages or of what royalty would be reasonable under the circumstances." *Id.* In order to receive lost profits in a patent case, the plaintiff generally makes a four-part showing: (1) demand for the patented product; (2) absence of acceptable non-infringing substitutes; (3) manufacturing and marketing capability to exploit the demand; and (4) the amount of the profit it would have made. *See Panduit Corp. v. Stahlin Bros. Fibre Works, Inc.*, 575 F.2d 1152, 1156 (6th Cir. 1978). This four-part showing establishes that the patent holder would have earned the lost profits "but for" the defendant's infringing activities.

98. In order to receive attorney's fees and costs in a patent case, the plaintiff must satisfy section 285 of the Patent Act, which states: "The court in exceptional cases may award reasonable attorney fees to the prevailing party." This provision can be invoked in cases of willful infringement or in other situations involving litigation conduct by either party that might warrant an award of fees and costs.

99. Reverse engineering means, generally speaking, inspecting and analyzing a product in order to learn what it contains, how it is made, how it functions, and the like. Reverse engineering a publicly available product does not violate trade secret law, and it serves as a defense or limitation on the scope of trade secret rights. Reverse engineering is a lawful means of competition and is not within "improper means" in trade secret law. Thus, a competitor is free to purchase a sample of a product and use a wide variety of analytical techniques to attempt to determine its composition, structure, chemical makeup, etc. Similarly, independent development is a lawful method of competition. In either case, the owner of the original trade secret has no cognizable claim under trade secret law, for either the reverse engineering or independent development itself or for the use of the information learned in manufacturing or selling a new product.

100. Reverse engineering a patented product can constitute a violation of patent law. The reverse engineering itself should not be infringing use of the product due to exhaustion. But if the competitor then proceeds to make, use, sell, offer to sell, or import new copies of the patented invention, these actions violate the exclusive rights of the patent owner. Similarly, there is no "independent development" defense in patent law.

101. **Answer (A) is correct.** Although a patent is presumed to be valid, *see* 35 U.S.C. § 282(a), invalidity is a defense provided in section 282(b)(2)–(3) of the Patent Act.

     Answer (B) is not correct. For a claim of infringement based on the defendant's making, using, or selling a patented invention, all of which are infringing under section 271(a), knowledge is irrelevant to liability (although relevant to the possible enhancement of damages under section 284). Knowledge is relevant to claims of inducement of infringement and contributory infringement under section 271(b)–(c). *See Aro Mfg. Co. v. Convertible Top Replacement Co.*, 377 U.S. 476 (1964) (contributory infringement); *Global-Tech Appliances, Inc. v. SEB S.A.*, 131 S. Ct. 2060 (2011) (inducement).

     Answer (C) is not correct. The Patent Act does not contain a statute of limitations. Section 286 limits monetary recovery to infringing acts committed within six years of filing of the claim of infringement, but it does not prevent a patent owner from suing for infringement that began more than six years before filing

     Answer (D) is not correct. See above.

102. **Answer (D) is correct.** If a medical practitioner makes use of a patented process in order to provide medical treatment, the physician is not liable because of statutory immunity for medical providers. Section 287(c) of the Patent Act immunizes medical practitioners for liability for the unauthorized use of medical and surgical procedures:

With respect to a medical practitioner's performance of a medical activity that constitutes an infringement under section 271(a) or (b) of this title, the provisions of sections 281, 283, 284, and 285 of this title shall not apply against the medical practitioner or against a related health care entity with respect to such medical activity.

The statute defines medical activity as

the performance of a medical or surgical procedure on a body, but shall not include (i) the use of a patented machine, manufacture, or composition of matter in violation of such patent, (ii) the practice of a patented use of a composition of matter in violation of such patent, or (iii) the practice of a process in violation of a biotechnology patent.

Under United States law, unlike that of some foreign nations, patents can be issued on medical procedures, such a new method for treating a physical ailment, as well as to medical devices. The statutory immunity prevents physicians from being liable for patent infringement when they provide medical treatment by using a patented treatment process. Note that the immunity applies to medical procedures, but not to the production or use of the underlying physical products that might be used in the course of medical treatment, such as a medical device or a pharmaceutical product. A medical practitioner is defined as "any natural person who is licensed by a State to provide the medical activity described in subsection (c)(1) or who is acting under the direction of such person in the performance of the medical activity." A *related health care entity* is "an entity with which a medical practitioner has a professional affiliation under which the medical practitioner performs the medical activity, including but not limited to a nursing home, hospital, university, medical school, health maintenance organization, group medical practice, or a medical clinic." The statute applies to treatment of "a human body, organ or cadaver, or a nonhuman animal used in medical research or instruction directly relating to the treatment of humans." Given this language, the law does not generally exempt veterinarians from liability. The statute is also inapplicable to patents filed prior to September 30, 1996.

Answer (A) is incorrect. As discussed above, the medical practitioner has statutory immunity.

Answer (B) is incorrect. As discussed above, the medical practitioner has statutory immunity.

Answer (C) is incorrect. As discussed above, the medical practitioner has statutory immunity.

103.   **Answer (D) is correct.** A prior user (who is acting in good faith) of a later-patented manufacturing process is not liable — in the statutorily prescribed circumstances — because of statutory immunity for good faith prior users of certain types of inventions. Section 273(a) of the Patent Act states:

A person shall be entitled to a defense under section 282(b) with respect to subject matter consisting of a process, or consisting of a machine, manufacture, or composition of matter used in a manufacturing or other commercial process, that would otherwise infringe a claimed invention being asserted against the person if—

(1) such person, acting in good faith, commercially used the subject matter in the United States, either in connection with an internal commercial use or an actual arm's

length sale or other arm's length commercial transfer of a useful end result of such commercial use; and

(2) such commercial use occurred at least 1 year before the earlier of either—

(A) the effective filing date of the claimed invention; or

(B) the date on which the claimed invention was disclosed to the public in a manner that qualified for the exception from prior art under section 102 (b).

35 U.S.C. § 273(a). Before the AIA, or America Invents Act, section 273 provided a narrower defense for certain good faith users of business methods that were patented by another after the good faith use began.

Answer (A) is incorrect. As discussed above, section 273(b) generally provides a defense in this situation.

Answer (B) is incorrect. If section 273(b) applies to the user of the process — here, Company B — then the sale by that user of a useful end result of the process — here, Company B's gasoline — exhausts the patent owner's rights under the patent as to that end result. *See* 35 U.S.C. § 273(d). The consumers' use of B's gasoline therefore would not infringe A's patent, and B could not be liable for inducing the (noninfringing) use of the gasoline.

Answer (C) is incorrect. There is no general defense of innocent infringement in patent cases. But as discussed above, section 273(b) generally provides a defense in this situation.

104. **Answer (D) is correct.** Company A, which licensed its patent to B, should not succeed with a patent infringement suit related to the fasteners manufactured by B under the license, because the license to B (which does not, on these facts, contain any limitation on the scope of the license) exhausts A's right to control the later sale and use of B's fasteners. Even though A seeks to sue C, not B, the exhaustion doctrine still applies to the licensed goods after they are sold to another party and combined with other parts. *See, e.g., Quanta Computer, Inc. v. LG Electronics, Inc.*, 553 U.S. 617 (2008).

Answer (A) is not correct. Although selling and using are indeed both infringing activities under section 271(a), and only B has an express license under the patent, the license to B exhausts A's use and sale rights with respect to the fasteners that B manufactures and sells under that license. A's right to control the making of new fasteners by other parties is not exhausted.

Answer (B) is not correct. Active inducement is a form of infringement, actionable under section 271(b), but on these facts C is not inducing B (although on other facts, a customer could induce a manufacturer to infringe a patent in the production of goods for that customer). Moreover, B has a license from A, so its making and selling of goods embodying the patent is noninfringing.

Answer (C) is not correct. This is a second-best answer. It is true that C is not making fasteners, and that C is not inducing B to manufacture them, but that is not the fundamental reason why A will not succeed. If C were not using B's licensed fasteners, then C's use and sale of other, unlicensed fasteners would infringe, even if C were not making them or inducing their manufacture.

105. The patent misuse doctrine is a defense to patent infringement. It can be asserted based on

a showing that the plaintiff has acted in a manner that is anticompetitive or otherwise inequitable. Conduct that is related to use of the patent or patent rights allegedly infringed and that violates the antitrust laws is likely to constitute patent misuse. Courts and commentators are divided on whether any conduct that does not violate antitrust laws can nonetheless constitute patent misuse. If patent misuse can be proven, the defendant is not liable for its otherwise infringing acts, at least until the patent owner is able to "purge" the effects of the misuse from the marketplace. One unique feature of the misuse doctrine is that the defendant can assert the defense even if the defendant itself was not the target of the conduct alleged to be misuse.

106. **Answer (D) is correct.** Trademark law is designed to further all three of the following policies: (1) promoting competition in the marketplace; (2) preventing consumer confusion or deception; and (3) protection of the goodwill and reputation of sellers.

    Answer (A) is incorrect. Trademark law serves all three purposes identified in this question.

    Answer (B) is incorrect. As noted above, trademark law serves all three purposes identified in this question.

    Answer (C) is incorrect. As noted above, trademark law serves all three purposes identified in this question.

107. The treatment of generic terms in trademark law plays an important role in limiting the scope of trademark rights. In order for a brand name to serve as a trademark, it must be capable of identifying a particular producer or source of the goods in question. A generic term cannot qualify as a trademark, because it is the name of a product (or service) in the consuming public's mind, not indication of the source of that product (or service). In other words, the term identifies the product (or service) itself, rather than serving as a brand name. A generic term thus fails to identify a particular source or producer. A term can be generic because it has always been a product name or category, such as coffee, diapers, or deep-dish pizza. If trademark law allowed one producer to have exclusive trademark rights to such a generic term, it would place competitors at a considerable disadvantage. Competitors would have difficulty marketing a product such as a laser printer if they were precluded from using the term "laser printer" in advertisements, on product packaging, or on the Internet, where searches are often conducted using key words. A term can also start out as a source-identifying brand name, but the brand can become so successful and dominant in consumer's minds that it eventually comes to be known to the consuming public as the product name itself. Historic examples of this phenomenon, known as "genericide," include Aspirin, Cellophane, and Thermos. Each of these terms began as a brand name but eventually came to be used as a name for the product itself. Thus, even a well-established trademark, including a fanciful mark, can sometimes be challenged on the ground that it has become generic. To assess whether a term has become generic, courts generally consider consumer surveys, as well as trade publications, media reports, and other sources.

108. **Answer (B) is correct.** The source of Congress' authority to enact the Lanham Act (trademark law) is the Commerce Clause, which gives Congress the power to regulate interstate and foreign commerce. The Intellectual Property Clause (Art. I, sec. 8, cl. 8) provides authority for the enactment of patents and copyrights for limited times but does not provide for protection of trademarks.

    Answer (A) is incorrect. As noted above, the Intellectual Property Clause provides authority for the enactment of patents and copyrights but does not provide for protection of trademarks.

Answer (C) is incorrect. The First Amendment is a limitation on the scope of Congress' power, not a grant of authority to it.

Answer (D) is incorrect. The Impeachment Clause has no particular relevance to intellectual property law.

109.   An arbitrary trademark involves the use of a common word applied in an unfamiliar way. In other words, the mark must have no connection to the underlying product, such as "Apple" for computer products.

110.   A fanciful trademark is a word invented solely to be used as a trademark. In other words, fanciful marks are words that have been coined or made up to serve as a mark — not a word previously in existence but with an alternate meaning. An example of a fanciful mark would be "Kodak," which was coined for use in connection with photographic equipment.

111.   **Answer (A) is correct.** A trademark term that is a surname, such as "Dell" for computers (named for founder Michael Dell), is treated, for distinctiveness purposes, the same as a descriptive mark. *See* 15 U.S.C. § 1052 (e)–(f) (excluding from registration marks that are "merely descriptive" and those that are "primarily merely a surname," but allowing registration of either type of mark if it "has become distinctive of the applicant's goods in commerce"). To see why, first consider the full range of the "spectrum of distinctiveness," which refers to the degree to which a mark is distinctive and can thereby serve a source-indicating trademark function. The spectrum extends from unprotectable generic words at one end of the spectrum to descriptive terms (which can serve as a trademark, but only upon a showing of secondary meaning) to suggestive, arbitrary, and finally fanciful marks at the other end of the spectrum (which are considered the strongest type of marks). Marks are thus classified in categories of generally increasing distinctiveness. As set forth by Judge Friendly in *Abercrombie & Fitch Co. v. Hunting World, Inc.*, 537 F.2d 4 (2d Cir. 1976), marks can be (1) generic; (2) descriptive; (3) suggestive; (4) arbitrary; or (5) fanciful. Descriptive marks generally make some reference to a characteristic of the product, or service, or to its geographic location. Thus, a surname, which a consumer would often perceive as denoting the name of an individual connected to the product or the source, is considered, like terms describing a product characteristic, not to be inherently distinctive. It is therefore protected as a trademark only upon a showing of secondary meaning (i.e., acquired distinctiveness). Because the Dell trademark has been used for a long period of time and is very well known as a source of computer products, the Dell mark has sufficient secondary meaning to be protected under trademark law even though it is deemed to be not inherently distinctive.

Answer (B) is incorrect. To be suggestive, the mark must indirectly suggest a connection to the trademark (involving a leap of imagination); the mark in this scenario makes direct reference to the name of the founder of the company.

Answer (C) is incorrect. To be arbitrary, the mark must have no connection to the underlying product, such as "Apple" for computer products.

Answer (D) is incorrect. To be fanciful, the mark must be coined or "made up" for use as a trademark, such as Nikon cameras.

112. **Answer (C) is correct.** The trademark term "Camel" for cigarettes is arbitrary. To be arbitrary, the mark must have no connection to the underlying product, such as "Apple" for computer products. There is no particular connection between camels and cigarettes.

Answer (A) is incorrect. The term "camel" does not describe a characteristic of the cigarettes.

Answer (B) is incorrect. The term "camel" does not have an indirect connection to cigarettes involving a leap of imagination.

Answer (D) is incorrect. The term "camel" is not a coined term.

113. **Answer (D) is correct.** The trademark term "Exxon" for petroleum products is fanciful. It is a word coined specifically to be a trademark.

Answer (A) is incorrect. "Exxon" does not describe a characteristic of the gasoline.

Answer (B) is incorrect. The term "Exxon" does not have an indirect connection to gasoline.

Answer (C) is incorrect. Because "Exxon" is a coined term, it is not a preexisting word and has no connection to petroleum products.

114. **Answer (A) is correct.** The mark "7-Eleven," for a chain of convenience stores that were originally open during the hours of 7a.m.–11p.m. is descriptive. It describes a characteristic of the stores (at least at one time) — they were open from 7a.m. until 11p.m. Consider a business that wishes to open using the name "24/7" to describe the fact that it is open at all times — this too would be a descriptive term.

Answer (B) is incorrect. It does not take a leap of imagination to make the connection between the mark and the store hours.

Answer (C) is incorrect. The term "7-Eleven" does have a direct connection to a characteristic of the business, so it is not arbitrary.

Answer (D) is incorrect. The term "7-Eleven" is not a coined word.

115. **Answer (B) is correct.** The term "At-A-Glance" for calendars is suggestive — it suggests quick visibility but requires a small imaginative step to discern that the calendar might enable the buyer to see a given time period, such as a month, "at a glance." *See Cullman Ventures, Inc. v. Columbian Art Works, Inc.*, 717 F. Supp. 96, 119–20 (S.D.N.Y. 1989). This term is very nearly descriptive, but the best answer is (B).

Answer (A) is incorrect. As noted above, the term is suggestive, although this is the second-best answer.

Answer (C) is incorrect. The term "At-A-Glance" has an indirect connection to a characteristic of the business, so it is definitely not arbitrary.

Answer (D) is incorrect. The term "At-A-Glance" is not a coined word.

116. **Answer (D) is correct.** All three of these categories of marks are precluded from federal registration on the Principal Register: immoral marks, disparaging marks, and scandalous marks. Under the Lanham Act,

[n]o trademark by which the goods of the applicant may be distinguished from the goods of others shall be refused registration on the principal register on account of its nature unless it (a) consists of or comprises immoral, deceptive, or scandalous matter; or matter which may disparage or falsely suggest a connection with persons, living or dead, institutions, beliefs, or national symbols, or bring them into contempt, or disrepute. 15 U.S.C. § 1052(a).

Answer (A) is incorrect. As discussed above, the Lanham Act precludes registration of all three categories of marks identified in this question.

Answer (B) is incorrect. As discussed above, the Lanham Act precludes registration of all three categories of marks identified in this question.

Answer (C) is incorrect. As discussed above, the Lanham Act precludes registration of all three categories of marks identified in this question.

117.   **Answer (A) is correct.** The attempt to protect the color red for pills designed to treat blood conditions (that is, the pills themselves are red in color) presents a challenge in trademark law. This type of trademark application would most likely be unprotectable on grounds of functionality (i.e., aesthetically functional because the red color can help patients easily identify the type of medicine). The prohibition on functional trademarks was codified in the 1998 Trademark Amendments, but it had long been recognized in the case law. The trademark statute now states that "[i]n a civil action for trade dress infringement . . . for trade dress not registered on the principal register, the person who asserts trade dress protection has the burden of proving that the matter sought to be protected is not functional." 15 U.S.C. § 1125(a)(3). As the Court noted in *Inwood Laboratories, Inc. v. Ives Laboratories, Inc.*, 456 U.S. 844, 850 (1982), a product feature is deemed functional and cannot serve as a trademark, "if it is essential to the use or purpose of the article or if it affects the cost or quality of the article." In *Qualitex Co. v. Jacobson Products Co.*, 514 U.S. 159, 165 (1995), the Court added that a feature is functional if its exclusive use by one enterprise "would put competitors at a significant non-reputation-related disadvantage." In other words, a feature is functional, and thus unprotectable, if it is one of a limited number of efficient options available to competitors and therefore free competition would be unduly hindered by giving the design or feature trademark protection. The functionality doctrine helps prevent the stifling of competition by the exhaustion of a limited number of options for product packing or design. As the Court noted in *Qualitex*, at 164–65:

> The functionality doctrine prevents trademark law, which seeks to promote competition by protecting a firm's reputation, from instead inhibiting legitimate competition by allowing a producer to control a useful product feature. It is the province of patent law, not trademark law, to encourage invention by granting inventors a monopoly over new product designs or functions for a limited time, after which competitors are free to use the innovation. If a product's functional features could be used as trademarks, however, a monopoly over such features could be obtained without regard to whether they qualify as patents and could be extended forever (because trademarks may be renewed in perpetuity).

Answer (B) is incorrect. The color red, as discussed above, is likely functional for this product category and thus not protected under trademark law. Moreover, even if it were non-functional, a color standing alone has been deemed to be descriptive or otherwise non-inherently distinctive for purposes of trademark analysis. In *Qualitex Co. v. Jacobson*

Products Co., 519 U.S. 159, 164–65 (1995), the Court found that a green-gold color for dry cleaning and laundry press pads could qualify for trademark protection but only if it possessed secondary meaning. Owens Corning Co.'s pink fiberglass insulation would be an example of a nonfunctional and recognizable trademark consisting of a color alone.

Answer (C) is incorrect. The color red, as discussed above, is likely functional on these facts and thus not protected under trademark law.

Answer (D) is incorrect. As noted above, the color red is likely functional in this case. If it had been non-functional, then it would be analyzed like a descriptive mark because color alone is deemed not to be inherently distinctive. Thus, this is the second-best answer.

118.   **Answer (C) is correct.** Product packaging trade dress can be either non-inherently distinctive (and therefore protectable only upon a showing of secondary meaning) or inherently distinctive (protectable regardless of secondary meaning), just like an ordinary word mark. This rule is based on the Supreme Court's holdings in *Two Pesos, Inc. v. Taco Cabana, Inc.*, 505 U.S. 763 (1992), which held that the trade dress of a restaurant can be protected under section 43(a) of the Lanham Act if it is inherently distinctive, even in the absence of proof of secondary meaning (i.e., acquired distinctiveness) and in *Wal-Mart Stores, Inc., v. Samara Bros., Inc.*, 529 U.S. 205 (2000), which held that although packaging and restaurant trade dress can be (but are not always) inherently distinctive, product design trade dress is deemed never to be inherently distinctive. In *Two Pesos*, the Court offered two definitions of trade dress. In general, "[t]he 'trade dress' of a product is essentially its total image and overall appearance. It involves the total image of a product and may include features such as size, shape, color or color combinations, texture, graphics, or even particular sales techniques." A second definition, focusing on the particular restaurant setting at issue in that case, is

> the total image of the business. Taco Cabana's trade dress may include the shape and general appearance of the exterior of the restaurant, the identifying sign, the interior kitchen floor plan, the decor, the menu, the equipment used to serve food, the servers' uniforms and other features reflecting on the total image of the restaurant.

Id. at 764 n.1.

Answer (A) is incorrect. The basic holding of *Two Pesos v. Taco Cabana* is that product packaging trade dress is categorized in the same manner as other types of marks, such as word marks. Thus, the trade dress could fall anywhere on the spectrum of distinctiveness. It is therefore incorrect to state that they are always inherently distinctive.

Answer (B) is incorrect. As noted above, the basic holding of *Two Pesos v. Taco Cabana* is that product packaging trade dress is categorized in the same manner as other types of marks, such as word marks. Thus, the trade dress could fall anywhere on the spectrum of distinctiveness. It is therefore incorrect to state that packaging trade dress is never inherently distinctive. It is true that the Court in *Qualitex*, discussed above, did find that a color mark, standing alone, is considered non-inherently distinctive.

Answer (D) is incorrect. It is clear from the Court's rulings that packaging trade dress can be protected under an ordinary trademark analysis. Thus, it is incorrect to state that only trade dress that has become famous can be protected (and then only under a dilution theory).

119.   **Answer (B) is correct.** A product configuration or product design trade dress is never inherently distinctive; it is deemed never to be inherently distinctive, and hence protectable only upon a showing of secondary meaning. This statement of the law is based on the Supreme Court's holding in *Wal-Mart Stores, Inc. v. Samara Bros., Inc.*, 529 U.S. 205 (2000). The Court specifically held that a product design (in this instance, children's dress designs) cannot be inherently distinctive, and therefore can be protected (whether registered or unregistered) only upon a showing of secondary meaning (i.e., acquired distinctiveness). The Court distinguished *Two Pesos v. Taco Cabana* based on the differences between product design and packaging trade dress:

> It seems to us that design, like color, is not inherently distinctive. The attribution of inherent distinctiveness to certain categories of word marks and product packaging derives from the fact that the very purpose of attaching a particular word to a product, or encasing it in a distinctive packaging, is most often to identify the source of the product. Although the words and packaging can serve subsidiary functions — a suggestive word mark (such as "Tide" for laundry detergent), for instance, may invoke positive connotations in the consumer's mind, and a garish form of packaging (such as Tide's squat, brightly decorated plastic bottles for its liquid laundry detergent) may attract an otherwise indifferent consumer's attention on a crowded store shelf — their predominant function remains source identification. Consumers are therefore predisposed to regard those symbols as indication of the producer, which is why such symbols "almost automatically tell a customer that they refer to a brand," and "immediately . . . signal a brand or a product 'source.' " And where it is not reasonable to assume consumer predisposition to take an affixed word or packaging as indication of source — where, for example, the affixed word is descriptive of the product ("Tasty" bread) or of a geographic origin ("Georgia" peaches) — inherent distinctiveness will not be found. In the case of product design, as in the case of color, we think consumer predisposition to equate the feature with the source does not exist. Consumers are aware of the reality that, almost invariably, even the most unusual of product designs — such as a cocktail shaker shaped like a penguin — is intended not to identify the source, but to render the product itself more useful or more appealing. The fact that product design almost invariably serves purposes other than source identification not only renders inherent distinctiveness problematic; it also renders application of an inherent distinctiveness principle more harmful to other consumer interests. Consumers should not be deprived of the benefits of competition with regard to the utilitarian and esthetic purposes that product design ordinarily serves by a rule of law that facilitates plausible threats of suit against new entrants based upon alleged inherent distinctiveness.

Wal-Mart Stores v. Samara, 529 U.S. 205 (2000).

Answer (A) is incorrect. As discussed above, the Court's ruling in *Wal-Mart Stores v. Samara* directly contradicts the statement that product configurations are always inherently distinctive and are therefore protectable regardless of secondary meaning.

Answer (C) is incorrect. Although this statement is true as to product packaging trade dress cases, the Court's ruling in *Wal-Mart Stores v. Samara* specifically rejects this approach for product configurations or product design trade dress.

Answer (D) is incorrect. Although secondary meaning is required to protect a product configuration as a trademark, it is not necessary for it to achieve fame. The "fame" standard does apply to dilution cases, but product configurations are protectable on the ordinary showing of secondary meaning.

120.   **Answer (A) is correct.** FedEx Corp. offers shipping services, but it also sells large numbers of caps, pens, and t-shirts bearing its logo (some are given away as well). Accordingly, FedEx can obtain trademarks for the goods it sells, as well as service marks for its shipping business. The company is offering bona fide products for sale in commerce, as well as services. There is no prohibition on obtaining both types of registrations for marks used both in goods markets and service markets. This scenario can be distinguished from that found in *In re Dr. Pepper Co.*, 836 F.2d 508 (Fed. Cir. 1987), in which the Federal Circuit held that trademark owners who use a mark for purely promotional purposes are ineligible for service mark protection for that mark because they have not made a bona fide use of the mark to sell a service.

Answer (B) is incorrect. Neither the trademark nor the service mark qualifies as "collective marks," a term that is discussed below in the answer to Question 122.

Answer (C) is incorrect. As noted above, there is no prohibition on obtaining both types of registrations for marks used to make bona fide sales in both goods markets and service markets.

Answer (D) is incorrect. The facts indicate that the mark is used to sell goods, not merely for promotional purposes. Even though some goods are given away (and are thus promotional in nature), other goods are clearly sold for profit-making purposes.

121.   **Answer (B) is correct.** The trademark term "UL Listed" (Underwriter's Labs) is a certification mark. The Lanham Act defines a certification mark as a mark "used upon or in connection with the products or services of one or more persons other than the owner of the mark to certify regional or other origin, material, mode of manufacture, quality, accuracy or other characteristics of such goods or services." 15 U.S.C. § 1127. Here, the "UL Listed" mark serves to certify that products sold by third parties (i.e., not sold directly by Underwriter's Labs) meet certain safety standards set by UL. The Lanham Act provides that certification marks (as well as collective marks) may be registered:

> Subject to the provisions relating to the registration of trademarks, so far as they are applicable, collective and certification marks, including indications of regional origin, shall be registrable under this Act, in the same manner and with the same effect as are trademarks, by persons, and nations, States, municipalities, and the like, exercising legitimate control over the use of the marks sought to be registered, even though not possessing an industrial or commercial establishment, and when registered they shall be entitled to the protection provided herein in the case of trademarks, except in the case of certification marks when used so as to represent falsely that the owner or a user thereof makes or sells the goods or performs the services on or in connection with which such mark is used. Applications and procedure under this section shall conform as nearly as practicable to those prescribed for the registration of trademarks.

15 U.S.C. § 1054.

Answer (A) is incorrect. This mark is not deceptive under these limited facts (i.e., used to mislead consumers), though such a claim was made and rejected in *Midwest Plastic Fabricators, Inc. v. Underwriters Laboratories, Inc.*, 906 F.2d 1568 (Fed. Cir. 1990). At issue in that case was the sufficiency of UL's testing and quality assurance process.

Answer (C) is incorrect. Certification marks and collective marks are somewhat similar, but UL is not a collective organization, as discussed in the next question below.

Answer (D) is incorrect. UL does not offer services for sale, but rather offers certification of other companies' products.

122.   The Lanham Act states that a collective mark:

> means a trademark or service mark — (1) used by the members of a cooperative, an association, or other collective group or organization, or (2) which such cooperative, association, or other collective group or organization has a bona fide intention to use in commerce and applies to register on the principal register established by this Act, and includes marks indicating membership in a union, an association, or other organization.

15 U.S.C. § 1127. An example of a collective mark is the Professional Golfers Association ("PGA"). A key distinction between a collective mark and a certification mark is that the former involves a membership organization whose members offer goods or services for sale, whereas the latter does not offer any goods or services but instead serves as a neutral third party certifying or vouching for the goods or services of others.

123.   The trademark incontestability doctrine prevents challenges to the ownership and validity of trademarks (with certain exceptions), and it applies only to marks that have been registered and continuously used without successful challenge for five years, and for which an affidavit of incontestability has been filed. As stated in the Lanham Act,

> Except on a ground for which application to cancel may be filed at any time under paragraphs (3) and (5) of section 14 of this Act [15 U.S.C. § 1064(3), (5)], and except to the extent, if any, to which the use of a mark registered on the principal register infringes a valid right acquired under the law of any State or Territory by use of a mark or trade name continuing from a date prior to the date of registration under this Act of such registered mark, the right of the registrant to use such registered mark in commerce for the goods or services on or in connection with which such registered mark has been in continuous use for five consecutive years subsequent to the date of such registration and is still in use in commerce, shall be incontestable.

15 U.S.C. § 1065. The preserved defenses to a claim of infringement of an incontestable mark are provided in section 33(b). 15 U.S.C. § 1115(b). There are four qualifications that must be satisfied to attain incontestable status:

> (1) there has been no final decision adverse to registrant's claim of ownership of such mark for such goods or services, or to registrant's right to register the same or to keep the same on the register; and (2) there is no proceeding involving said rights pending in the Patent and Trademark Office or in a court and not finally disposed of; and (3) an affidavit is filed with the Director within one year after the expiration of any such five-year period setting forth those goods or services stated in the registration on or in connection with which such mark has been in continuous use for such five consecutive years and is still in use in commerce, and the other matters specified in paragraphs (1) and (2) of this section; and (4) no incontestable right shall be acquired in a mark which is the generic name for the goods or services or a portion

thereof, for which it is registered.

Id. More information on validity challenges to incontestable registrations can be found in the answer to Question 141 in Topic 12.

124. **Answer (A) is correct.** Under the common law, trademark rights are established through bona fide public use in the marketplace. The essence of trademark ownership is use of the mark in connection with goods or services in a manner that builds consumer recognition in the marketplace. As Judge Easterbrook suggested in *Scandia Down Corp. v. Euroquilt, Inc.*, 772 F.2d 1423, 1429–30 (7th Cir. 1985), "[t]rademarks help consumers to select goods."

   Answer (B) is incorrect. Registration with the state trademark or secretary of state's office can serve to register a claim to trademark rights, but the common law method of establishing ownership remains actual use in the marketplace.

   Answer (C) is incorrect. A successful suit for unfair competition against a competitor might be the result of establishing ownership rights in a mark, but it is not how trademark ownership is established as a preliminary matter.

   Answer (D) is incorrect. As discussed above, trademark rights are established through bona fide public use in the marketplace. Registration with a state can sometimes bolster those rights state-wide, and filing suit is a way to enforce those rights.

125. **Answer (C) is correct.** Priority over others as to trademark ownership under the Lanham Act can be attained through use in commerce or filing an application with bona fide intent to use (upon following the proper procedures to establish actual use in commerce). The amended language in the Lanham Act, codified at 15 U.S.C. § 1051(b) states as follows:

    > (1) A person who has a bona fide intention, under circumstances showing the good faith of such person, to use a trademark in commerce may request registration of its trademark on the principal register hereby established by paying the prescribed fee and filing in the Patent and Trademark Office an application and a verified statement, in such form as may be prescribed by the Director.

    > (2) The application shall include specification of the applicant's domicile and citizenship, the goods in connection with which the applicant has a bona fide intention to use the mark, and a drawing of the mark.

    > (3) The statement shall be verified by the applicant and specify—

    > (A) that the person making the verification believes that he or she, or the juristic person in whose behalf he or she makes the verification, to be entitled to use the mark in commerce;

    > (B) the applicant's bona fide intention to use the mark in commerce;

    > (C) that, to the best of the verifier's knowledge and belief, the facts recited in the application are accurate; and

(D) that, to the best of the verifier's knowledge and belief, no other person has the right to use such mark in commerce either in the identical form thereof or in such near resemblance thereto as to be likely, when used on or in connection with the goods of such other person, to cause confusion, or to cause mistake, or to deceive.

Except for applications filed pursuant to section 1126 of this title, no mark shall be registered until the applicant has met the requirements of subsections (c) and (d) of this section.

(4) The applicant shall comply with such rules or regulations as may be prescribed by the Director. The Director shall promulgate rules prescribing the requirements for the application and for obtaining a filing date herein.

Answer (A) is incorrect. Traditionally, use in commerce was the only method of obtaining priority under federal trademark law, but this has been altered with the intent-to-use process.

Answer (B) is incorrect. Priority under the intent-to-use application is not fully established until actual use in commerce takes place, a statement of use is properly filed and accepted, and a registration issues.

Answer (D) is incorrect. As noted above, priority under the intent-to-use application is not fully established until actual use in commerce takes place, a statement of use is properly filed and accepted, and a registration issues.

126.   **Answer (C) is correct.** Company B will own the rights to the mark because it filed the intent-to-use application before A used the mark and ultimately received the notice of allowance. This is true even though Company A developed the coined trademark first and used the mark before Company B used it. The critical facts are that Company B filed an intent-to-use (or "ITU") application before any use in commerce by Company A. Given that Company B received a notice of allowance and proceeded to make its own use in commerce in timely fashion, it has perfected its rights under the ITU application process and will receive all rights to the mark under federal law. Moreover, there is no evidence that Company B acted in bad faith.

Answer (A) is incorrect. Neither the common law nor the Lanham Act gives priority for simply coming up with a mark, though a new user of a mark in a market is often given a window in which to develop trademark rights before others can appropriate it. Even this narrow window is limited in time and scope under the common law. *See generally Galt House, Inc. v. Home Supply, Inc.*, 483 S.W.2d 107 (Ky. Ct. App. 1972). The ITU provisions here would trump any common law claim on these facts.

Answer (B) is incorrect. Under the common law and traditional trademark principles, Company A would have obtained the rights, at least on the West Coast, because it was the first to make bona fide use of the trademark there. *See, e.g., Blue Bell, Inc. v. Farah Manufacturing Co.*, 508 F.2d 1260 (5th Cir. 1975). As discussed above, however, the ITU process changes this analysis when another party has properly and in good faith made use of its provisions, as in this case.

Answer (D) is incorrect. No division of rights would be available in this situation. In this situation, the ITU provision would definitively assign the rights across the U.S. to Company B.

127. **Answer (C) is correct.** Company A obtains all rights to the trademark nationwide, except that Company B has exclusive rights state-wide in Arkansas and Tennessee. These facts present an illustration of the limited-area exception under the Lanham Act. The critical facts in this case are that Company A was both first to use the mark and then file to federally register in 2010, at which point Company B had only state-wide operations in Arkansas and Tennessee, which it began in good faith without knowledge or A's mark. The Lanham Act gives Company A nationwide priority, except for geographic areas in which Company B already had ongoing operations at the time of the registration. Company B, therefore, enjoys the benefit of the limited-area exception, which allows it to continue doing business in the geographic areas where it had established goodwill — in this instance, the entire states of Arkansas and Tennessee. Company B is not permitted to expand its operations into other parts of the country and is effectively frozen into its present locations. (If Company B had only been actively doing business in a smaller area, such as the Nashville, Tennessee metropolitan area, then it would be limited to that smaller area.) The governing provision of the Lanham Act states:

> To the extent that the right to use the registered mark has become incontestable under section 15, the registration shall be conclusive evidence of the validity of the registered mark and of the registration of the mark, of the registrant's ownership of the mark, and of the registrant's exclusive right to use the registered mark in commerce. . . . Such conclusive evidence of the right to use the registered mark shall be subject to proof of infringement as defined in section 32, and shall be subject to the following defenses or defects:
>
> . . . .
>
> (5) That the mark whose use by a party is charged as an infringement was adopted without knowledge of the registrant's prior use and has been continuously used by such party or those in privity with him from a date prior to (A) the date of constructive use of the mark established pursuant to section 7(c), (B) the registration of the mark under this Act if the application for registration is filed before the effective date of the Trademark Law Revision Act of 1988, or (C) publication of the registered mark under subsection (c) of section 12 of this Act: Provided, however, That this defense or defect shall apply only for the area in which such continuous prior use is proved.

15 U.S.C. § 1115(b). Although Company A's mark is not noted to be incontestable, it will be subject to at least those defenses to which an incontestable mark is subject.

Answer (A) is incorrect. As discussed above, there is a carve-out based on the limited-area exception for Company B, which was doing business in two states before A's federal registration.

Answer (B) is incorrect. The limited-area exception gives Company B exclusive rights in its market area — to allow both companies to operate in the same geographic and product market would cause significant consumer confusion.

Answer (D) is incorrect. This answer ignores the nationwide rights that Company A obtains by virtue of its registration, except for areas within the limited-area exception. This answer would have been correct under the common law, without any federal filings.

128. **Answer (D) is correct.** The term of protection for trademarks under the Lanham Act can be

perpetual as long as the trademark has not been abandoned and has not become generic. Subject to requirements for trademark registration renewal, there is no time limit on the duration of a trademark. Essentially, as long as it continues to function as a source indicator, it is eligible for continued protection. Unlike patents and copyrights, which have a Constitutional restriction on their duration (the "limited times" provision of the Intellectual Property Clause), there is no similar limit on congressional authority under the Commerce Clause — the constitutional basis for trademark protection. Despite this potential for perpetual protection, a trademark can always be challenged on grounds that it has been abandoned or has become generic. *See* 15 U.S.C. §§ 1059 (providing no limit on the number of times a registration may be renewed), 1064(3) (allowing a cancellation petition to be filed at any time if the mark has become generic or is abandoned), & 1115 (preserving abandonment and genericness as defenses to any action for infringement of a registered trademark).

Answer (A) is incorrect. There is no 50-year "term" for trademark protection.

Answer (B) is incorrect. This statement overstates the potentially perpetual existence of trademarks, particularly because a trademark can always be challenged on grounds that it has been abandoned or has become generic.

Answer (C) is incorrect. This statement is the second-best answer, but it ignores the potential challenge that can be made if a trademark has become generic.

129.   **Answer (D) is correct.** A trademark becomes incontestable under the Lanham Act when it is registered under federal law and continuously used for five years and an affidavit of incontestability has been filed. These points are found in the plain language of the statute:

> The right of the owner to use such registered mark in commerce for the goods or services on or in connection with which such registered mark has been in continuous use for five consecutive years subsequent to the date of such registration and is still in use in commerce, shall be incontestable, provided that . . . (3) an affidavit is filed within one year after the expiration of any such five-year period setting for the [certain required information related to use and lack of legal proceedings adverse to the claim of ownership].

15 U.S.C. § 1065.

Answer (A) is incorrect. The focus of incontestability is registration, not merely use.

Answer (B) is incorrect. As noted above, the focus of incontestability is registration, not merely use.

Answer (C) is incorrect. By its terms, as noted above, the statute requires five years of registration and continuous use, as well as the filing of the required affidavit.

130.   The typical elements of the likelihood of confusion test are found in the Second Circuit's decision in *Polaroid Corp. v. Polarad Electronics Corp.*, 287 F.2d 492, 495 (2d Cir. 1961), which set forth a multi-factor balancing test for determining the likelihood of confusion: (1) the strength of the mark; (2) the degree of similarity between the two marks; (3) the marketplace proximity of the two marks; (4) the likelihood that the senior user of the mark will bridge the gap; (5) evidence of actual confusion; (6) the junior user's bad faith in adopting the mark; (7) the quality of the junior user's mark; and (8) the sophistication of the relevant consumer group. Other circuits apply varying formulations of the balancing test, with most of the same *Polaroid* factors included in the analysis. Additional factors considered by some circuits include the degree of purchaser care and the similarity of marketing channels. In order to establish a claim of unfair competition or trademark infringement, the trademark owner must ultimately show a likelihood that ordinary purchasers will be confused regarding the source, sponsorship, or origin of the goods or services in question. This crucial standard applies to cases of infringement of registered trademarks (under section 32 of the Lanham Act, 15 U.S.C. § 1114) and of unregistered trademarks, which are protected under section 43(a) of the Lanham Act, 15 U.S.C. § 1125. The likelihood of confusion standard is also frequently applied in cases of unfair competition and other state law trademark theories.

131.   **Answer (D) is correct.** Circuits are split on whether the analysis of likelihood of confusion is a question of fact or a "mixed question of law and fact." If it is an issue of fact, then an assessment of the individual factors and the overall balancing of all factors is left to the fact-finder, ordinarily a jury. If it is a mixed question of law and fact, then each of the individual confusion factors are fact issues, while the final weighing or balancing of the factors is an issue of law for the court. It is important to note that the standard of review for appeals of likelihood of confusion determinations is also affected by this issue. If it is a fact issue, then district court determinations will only be overturned if clearly erroneous. On the other hand, if it is a mixed question of law and fact, then the appellate court would review the legal determination de novo, with no deference given to the lower court's judgment on the ultimate issue of law — the balancing of the factors.

   Answer (A) is incorrect. As discussed above, courts are split on this issue.

   Answer (B) is incorrect. No court has taken the view that the standard is purely a matter of law, given that the underlying confusion factors clearly involve factual determinations.

   Answer (C) is incorrect. As discussed above, courts are split on this issue.

132.   **Answer (C) is correct.** Proof of actual confusion in trademark cases is not required, but if it is proven it is persuasive evidence of a likelihood of confusion. Actual confusion can be shown directly by proof that consumers were in fact confused as to the source or sponsorship of the

goods or services or indirectly through the use of survey evidence. Thus, if the trademark plaintiff can bring forward this type of evidence, it is a persuasive indicator of the likelihood of confusion. On the other hand, the plaintiff is not required to prove actual confusion, as the ultimate question is whether there is a likelihood of confusion among ordinary consumers.

Answer (A) is incorrect. As discussed above, the plaintiff is not required to prove actual confusion, as the ultimate question is whether there is a likelihood of confusion among ordinary consumers.

Answer (B) is incorrect. Actual confusion is not one of the less important factors in a likelihood of confusion analysis. As discussed above, it can be highly probative of a likelihood of confusion.

Answer (D) is incorrect. In most cases, actual confusion is not easily shown. It requires rather precise testimony from consumers (which can only occur if the defendant has already begun selling in the marketplace) or quite expensive and intricately designed survey evidence. A single instance of actual confusion, a poorly constructed survey, or a survey showing very low percentages of confusion (such as five percent) would be insufficient to show actual confusion.

133.   A trademark plaintiff can prove actual confusion directly by presenting evidence that consumers were in fact confused as to the source or sponsorship of the goods or services, via affidavit, deposition, or live testimony by those consumers, depending on the circumstances, or indirectly through the use of survey evidence. The central point is that if a substantial number of consumers were in fact confused, then there is a high likelihood of actual confusion. Thus, if the plaintiff can show a meaningful number of instances in which consumers did in fact have confusion as to the source or sponsorship of the goods or services, actual confusion is established. If this proof is absent, as is often the case for a variety of reasons, the plaintiff can conduct a survey of ordinary and relevant potential purchasers. The survey must have a meaningful number of participants who are potential purchasers. Moreover, the survey must be written and conducted properly so as to elicit useful responses — for example, it should not have leading questions. It is unsettled whether any particular percentage of consumers in a survey must be shown to have been confused as to source or sponsorship to establish actual confusion. Valid surveys showing more than 25% confusion are given great weight. *See, e.g., Piper Aircraft Corp. v. WagAero, Inc.*, 741 F.2d 925 (7th Cir. 1984) (45%); *Union Carbide Corp. v. Ever-Ready, Inc.*, 531 F.2d 366 (7th Cir.) (over 50%), *cert. denied*, 429 U.S. 830 (1976); *A.T. Cross Co. v. TPM Distributing, Inc.*, 1985 U.S. Dist. LEXIS 18805 (D. Minn. June 19, 1985) (34–43%); *McDonald's Corp. v. McBagel's, Inc.*, 649 F. Supp. 1268 (S.D.N.Y. 1986) (25%). Some courts have found relatively low percentages to be sufficient to show confusion, including percentages as low as 11, 15, 16, and 20%. *See RJR Foods, Inc. v. White Rock Corp.*, 603 F.2d 1058 (2d Cir. 1979) (15 to 20%); *James Burrough, Ltd. v. Sign of Beefeater, Inc.*, 540 F.2d 266 (7th Cir. 1976) (15%); *Humble Oil & Refining Co. v. American Oil Co.*, 405 F.2d 803 (8th Cir.), *cert. denied*, 395 U.S. 905 (1969); *Quality Inns International, Inc. v. McDonald's Corp.*, 695 F. Supp. 198 (D. Md. 1988) (16%). Surveys showing less than 10% confusion have generally been deemed insufficient to show actual confusion (and are likely to be adduced by the defendant in order to negate actual confusion). *See, e.g., Henri's Food Products Co. v. Kraft, Inc.*, 717 F.2d 352 (7th Cir. 1983) (7.6% confusion found in defendant's survey; plaintiff did not present survey evidence); *Weight Watchers International, Inc. v. Stouffer Corp.*, 744 F. Supp. 1259 (S.D.N.Y. 1990) (nine percent confusion deemed insufficient); *G. Heileman Brewing Co. v. Anheuser-Busch,*

Inc., 676 F. Supp. 1436 (E.D. Wis. 1987) (survey showing 4.5% actual confusion weighs against finding likelihood of confusion), *aff'd*, 873 F.2d 985 (7th Cir. 1989); *Wuv's International, Inc. v. Love's Enterprises, Inc.*, 1980 U.S. Dist. LEXIS 16512 (D. Colo. Nov. 4, 1980) (9% insufficient). As noted above, if the trademark plaintiff can bring forward this type of evidence of actual confusion, it is a persuasive indicator of the likelihood of confusion.

134. **Answer (D) is correct.** A trademark owner that has not obtained federal registration for its trademark can bring suit for all relief available under section 43(a) of the Lanham Act, 15 U.S.C. § 1125, but does not have other statutory rights that a registered trademark holder would have. Claims for infringement of a registered trademark can be brought under section 32 of the Lanham Act, 15 U.S.C. § 1114, but section 43(a) permits claims for both registered and unregistered trademarks. Section 43(a) states in relevant part:

> Any person who, on or in connection with any goods or services, or any container for goods, uses in commerce any word, term, name, symbol, or device, or any combination thereof, or any false designation of origin, false or misleading description of fact, or false or misleading representation of fact, which—
>
> (A) is likely to cause confusion, or to cause mistake, or to deceive as to the affiliation, connection, or association of such person with another person, or as to the origin, sponsorship, or approval of his or her goods, services, or commercial activities by another person, or
>
> (B) in commercial advertising or promotion, misrepresents the nature, characteristics, qualities, or geographic origin of his or her or another person's goods, services, or commercial activities,
>
> shall be liable in a civil action by any person who believes that he or she is or is likely to be damaged by such act.

15 U.S.C. § 1125. A plaintiff bringing suit under section 43(a) can recover monetary and injunctive relief. There are statutory benefits to federal registration of a trademark, including evidentiary benefits under section 33(a) of the Lanham Act (15 U.S.C. § 1115(a)), nationwide constructive use under section 7 (15 U.S.C. § 1057), and incontestability under section 15 (15 U.S.C. § 1065). A registration serves as prima facie evidence of the mark's validity, the registrant's ownership of the mark, and the registrant's exclusive right to use the mark in commerce in connection with the listed goods or services. The constructive use provision provides nationwide priority in the mark as of the filing date, and the constructive notice provision, 15 U.S.C. § 1072, means that the registration serves as notice to all junior (i.e., subsequent) users as of the registration date. The federal registrant secures rights to its mark throughout the country, enabling it to bar any later users, as well as to "freeze" any prior users in their then-existing markets under the limited-area exception. See answer to Question 127 in Topic 10. The benefits of incontestability are addressed in the answers to Question 123 in Topic 9 and Question 141 in Topic 12.

Answer (A) is incorrect. The trademark owner does not have the statutory benefits to federal registration, including constructive notice and incontestability.

Answer (B) is incorrect. The trademark owner is not limited to injunctive relief; monetary remedies are available as well.

Answer (C) is incorrect. Registration of the mark is not a condition precedent to suit in trademark litigation under section 43(a).

135.   **Answer (D) is correct.** The following statement most accurately describes the approach taken by federal trademark law to questions of remedies — injunctive relief is frequently granted, and money damages are available upon a showing of bad faith or actual harm. Injunctive relief is available under section 34 of the Lanham Act, 15 U.S.C. § 1116(a), which states:

> The several courts vested with jurisdiction of civil actions arising under this chapter shall have power to grant injunctions, according to the principles of equity and upon such terms as the court may deem reasonable, to prevent the violation of any right of the registrant of a mark registered in the Patent and Trademark Office or to prevent a violation under subsection (a), (c), or (d) of section 1125 of this title.

The Lanham Act also provides for monetary relief:

> When a violation of any right of the registrant of a mark registered in the Patent and Trademark Office, or a violation under section 1125(a) of this title, shall have been established in any civil action arising under this chapter, the plaintiff shall be entitled, subject to the provisions of sections 1111 and 1114 of this title, and subject to the principles of equity, to recover (1) defendant's profits, (2) any damages sustained by the plaintiff, and (3) the costs of the action. The court shall assess such profits and damages or cause the same to be assessed under its direction. In assessing profits the plaintiff shall be required to prove defendant's sales only; defendant must prove all elements of cost or deduction claimed. In assessing damages the court may enter judgment, according to the circumstances of the case, for any sum above the amount found as actual damages, not exceeding three times such amount. If the court shall find that the amount of the recovery based on profits is either inadequate or excessive the court may in its discretion enter judgment for such sum as the court shall find to be just, according to the circumstances of the case. Such sum in either of the above circumstances shall constitute compensation and not a penalty.

15 U.S.C. § 1117(a). The basic principle of causation serves to limit "any damages sustained by the plaintiff" to require proof of actual harm. Courts have also generally interpreted "subject to the principles of equity" to mean that "defendant's profits" are only obtainable when the trademark owner has shown actual confusion (in which case it is reasonable to presume defendant's profits were the result of the confusion and should be paid to the plaintiff) or bad faith (which makes it appropriate to award the profits to the plaintiff owner of the mark).

Answer (A) is incorrect. There is no presumption in favor of monetary relief, and injunctions are frequently granted.

Answer (B) is incorrect. There is no presumption in favor of injunctive relief, and money damages are awarded when the evidence supports it — and not only in "exceptional" cases. Attorney's fees, on the other hand, are only available "in exceptional cases." 15 U.S.C. § 1117 (a).

Answer (C) is incorrect. As noted above, monetary damages are available upon a showing of bad faith or actual harm.

136.   Corrective advertising is a form of damages recoverable by plaintiffs in order to correct any false and misleading impression created by the defendant's false or confusingly similar advertising. For example, in *U-Haul International, Inc. v. Jartran, Inc.*, 793 F.2d 1034 (9th

Cir. 1986), the plaintiff recovered $13.6 million in corrective advertising, which easily exceeded the original $6 million expended by the defendant in its alleged false advertising campaign. The court concluded that the role of the expensive advertising campaign was needed to correct harm that had been done to the U-Haul trademark. In *ALPO Petfoods, Inc. v. Ralston Purina Co.*, 997 F.2d 949 (D.C. Cir. 1993), the court upheld a $3.6 million award for corrective advertising to compensate for the cost of reasonably responding to the defendant's advertisements.

137.   Under the Lanham Act, attorney's fees can be obtained in trademark litigation as follows: "The court in exceptional cases may award reasonable attorney fees to the prevailing party." 15 U.S.C. § 1117(a). Thus, attorney's fees are typically awarded in cases of intentional or willful conduct, fraud, or litigation misconduct. *See, e.g., Taco Cabana International, Inc. v. Two Pesos, Inc.*, 932 F.2d 1113, 1127–28 (5th Cir. 1991) (awarding $940,000 in attorney's fees for intentional copying of trade dress).

138.   **Answer (D) is correct.** The strongest theory for infringement of a long-standing and widely known trademark such as "Nike" when used by someone in a totally unrelated field of enterprise, such as a taco stand, is dilution by blurring. Because of the wide disparity in the product markets in this situation, proving a likelihood of confusion is difficult. A theory of dilution resulting from blurring the selling power of the famous Nike mark is therefore a stronger claim than the theory that there was confusion as to source or sponsorship of the defendant's taco stand. Even if the ordinary consumer would not be confused, the distinctive quality of the plaintiff's famous brand name is damaged when the name is used to market unrelated products or services. Over time, if these uses were allowed to proceed unabated, the term Nike, when used as a mark, would no longer automatically bring to mind the maker of athletic shoes and accessories. To address the potential loss of selling power of marks in these situations, some states enacted trademark dilution statutes, allowing relief when a distinctive or famous trademark was blurred or tarnished by the use of a substantially similar or identical mark, even in the absence of a showing of consumer confusion or direct competition in the plaintiff's market. In 1995, Congress enacted the federal Trademark Dilution Act, which made the dilution doctrine a matter of federal trademark law. The federal act requires that a mark be "famous" in order to receive protection from dilution. Some states also require fame, but only within the state, while others do not include "famous" mark status in the statute (although judges typically still view unusual mark strength as a requirement. *See, e.g., Sally Gee, Inc. v. Myra Hogan, Inc.*, 699 F. 2d 621, 625 (2d Cir. 1983) (stating that New York antidilution law protected "only extremely strong marks"). The federal dilution law, as amended in 2006, states:

> Subject to the principles of equity, the owner of a famous mark that is distinctive, inherently or through acquired distinctiveness, shall be entitled to an injunction against another person who, at any time after the owner's mark has become famous, commences use of a mark or trade name in commerce that is likely to cause dilution by blurring or dilution by tarnishment of the famous mark, regardless of the presence or absence of actual or likely confusion, of competition, or of actual economic injury.

15 U.S.C. § 1125(c)(1).

Answer (A) is incorrect. A state law unfair competition claim is clearly not the strongest claim on these facts — it generally requires a showing of a likelihood of confusion and may offer less satisfactory remedies than a federal claim (depending on applicable state law). Given the wide disparity in the product markets at issue here, proving a likelihood of confusion is difficult.

Answer (B) is incorrect. A federal trademark infringement claim is not the strongest claim on these facts — it requires a showing of a likelihood of confusion, as discussed above.

Answer (C) is incorrect. A claim of dilution by tarnishment requires a negative association with the famous mark, which is unlikely to be shown on these facts.

139.   Section 43(c)(2)(A) of the Lanham Act sets forth factors for determining whether a mark is famous for purposes of federal dilution law:

> For purposes of paragraph (1), a mark is famous if it is widely recognized by the general consuming public of the United States as a designation of source of the goods or services of the mark's owner. In determining whether a mark possesses the requisite degree of recognition, the court may consider all relevant factors, including the following:

> (i) The duration, extent, and geographic reach of advertising and publicity of the mark, whether advertised or publicized by the owner or third parties.

> (ii) The amount, volume, and geographic extent of sales of goods or services offered under the mark.

> (iii) The extent of actual recognition of the mark.

> (iv) Whether the mark was registered under the Act of March 3, 1881, or the Act of February 20, 1905, or on the principal register.

15 U.S.C. § 1125(c)(2)(A). Under this standard for fame, a mark must be widely known by the general consuming public in the U.S., not within a narrow group of specialty consumers or in a small geographic area, in order to receive protection against dilution. *See, e.g., Cosi, Inc. v. WK Holdings, LLC.*, 2007 U.S. Dist. LEXIS 31990 (D. Minn. May 1,) (Cosi restaurant mark not sufficiently famous); *Milbank Tweed Hadley & McCoy LLP v. Milbank Holding Corp.*, 82 U.S.P.Q.2D 1583 (C.D. Cal. 2007) (Milbank Tweed law firm's Milbank mark not sufficiently famous).

140.   Claims of trademark dilution by tarnishment and dilution by blurring are distinct, although both are actionable under the federal TDRA and under most state dilution statutes. A theory of dilution resulting from blurring the selling power of a famous mark involves damage to the distinctive quality of the plaintiff's famous brand name when the name is used to market unrelated products or services. Over time, if these uses were allowed to proceed unabated, the famous mark would no longer automatically bring to mind the plaintiff, with a resulting loss of selling power. The TDRA delineates the factors relevant to a blurring claim:

> For purposes of paragraph (1), "dilution by blurring" is association arising from the similarity between a mark or trade name and a famous mark that impairs the distinctiveness of the famous mark. In determining whether a mark or trade name is likely to cause dilution by blurring, the court may consider all relevant factors, including the following:

> (i) The degree of similarity between the mark or trade name and the famous mark.

> (ii) The degree of inherent or acquired distinctiveness of the famous mark.

(iii) The extent to which the owner of the famous mark is engaging in substantially exclusive use of the mark.

(iv) The degree of recognition of the famous mark.

(v) Whether the user of the mark or trade name intended to create an association with the famous mark.

(vi) Any actual association between the mark or trade name and the famous mark.

15 U.S.C. § 1125(c)(2)(B). A claim of dilution by tarnishment, on the other hand, requires a harmful negative association with the famous mark: "For purposes of paragraph (1), 'dilution by tarnishment' is association arising from the similarity between a mark or trade name and a famous mark that harms the reputation of the famous mark." 15 U.S.C. § 1125(c)(2)(C). Tarnishment cases can involve use of the famous mark in settings involving illegal drugs, pornography, and other unsavory material. *See generally Coca-Cola Co. v. Gemini Rising, Inc.*, 346 F. Supp. 1183 (E.D.N.Y. 1972) (state law dilution claim involving "Enjoy Cocaine" poster, which elicited the Coca-Cola brand and color scheme). The tarnishment claim can involve other types of unfavorable or negative associations. For example, even though gambling was not characterized by the court as unsavory, the Second Circuit in *New York Stock Exchange, Inc., v. New York, New York Hotel, LLC*, 293 F.3d 550 (2d Cir. 2002), reversed a grant of summary judgment for the defendant casino on the stock exchange's tarnishment claim, noting that tarnishment was not limited to "seamy" conduct and that the exchange might be able to demonstrate that its reputation for integrity might be harmed by the connection to gambling, which many consumers believe to involve odds that are stacked in favor of the casino.

141. **Answer (D) is correct.** The validity of an incontestable registration can be challenged by an accused infringer on the ground that the mark is either generic or disparaging, but no challenge based on descriptiveness can be mounted. As discussed previously, the trademark incontestability doctrine prevents challenges to the ownership and validity of trademarks (with certain exceptions) that have been registered and continuously used without successful challenge for five years, if an affidavit of incontestability is filed. Challenges based on descriptiveness or lack of secondary meaning are precluded. With regard to disparaging marks (as well as other marks precluded from registration in 15 U.S.C. § 1064(3)), challenges can still be made at any time. The incontestability provision carves out certain bases for challenge: "Except on a ground for which application to cancel may be filed at any time under paragraphs (3) and (5) of section 14 of this Act, . . . the right of the registrant to use such registered mark . . . shall be incontestable." 15 U.S.C. § 1065. Paragraph (3) of section 14 of the Lanham Act (which governs cancellations) provides for challenges:

> [a]t any time if the registered mark becomes the generic name for goods or services, or a portion thereof, for which it is registered, or is functional, or has been abandoned, or its registration was obtained fraudulently or contrary to Section 4 [certification and collective marks] or of subsection (a), (b), or (c) of section 2 [trademark and service marks] for a registration under this Act.

15 U.S.C. § 1064 (3). Marks that disparage "persons, living or dead, institutions, beliefs or national symbols", as well as "immoral, deceptive, or scandalous matter" are unregisterable under section 2(a). 15 U.S.C. § 1052 (a).

A widely publicized recent attempt to cancel an inconstestable mark involves the long-held Washington Redskins trademarks, which have been challenged on the ground that they allegedly disparage Native Americans. *See Harjo v. Pro Football, Inc.*, 30 U.S.P.Q.2D 1828 (T.T.A.B. 1994), later proceeding, 50 U.S.P.Q.2D 1705 (T.T.A.B. 1999), *reversed by* 284 F. Supp. 2d 96 (D.D.C. 2003), *remanded by* 415 F.3d 44 (D.C. Cir. 2005), *summary judgment granted* 567 F. Supp. 2d 46 (D.D.C. 2008), *affirmed by* 565 F.3d 880 (D.C. Cir. 2009). *See also Blackhorse v. Pro Football, Inc.*, Cancellation Proceeding No. 92046185. As for challenges based on genericness, the Lanham Act specifically states that "no incontestable right shall be acquired in a mark which is the generic name for the goods or services or a portion thereof, for which it is registered." 15 U.S.C. § 1065.

Answer (A) is incorrect. As discussed previously, the trademark incontestability doctrine prevents challenges based on descriptiveness or lack of secondary meaning.

Answer (B) is incorrect. The trademark incontestability doctrine does not preclude challenges based on the mark's being generic, but it also allows challenges for being disparaging.

Answer (C) is incorrect. As discussed previously, the trademark incontestability doctrine allows challenges based on the mark's being disparaging, but it also allows challenges for being generic.

142.   **Answer (D) is correct.** Any of the following would be a basis for a trademark abandonment defense: naked licensing, nonuse with no intent to resume use, or assignment in gross. Trademark owners can involuntarily lose or voluntarily abandon their trademark rights in several ways. Under the Lanham Act, a mark is deemed to be abandoned in the following circumstances:

> (1) When its use has been discontinued with intent not to resume such use. Intent not to resume may be inferred from circumstances. Nonuse for 3 consecutive years shall be prima facie evidence of abandonment. "Use" of a mark means the bona fide use of such mark made in the ordinary course of trade, and not made merely to reserve a right in a mark.

> (2) When any course of conduct of the owner, including acts of omission as well as commission, causes the mark to become the generic name for the goods or services on or in connection with which it is used or otherwise to lose its significance as a mark. Purchaser motivation shall not be a test for determining abandonment under this paragraph.

15 U.S.C. § 1127. A firm might simply abandon its mark voluntarily because it decides to change its name or to liquidate its business. It might also abandon the mark by sheer inactivity or nonuse. Another basis for abandonment is naked licensing — the failure to exercise control over the licensing of a mark, resulting in uncontrolled or indiscriminate use of the mark in a manner that can deceive consumers. Uncontrolled use of a mark causes it to lose its source significance or "otherwise to lose its significance as a mark." Abandonment can thus result involuntarily through naked licensing, although such instances are rare. *See TMT North America, Inc. v. Magic Touch GmbH*, 124 F.3d 876, 885–86 (7th Cir. 1997); *Exxon Corp. v. Oxxford Clothes, Inc.*, 109 F.3d 1070 (5th Cir. 1997). *See generally* MCCARTHY ON TRADEMARKS §§ 18:42, 18:48 (1995). Finally, a trademark can only be assigned with the goodwill associated with the mark. The assignment of a mark without its associated goodwill is prohibited as an "assignment in gross." *See Sugar Busters LLC v. Brennan*, 177 F.3d 258 (5th Cir. 1999). Like naked licensing, separation of a mark from its goodwill by assignment in gross causes the mark "otherwise to lose its significance as a mark."

Answer (A) is incorrect. As discussed above, any of the grounds can establish abandonment.

Answer (B) is incorrect. As discussed above, any of the grounds can establish abandonment.

Answer (C) is incorrect. As discussed above, any of the grounds can establish abandonment.

143.   The basic elements of the trademark fair use defense are (1) use of the term other than as a mark, (2) good faith, and (3) use of the term descriptively. The Lanham Act describes the trademark fair use defense as follows:

> That the use of the name, term, or device charged to be an infringement is a use, otherwise than as a mark, of the party's individual name in his own business, or of the

individual name of anyone in privity with such party, or of a term or device which is descriptive of and used fairly and in good faith only to describe the goods or services of such party, or their geographic origin.

15 U.S.C. § 1115(b)(4). Under this defense, a producer of canned vegetables would be permitted to describe its goods as being "green" in color or "giant" in size without infringing on the "Green Giant" trademark, as long as the elements of the fair use test are satisfied. In *KP Permanent Make-Up, Inc. v. Lasting Impression I, Inc.*, 543 U.S. 111 (2004), the Supreme Court addressed the fair use defense in a case involving two producers of permanent makeup, both using the term "micro color" in the marketing and sale of their products. The Court held that a defendant asserting trademark fair use defense is not required to negate or disprove that its actions cause a likelihood of confusion. Thus, even if some likelihood of confusion might take place, the defendant can prevail if it has proven the requisite elements of the fair use defense.

144. **Answer (D) is correct.** In this scenario, Company A wishes to make reference to Company B's competing product in a television commercial. Company B's name can be used in the commercial as comparative advertising, but only if the advertisement is truthful and non-misleading. Thus, although many companies avoid directly identifying competitor brands as a matter of policy or for pragmatic reasons, the comparative advertising defense does permit such references in limited circumstances. *See R.G. Smith v. Chanel, Inc.*, 402 F.2d 562 (9th Cir. 1968); *see also Pebble Beach Co. v. Tour 18 I Limited*, 155 F.3d 526 (5th Cir. 1998) (nominative use).

Answer (A) is incorrect. As long as the comparative advertising is truthful and non-misleading, it is not actionable as either trademark infringement or dilution.

Answer (B) is incorrect. As long as the comparative advertising is truthful and non-misleading, it is not actionable as either trademark infringement or dilution.

Answer (C) is incorrect. If the attempt at comparative advertising is either false or misleading, it is actionable and is not shielded by this defense.

145. **Answer (B) is correct.** In this scenario, Cochran Industries purchases old sunglasses in which the lens has been broken or scratched, puts a new lens into them, and sells them in mass quantities under the original brand name on the sunglasses. The sunglasses can be sold under the original brand name as long as they are clearly marked as reconditioned and assuming that replacing the lens is not considered unlawful reconstruction. In the landmark case of *Champion Spark Plug Co. v. Sanders*, 331 U.S. 125 (1947), the Supreme Court held that repaired or reconditioned products can continue to be sold under the trademark of the original seller, as long as the following provisos are met: (1) the identity of the repairer must be clear, (2) the product must be clearly marked as repaired, used, or reconditioned, and (3) the repair must not be so extensive as to make any reference to the original manufacturer misleading (i.e., it cannot constitute a complete reconstruction of the product). The Lanham Act provides no relief to the original manufacturer if these conditions are met.

Answer (A) is incorrect. As discussed above, repaired or reconditioned products can be lawfully sold, but the identity of the repairer must be clearly marked and the product must be clearly labeled as repaired, used, or reconditioned.

Answer (C) is incorrect. As discussed above, repaired or reconditioned products can be sold as long as the conditions set forth in *Champion Spark Plug Co. v. Sanders* are met. Used goods provide a valuable form of competition in the marketplace for new trademarked goods, which is beneficial to consumers and which increases the amount of competition in the marketplace.

Answer (D) is incorrect. The doctrine of reverse palming off is not a defense and has no bearing on this fact scenario.

```
┌─────────────────────────────────────────────────────────────────────────┐
│  TOPIC 13:                                              ANSWERS           │
│  RIGHT OF PUBLICITY & IDEA PROTECTION                                     │
└─────────────────────────────────────────────────────────────────────────┘
```

146.   **Answer (D) is correct.** The use of personal information in a book written by a famous individual would not be protected under the right of publicity. The expression in the book would be the subject of copyright protection, although the facts therein would not be. On the other hand, a sound-alike performance, a look-alike performance, and most clearly a signature can give rise to liability for a violation of the right of publicity, depending upon applicable state law. Signatures are commonly protected under standard formulations of the right of publicity, and some courts have expanded the right to cover sound-alike performance and look-alike performances. *See, e.g., Midler v. Ford Motor Co.*, 849 F.2d 460 (9th Cir. 1988) (sound-alike Bette Midler commercial for Ford automobiles); *Wendt v. Host International, Inc.*, 125 F.3d 806 (9th Cir. 1997) (animatronic, life-size figures resembling Cliff and Norm from television series *Cheers*, and therefore also resembling the individuals who played those roles). *See also White v. Samsung Electronics America, Inc.*, 989 F.2d 1512 (9th Cir. 1993) (robot evoking Vanna White found potentially actionable).

   Answer (A) is incorrect. As discussed above, the right of publicity can encompass this claim, depending on state law.

   Answer (B) is incorrect. As discussed above, the right of publicity can encompass this claim, depending on state law. *See also Onassis v. Christian Dior–New York, Inc.*, 122 Misc. 2d 603 (N.Y. Sup. Ct. 1984) (Jacqueline Kennedy Onassis look-alike in advertisement).

   Answer (C) is incorrect. As discussed above, the right of publicity is very likely to encompass this claim, depending on state law.

147.   **Answer (A) is correct.** The right of publicity can be viewed as both a personal privacy right and a commercial right. With regard to personal privacy foundations, Warren & Brandeis in their 1890 article identified the right of publicity as one of the four privacy torts. *See* Samuel D. Warren & Louis D. Brandeis, *The Right To Privacy*, 4 HARV. L. REV. 193 (1890). Thus, the right of publicity originated as a personal right, akin to defamation, but it has developed in more recent years into a significant commercial right. The RESTATEMENT (THIRD) OF UNFAIR COMPETITION § 46 focused on the commercial aspects of this tort: "One who appropriates the commercial value of a person's identity by using without consent the person's name, likeness, or other indicia of identity for purposes of trade is subject to liability for the relief appropriate under the rules stated in §§ 48 and 49."

   Answer (B) is incorrect. As discussed above, the right of publicity can be viewed as either a personal privacy right or a commercial right.

   Answer (C) is incorrect. As discussed above, the right of publicity can be viewed as either a personal privacy right or a commercial right.

   Answer (D) is incorrect. The right of publicity is not constitutionally protected. Although it is a form of privacy protected under state tort law, this type of privacy claim is analytically distinct from the line of United States Supreme Court cases addressing a "constitutional right of privacy."

148. Whether the right of publicity survives the death of the person whose name or likeness was used for commercial purposes in that state depends upon state law and on the primary policy underpinnings of the right of publicity claim. States are split on this issue, and a small number of states address this issue by statute. States that view the right of publicity as primarily a commercial right deem it to survive death, whereas states that view the claim as primarily a personal tort (akin to a defamation or invasion of privacy claim) often hold that the claim does not survive death. In some states, the posthumous right of publicity is only available if the person's identity has commercial value at or after death. For representative cases finding the right of publicity to survive death, *see State ex rel. Elvis Presley International Memorial Foundation v. Crowell*, 733 S.W.2d 89 (Tenn. Ct. App. 1987) (Tennessee law); *McFarland v. Miller*, 14 F.3d 912 (3d Cir. 1994) (New Jersey law); *Martin Luther King, Jr. Center for Social Change, Inc. v. American Heritage Products, Inc.*, 694 F.2d 674 (11th Cir. 1983) (Georgia law); *Joplin Enterprises v. Allen*, 795 F. Supp. 349 (W.D. Wash. 1992) (California law). For cases holding that the right of publicity does not survive death, *see Pirone v. MacMillan, Inc.*, 894 F.2d 579 (2d Cir. 1990) (New York law); *Southeast Bank, N.A. v. Lawrence*, 489 N.E.2d 744 (N.Y. 1985) (Florida law); *Reeves v. United Artists Corp.*, 765 F.2d 79 (6th Cir. 1985) (Ohio law).

149. **Answer (A) is correct.** An ordinary citizen (i.e., not a celebrity) is photographed while walking down a public street. The person's image is then used in a cellular phone advertisement without his or her consent. The best intellectual property claim to assert in this situation is the right of publicity. It might appear to be counterintuitive that any claim case be asserted on these facts because the individual photographed was not a celebrity and was photographed on a public street. Neither of these considerations, standing alone, would vitiate a right of publicity claim. First, ordinary persons who are not public figures or celebrities are entitled to protection under the right of publicity, as are celebrities and other public figures. In some states, the posthumous right of publicity is only available if the person's identity has commercial value at or after death. Most right of publicity cases happen to involve well-known persons because their images are often used in advertising and because they will have much higher potential recoveries for compensatory damages than ordinary persons. Second, the presence of a person on a public street does not serve as implied consent to the use of their image for advertising or commercial purposes.

      Answer (B) is incorrect. Trade secret law would not provide a right of action for this type of photography in a public setting and use of those images for commercial purposes.

      Answer (C) is incorrect. Copyright law would not provide a right of action for this situation; the photographer did not take any creative expression owned by another.

      Answer (D) is incorrect. False endorsement under the Lanham Act would require proof of a likelihood of confusion as to the person's endorsement of the product being advertised (not mere confusion as to whether the person was a paid model). This generally restricts false endorsement claims to famous persons. *See, e.g., Albert v. Apex Fitness, Inc.*, 1997 U.S. Dist. LEXIS 8535 (S.D.N.Y. June 12, 1997).

150. **Answer (D) is correct.** A copyright law theory of recovery will not provide relief for the unauthorized use of an idea. Section 102(b) of the Copyright Act of 1976 expressly precludes copyright protection for an idea: "In no case does copyright protection for an original work

of authorship extend to any idea, procedure, process, system, method of operation, concept, principle, or discovery, regardless of the form in which it is described, explained, illustrated, or embodied in such work." 17 U.S.C. § 102(b). On the other hand, state law claims for breach of express or implied contract or for quasi-contract or unjust enrichment can protect ideas in certain circumstances, depending upon applicable state law.

Answer (A) is incorrect. A quasi-contract claim or unjust enrichment claim can be asserted. In *Matarese v. Moore-McCormack Lines, Inc.*, 158 F.2d 631 (2d Cir. 1946), where the defendant sought the disclosure by the plaintiff, defendant promised compensation, the idea disclosed was specific and novel (and in the case, patentable), and the defendant subsequently used the idea without compensating the plaintiff, the court ruled for the plaintiff on his claim for the defendant's unjust enrichment. Some states also provide for a claim of misappropriation of an idea, while others do not. Where such a claim exists, it will generally require proof of the idea's novelty, disclosure of the idea in confidence, and defendant's use of the idea, and novelty will be fairly strictly judged. *See, e.g., Baer v. Chase*, 392 F.3d 609 (3d Cir. 2004); *Nadel v. Play-by-Play Toys & Novelties, Inc.*, 208 F.3d 368 (2d Cir. 2000).

Answer (B) is incorrect. An express contact can protect the disclosure of an idea in some circumstances, *see Nadel v. Play-by-Play Toys & Novelties, Inc.*, 208 F.3d 368 (2d Cir. 2000) (exploring the level of novelty of an idea that will support a claim of breach of contract), but a court will generally not waive any of the usual requirements for the formation of a contract, including mutual intent to contract, an exchange of promises, and definiteness. *See Smith v. Recrion Corp.*, 541 P.2d 663 (Nev. 1975) (explaining that even when related to the disclosure of an idea, a contract requires an exchange of promises (whether implied via conduct or expressly in words) and mutual intent to enter into a contract). *See also Baer v. Chase*, 392 F.3d 609 (3d Cir. 2004) (rejecting, for lack of definiteness, a contract-based claim related to disclosure of ideas to the producer and writer of *The Sopranos*).

Answer (C) is incorrect. As discussed above, an implied contact can protect the disclosure of an idea in some circumstances, if the idea purveyor can prove the usual requirements for the creation of a contract.

151. **Answer (B) is correct.** Protection of intellectual property rights can be described as solving a public goods problem. The standard public goods problem involves a product or service that has a number of basic characteristics. In a state of nature (i.e., without legal protections), a public good created by one person can easily be appropriated by another, which can lead to "free rider" problems. In other words, people can make use of the efforts of others without compensating them. Because of this problem, there is underinvestment in public goods absent property rights or another mechanism to reward innovation. Ironically, another feature of a public good such as intellectual property is that it is not exhaustible. The use of the good (or service) by some does not diminish the ability of others to enjoy the substance of the good (or service). If one person reads a book or listens to a song, that action does not prevent another person from enjoying it — as the wave of music file-sharing has shown, sharing music is now almost costless. The classic example of a public good in the standard economics text is the provision of national defense. Once a nuclear arsenal is created to protect persons in a nation, everyone in that nation benefits from it; in addition, once national defense is established, more people can be protected by the arsenal with few to no additional costs (within the same geographic area). For this reason, the government provides national defense because it would not likely be produced in a completely free market. Similarly, intellectual property law solves the free rider problem by giving property rights to inventions and creative works. Patents and copyrights provide incentives for investment in research and development or creative endeavor, and unauthorized use can diminish the economic returns available to the creator by diminishing the ability of the creator to charge for access or use. Yet like other public goods, once the invention or creative work has been made, the unauthorized use of that intellectual property by others does not diminish its creator's enjoyment of its substance (e.g., the quality of the music or the function of the device).

Answer (A) is incorrect. Moral hazard is an economic problem involving the likelihood that someone who is insulated from risks will change their behavior, particularly by taking greater risks than they would otherwise. A classic illustration is insurance coverage, because coverage against losses might increase the risk-taking behavior of the insured. Thus, a contract or a government action that insulates parties from risks can lead to greater risky behavior. The moral hazard problem, however, does not have any particular relevance to intellectual property.

Answer (C) is incorrect. Protection of intellectual property does not solve a monopoly problem. An economic monopoly exists when there are, practically, no available substitutes for a particular product or service, and thus the seller is able to control prices and obtain unusually high profits. It is often stated that intellectual property rights confer a legal monopoly, although whether this right to exclude is truly an economic monopoly depends on the existence of practically available and acceptable substitutes in the marketplace.

Answer (D) is incorrect. As discussed above, moral hazard and monopoly problems are not generally solved by providing intellectual property rights.

152.   **Answer (B) is correct.** The strongest form of intellectual property protection (i.e., offering the greatest exclusivity) is a patent. The central point of this question is to focus on which intellectual property right offers the greatest exclusivity. Patents offer a broad right to exclude others from making, using, selling, offering to sell, or importing the patented invention for the term of the patent. There is no reverse engineering or independent development defense.

   Answer (A) is incorrect. Trademarks do not offer the right to exclude competitors from offering competitive goods or services, but instead only the right to prevent the use of confusingly similar marks. *See William R. Warner & Co. v. Eli Lilly & Co.*, 265 U.S. 526 (1924).

   Answer (C) is incorrect. Copyrights do offer some exclusivity as to the rights of copyright owners, but these rights are limited by a large range of defenses including independent creation, the idea/expression distinction, and the fair use defense.

   Answer (D) is incorrect. Trade secret protection does offer some exclusivity, but the owner of a trade secret can only exclude competitors who obtain the information by breach of confidence, improper means, or other similar conduct. Moreover, trade secret claims do not prevent reverse engineering or independent development.

153.   **Answer (D) is correct.** All three listed forms of intellectual property protection are available for computer software — patents, copyrights, and trade secret law. As long as the software satisfies the applicable requirements of a utility or design patent, it can be patented. *See generally Gottschalk v. Benson*, 409 U.S. 63 (1972); *Diamond v. Diehr*, 450 U.S. 175 (1981). Software code and user interfaces can also be copyrightable subject matter, as either a literary work or an audio-visual work. Finally, software can be maintained by a firm as a trade secret. *See, e.g., Justmed, Inc. v. Byce*, 600 F. 3d 1118 (9th Cir. 2010) (discussing trade secret protection for software code under Idaho law and under the Copyright Act).

   Answer (A) is incorrect. As discussed above, all three listed forms of intellectual property protection are available for computer software.

   Answer (B) is incorrect. As discussed above, all three listed forms of intellectual property protection are available for computer software.

   Answer (C) is incorrect. As discussed above, all three listed forms of intellectual property protection are available for computer software.

154.   **Answer (A) is correct.** Functional aspects of a product can be protected under utility patent law, which protects useful inventions. Copyright law does not offer protection for functional or useful features of a product, but instead only for aspects of the product that are non-functional and conceptually separable from the useful aspects of the product. *See Brandir Int'l., Inc. v. Cascade Pacific Lumber Co.*, 834 F.2d 1142 (2d Cir. 1987) (bike rack features deemed functional and thus not copyrightable). Design patent law also does not offer protection for functional or useful features of a product, but instead only for its ornamental aspects.

   Answer (B) is incorrect. As discussed above, copyright law does not offer protection for functional or useful features of a product.

Answer (C) is incorrect. As discussed above, design patent law does not offer protection for functional or useful features of a product.

Answer (D) is incorrect. As discussed above, functional features are protected by utility patents, but not by design patents.

155.   **Answer (B) is correct.** A short phrase or slogan can be protected under trademark law if the phrase or slogan is used in commerce to promote goods or services and becomes a source indicator. Thus, the phrase or slogan is eligible to be protected as a trademark, just as a work, symbol, device, sound, or color might be. The Copyright Office prohibits the registration of short names, phrases, or expressions such as the name of a product or service, even if it is novel or distinctive. *See* 37 C.F.R. § 202.1 (short phrases, names, and similar material not subject to copyright protection); Copyright Office Circular 34 (*available at* http://www.copyright.gov/circs/circ34.pdf). Finally, the phrase or slogan would not satisfy the substantive requirements of patent law and would probably also be precluded by the "printed matter" doctrine.

Answer (A) is incorrect. As discussed above, copyright law would not protect the short phrase or slogan.

Answer (C) is incorrect. As discussed above, patent law would not protect the short phrase or slogan.

Answer (D) is incorrect. As discussed above, copyright law would not protect the short phrase or slogan, but trademark law would do so.

156.   **Answer (A) is correct.** Copying a competitor's unpatented product and selling a duplicate of it at a lower price is not actionable under intellectual property law. This form of competition is indeed the essence of free market competition, which benefits consumers through lower prices and increased alternative sources of supply. Unfair competition law does not prevent copying of a competitor's product, only the use of a confusingly similar mark. *See William R. Warner & Co. v. Eli Lilly & Co.*, 265 U.S. 526 (1924). Trade secret law does not prevent duplication of a product by reverse engineering or independent development, although it would prevent duplication by breach of confidence or improper means. The right of publicity does not protect products, but rather aspects of personal identity such as name or likeness.

Answer (B) is incorrect. As discussed above, unfair competition law does not prevent copying of a competitor's product, only the use of a confusingly similar mark.

Answer (C) is incorrect. As discussed above, trade secret law does not prevent duplication of a product by reverse engineering or independent development.

Answer (D) is incorrect. As discussed above, the right of publicity does not protect products, but rather aspects of personal identity such as name or likeness.

157.   Under present United States copyright law, a work must have been published before 1923 in order for it to be in assuredly in the public domain (because its maximum term of 28 years plus a 47-year renewal would have expired before all terms were extended by 20 years in the 1998 CTEA). Copyrights for works published after that date but before January 1, 1978 are governed by the Copyright Act of 1909, with extensions provided by later amendments, for a maximum of 95 years from publication (28-year initial term plus 67 years in the renewal

term). Works published under the 1909 Act, which provided for renewal terms, can thus still be copyrighted as long as the copyright renewal was effectuated. Works published on or after January 1, 1978 are governed by the Copyright Act of 1976.

158.   The four typical requirements for enforcement of a covenant not to compete in employment settings are that the covenant: (1) must promote a legitimate interest of the employer, (2) must be reasonable in duration and scope, (3) must not unduly burden the employee, and (4) must not be contrary to public policy. Public policy considerations include whether the covenant creates a monopoly or interferes with other important public policies, such as the attorney-client or physician-patient relationship. *See* GARY MYERS, PRINCIPLES OF INTELLECTUAL PROPERTY LAW 372–74 (2d ed. 2013). Covenants not to compete related to the sale of business are generally viewed more favorably by the courts, but employment non-compete agreements are disfavored and narrowly construed.

159.   **Answer (A) is correct.** The "Berne Convention" addresses protection under copyright law. The Berne Convention for the Protection of Literary and Artistic Works is an international treaty to which the United States has adhered and which sets forth minimum copyright protections and limits the types of formalities that can be imposed on copyright owners. Congress ratified the Berne Convention Implementation Act of 1988, which dispensed with the requirement of copyright notice for works created after the effective date of the Act. Adherence to the Berne Convention has also resulted in increased protection for moral rights, as reflected in the Visual Artists Rights Act of 1990 ("VARA").

    Answer (B) is incorrect. As discussed above, the Berne Convention addresses protection under copyright law, not patent law.

    Answer (C) is incorrect. As discussed above, the Berne Convention addresses protection under copyright law, not trade secret law.

    Answer (D) is incorrect. As discussed above, the Berne Convention addresses protection under copyright law, not trademark law.

160.   **Answer (C) is correct.** The McDonald's "golden arches" can be protected under trademark law. Under the Lanham Act, trademarks:

> Include[] any word, name, symbol, or device, or any combination thereof — (1) used by a person, or (2) which a person has a bona fide intention to use in commerce and applies to register on the principal register established by this chapter, to identify and distinguish his or her goods, including a unique product, from those manufactured or sold by others and to indicate the source of the goods, even if that source is unknown.

15 U.S.C. § 1127. The "golden arches" are clearly source-indicating symbols for McDonald's restaurant services.

    Answer (A) is incorrect. Patent law does not protect brand names or symbols.

    Answer (B) is incorrect. Copyright law does not protect brand names or basic symbols, although it might protect more complex design logos, visual depictions, or marketing materials. For purposes of this question, trademark law is clearly the more directly relevant form of intellectual property.

    Answer (D) is incorrect. Trade secret law does not protect brand names or symbols, which by definition must be used publicly to develop good will. Trade secret law might protect a marketing campaign prior to its public announcement.

161.   In the pre-Copyright Act of 1976 case of *International News Service v. Associated Press*, 248 U.S. 215 (1918), the Supreme Court recognized a broad claim for unfair competition when a competitor appropriates current news stories from a news wire service for use in direction competition. The elements of a "hot news" claim of misappropriation under *INS v. AP* and its progeny have been summarized in the Second Circuit's opinion *National Basketball Association v. Motorola, Inc.*, 105 F.3d 841 (2d Cir. 1997). The court rejected a misappropriation claim brought by the National Basketball Association (NBA) against the manufacturer of a hand-held pager, which transmitted NBA basketball scores during games without authorization from the NBA. The court concluded that only a very limited "hot news" misappropriation claim survived preemption by the Copyright Act of 1976, 17 U.S.C. § 301. The court identified five elements that must be shown in order to prove a "hot news" misappropriation claim: (1) the plaintiff generates or gathers information at some cost; (2) the information is time sensitive; (3) the defendant's use of the information constitutes free riding upon the plaintiff's investment; (4) the defendant is in direct competition with the plaintiff; and (5) the free rider problem will so reduce incentives to produce the information that its existence or quality of the information would be substantially threatened.

162.   **Answer (A) is correct.** Boat hull designs and semiconductor products (mask works) receive *sui generis* protection under current federal law, but databases do not. Boat hull designs are protected under the Vessel Hull Design Protection Act of 1998, Title 17, Chapter 13 of the United States Code, which provides *sui generis* protection for original designs of vessel hulls. Semiconductor products, also known as mask works, receive protection under the Semi-Conductor Chip Protection Act of 1984, which protects original mask works and related semiconductor products that are registered with the Copyright Office. A mask work is a two- or three-dimensional layout or topography of an integrated circuit, i.e. the arrangement on a computer "chip" of various semiconductor devices (e.g., transistors and resistors). *See* GARY MYERS, PRINCIPLES OF INTELLECTUAL PROPERTY LAW 389–90 (2d ed. 2013).

Answer (B) is incorrect. Databases do not currently receive protection under United States intellectual property law. In *Feist Publications, Inc. v. Rural Telephone Service Co.*, 499 U.S. 340 (1991), the Supreme Court concluded that copyright law does not protect laboriously gathered and maintained factual compilations if they do not possess a minimum level of creativity in their selection or arrangement. In light of *Feist*, most factual databases do not qualify for copyright protection. Although bills that have been regularly introduced in Congress to provide *sui generis* protection to the creators of databases, they have not been enacted thus far. Factual databases are eligible for protection in some foreign countries, for example pursuant to the European Union's Database Directive.

Answer (C) is incorrect. As discussed above, databases do not currently receive protection under United States law.

Answer (D) is incorrect. As discussed above, databases do not currently receive protection under United States law.

163.   Cybersquatting is the practice of registering a domain name or otherwise establishing an Internet presence making use, in bad faith, of well-established trademarks owned by others. This practice became very common with the advent of widespread use of the Internet in the

1990s. In early cases, trademark owners brought suit using traditional theories of trademark infringement and dilution. These cases were generally successful, but traditional trademark remedies were not completely effective because many infringing websites were located in countries outside the reach of United States law, which made enforcement of judgments difficult. Congress enacted the Anticybersquatting Consumer Protection Act of 1999 (the "ACPA"), which provides specific remedies to address the problem of cybersquatting. *See Sporty's Farm, L.L.C. v. Sportsman's Market, Inc.*, 202 F.3d 489 (2d Cir. 2000). The ACPA added a new section 43(d) to the Lanham Act, 15 U.S.C. § 1125(d), with remedies for cybersquatting. The ACPA provides remedies against the bad faith registration, trafficking, or use of a domain name when the domain name dilutes a famous mark, or is confusingly similar to the mark of another. The primary remedies of the Lanham Act, injunctive relief and monetary damages, are available for violations of section 43(d), *see* 15 U.S.C. §§ 1116(a), 1117 (a), and 1125 (d) (3), and a court may also "order the forfeiture or cancellation of the domain name or the transfer of the domain name to the owner of the mark." 15 U.S.C. § 1125(d)(1)(C).

164.   **Answer (D) is correct.** Unauthorized music file-sharing can be a violation of copyright protections against reproduction or distribution. 17 U.S.C. § 106. At first blush, it would appear that music file-sharing is primarily a problem of reproduction — making unauthorized copies of musical works. In fact, however, the uploading of a song constitutes a distribution of that song (by the person having a lawful or unauthorized copy of it), if another person ultimately downloads that file, and the unauthorized downloading of the song by the recipient is a reproduction of that work. *See, e.g., Atlantic Recording Corp. v. Howell*, 554 F. Supp. 2d 976, 981–985, (D Ariz. 2008); *Capitol Records, Inc. v. Thomas*, 579 F. Supp. 2d 1210, 1214–25 (D. Minn. 2008). Thus, both rights can be implicated by unauthorized music file-sharing.

   Answer (A) is incorrect. Public performance rights are not implicated by the mere act of file-sharing of music because the music is not being "performed." Under 17 U.S.C. § 101, performing a work "means to recite, render, play, dance, or act it, either directly or by means of any device or process or, in the case of a motion picture or other audiovisual work, to show its images in any sequence or to make the sounds accompanying it audible."

   Answer (B) is incorrect. As discussed above, both reproduction and distribution rights can be violated by music file-sharing.

   Answer (C) is incorrect. As discussed above, both reproduction and distribution rights can be violated by music file-sharing.

165.   **Answer (D) is correct.** None of the listed defenses are likely to succeed in a music file-sharing case. In *A&M Records, Inc. v. Napster, Inc.*, 239 F.3d 1004, 1014 (9th Cir. 2001), the Ninth Circuit found no defense or limitation in the Copyright Act offered a viable defense to the copyright claims brought by the music industry. The court's opinion includes a detailed analysis and rejection of the fair use defense and a brief preliminary rejection of the copyright misuse defense. The first sale doctrine would not be a viable defense because file-sharing does not involve the physical transfer of a lawfully obtained copy of the song, but rather the making of additional copies of the copyrighted song.

   Answer (A) is incorrect. As discussed above, the court rejected the copyright misuse defense.

Answer (B) is incorrect. As discussed above, the first sale doctrine would not be a viable defense.

Answer (C) is incorrect. As discussed above, the court rejected the fair use defense.

166.   The test for determining whether a mark is deceptive under the Lanham Act is set forth in *In re Budge Manufacturing Co.*, 857 F.2d 773, 775 (Fed. Cir. 1988): "(1) Is the term misdescriptive of the character, quality, function, composition or use of the goods? (2) If so, are prospective purchasers likely to believe that the misdescription actually describes the goods? (3) If so, is the misdescription likely to affect the decision to purchase?" Deceptive marks are precluded from trademark registration. 15 U.S.C. § 1052.

167.   **Answer (A) is correct.** The presence of the defendant's commercial or profit-making purpose weighs against fair use but is only one of the relevant factors. In *Campbell v. Acuff-Rose Music Inc.*, 510 U.S. 569 (1994), the Supreme Court held that a commercial purpose (such as selling CDs for profit) was not determinative of fair use and did not give rise to a presumption against fair use. The presumption against fair use for commercial uses was found in dictum in the earlier decision in *Sony Corp. v. Universal City Studios*, 464 U.S. 417 (1984), but the Court in *Campbell* specifically rejected the idea that such a presumption exists.

Answer (B) is incorrect. As discussed above, the Court in *Campbell* specifically rejected the idea that such a presumption should be applied.

Answer (C) is incorrect. The Court in *Campbell* also rejected the idea that a commercial use should presumed to be harmful:

> No "presumption" or inference of market harm that might find support in *Sony* is applicable to a case involving something beyond mere duplication for commercial purposes. *Sony's* discussion of a presumption contrasts a context of verbatim copying of the original in its entirety for commercial purposes, with the noncommercial context of *Sony* itself (home copying of television programming). In the former circumstances, what Sony said simply makes common sense: when a commercial use amounts to mere duplication of the entirety of an original, it clearly "supersede[s] the objects" of the original and serves as a market replacement for it, making it likely that cognizable market harm to the original will occur. But when, on the contrary, the second use is transformative, market substitution is at least less certain, and market harm may not be so readily inferred. Indeed, as to parody pure and simple, it is more likely that the new work will not affect the market for the original in a way cognizable under this factor, that is, by acting as a substitute for it ("supersed[ing] [its] objects"). This is so because the parody and the original usually serve different market functions.

Campbell v. Acuff-Rose Music Inc., 510 U.S. 569, 591 (1994).

Answer (D) is incorrect. As discussed above, a commercial purpose is a factor weighing against fair use in the overall balancing test.

168.   **Answer (B) is correct.** Customer goes to a photography studio and has portraits made. The customer pays for 10 prints from the photographer. The customer scans a photograph onto a disk, removes the copyright notice placed on the photo using photo editing software, and makes 20 extra prints of the photo without the copyright notice. The extra prints are kept in

the customer's home office drawer. In a copyright suit brought by the photographer, the court will likely find that the customer violated the photographer's reproduction rights, as well as the Digital Millennium Copyright Act ("DMCA"). The reproduction of the photograph is a straightforward violation of the section 106 reproduction right in this case. The DMCA violation involves removal of copyright management information:

> Removal or Alteration of Copyright Management Information.— No person shall, without the authority of the copyright owner or the law—

> (1) intentionally remove or alter any copyright management information,

> (2) distribute or import for distribution copyright management information knowing that the copyright management information has been removed or altered without authority of the copyright owner or the law, or

> (3) distribute, import for distribution, or publicly perform works, copies of works, or phonorecords, knowing that copyright management information has been removed or altered without authority of the copyright owner or the law, knowing, or, with respect to civil remedies under section 1203, having reasonable grounds to know, that it will induce, enable, facilitate, or conceal an infringement of any right under this title.

17 U.S.C. § 1202(b). Removal of the copyright notice can violate this provision of the DMCA.

Answer (A) is incorrect. On these facts, there was no distribution or public display of the work.

Answer (C) is incorrect. As noted above, there is also a potential violation of the DMCA on this set of facts.

Answer (D) is incorrect. Ownership of the copy of the photograph does not excuse reproduction of the work or the potential DMCA violation. The first sale defense does not apply to these types of violations.

169.   **Answer (C) is correct.** Both patent claims and federal copyright claims can only be brought in federal court (i.e., there is no concurrent state court jurisdiction). *See* 28 U.S.C. § 1338(a). For Lanham Act claims, on the other hand, there is concurrent state court jurisdiction. *Id.*

Answer (A) is incorrect. As noted above, federal courts have original and exclusive jurisdiction over both patent and copyright claims.

Answer (B) is incorrect. As noted above, federal courts have original and exclusive jurisdiction over both patent and copyright claims.

Answer (D) is incorrect. As noted above, federal courts have original and exclusive jurisdiction over both patent and copyright claims.

170.   **Answer (B) is correct.** A patent owner who imposes a tying arrangement on customers who purchase its patented product (requiring that they also purchase a second, unpatented product) is likely to have committed patent misuse, if the patent owner has market power. This is a classic illustration of a situation in which patent misuse can be asserted. In light of amendments in the Patent Misuse Reform Act of 1988, market power must be shown to establish misuse on grounds of tying:

> No patent owner otherwise entitled to relief for infringement or contributory infringement of a patent shall be denied relief or deemed guilty of misuse or illegal

extension of the patent right by reason of his having done one or more of the following: . . . (5) conditioned the license of any rights to the patent or the sale of the patented product on the acquisition of a license to rights in another patent or purchase of a separate product, unless, in view of the circumstances, the patent owner has market power in the relevant market for the patent or patented product on which the license or sale is conditioned.

35 U.S.C. § 271(d).

Answer (A) is incorrect. On these facts, there is possible misuse, but not waiver.

Answer (C) is incorrect. As noted above, market power must be shown to prove misuse by tying.

Answer (D) is incorrect. This doctrine does not apply to this set of facts.

171. **Answer (A) is correct.** If a computer manufacturer wished to obtain trademark protection for the color dark green (standing alone) for use on the outer surface of all of its laptop computers, this green trademark would most likely be found protected once secondary meaning is shown, because it is not inherently distinctive. The color green does not appear to serve an aesthetic or functional purpose as to laptop computers and thus can receive trademark protection upon a showing of secondary meaning. *See Qualitex Co. v. Jacobson Products Co.*, 514 U.S. 159 (1995) (color marks are protectable if non-functional and if they develop secondary meaning).

Answer (B) is incorrect. In light of *Qualitex*, a mark consisting of a color standing alone must have secondary meaning to be protected.

Answer (C) is incorrect. As noted above, the color green does not appear to serve an aesthetic or functional purpose as to laptop computers.

Answer (D) is incorrect. As noted above, under *Qualitex* a color can be a trademark in the proper circumstances.

172. **Answer (C) is correct.** Independent creation of the accused work, meaning that the accused infringer had no access to the copyright owner's protected work, is a complete defense to a claim of copyright infringement. *See, e.g., Arnstein v. Porter*, 154 F.2d 464 (2d Cir. 1946) (explaining that proof of copying, either by direct evidence or circumstantial evidence consisting of access and striking similarity, is required before the question of unlawful appropriation will be addressed).

Answer (A) is incorrect. Independent creation, invention, or development is not a defense to patent infringement, standing alone. The AIA did create a the good-faith prior user defense for "a process, or consisting of a machine, manufacture, or composition of matter used in a manufacturing or other commercial process" if (with certain other requirements) the accused infringer's good faith, commercial use began at least a year before the effective filing date of the claimed invention (or its public disclosure as set forth in section 102(b)). *See* 35 U.S.C. § 273(a). A good-faith prior use defense is not, however, the same as an independent creation defense; however, independent creation might be a factor in the defense, since an accused infringer is barred from raising the defense if "the subject matter on which the defense is based was *derived from the patentee or persons in privity with the patentee.*" 35 U.S.C. § 273(e)(2).

Answer (B) is incorrect. Independent creation could show that an accused trademark infringer acted in good faith, or without intent to confuse consumers, but the accused infringer's intent or bad faith is but one of many factors considered in the likelihood of confusion analysis. *See, e.g., Polaroid Corp. v. Polarad Electronics Corp.*, 287 F.2d 492, 495 (2d Cir. 1961). It is not determinative.

Answer (D) is incorrect. Independent creation is a defense to a claim of copyright infringement.

173.   **Answer (D) is correct.** As explained below, none of the listed options would apply on these facts.

Answer (A) is incorrect. The facts do not indicate that Paula Pilot has fixed a work of authorship in a tangible medium of expression (or, if she did, that Steven Screenwriter had access to that work). *See* 17 U.S.C. § 102(a). Moreover, the facts outlined above indicate that what Paula Pilot shared with Steven Screenwriter and what he used was in the nature of facts or ideas, rather than her particular expression of those facts or ideas.

Answer (B) is incorrect. The facts do not indicate that Paula Pilot extended any kind of offer to Steven Screenwriter that he could accept by word or action, and indeed it appears that Pilot provided information to Screenwriter entirely of her own accord, without any invitation by Screenwriter. *See, e.g., Smith v. Recrion Corp.*, 541 P.2d 663 (Nev. 1975) (explaining that even when related to the disclosure of an idea, a contract requires an exchange of promises (even if implied via conduct rather than expressly in words) and mutual intent to enter into a contract). Moreover, Steven Screenwriter's statement, "Nice meeting you. Sounds like a great movie. I'll see what I can do with it and will get you in touch with the right people," even if it were a promise of compensation specific enough for enforcement (which it is not), came *after* Pilot's disclosure and would generally be unenforceable for lack of consideration. *See id.* Another useful case to consider might be *Baer v. Chase*, 392 F.3d 609 (3d Cir. 2004) (rejecting, for lack of definiteness, a contract-based claim related to disclosure of ideas to the producer and writer of *The Sopranos*, and also rejecting a misappropriation claim for lack of novelty of the ideas).

Answer (C) is incorrect. The facts do not support a claim of trade secret misappropriation. Although Paula Pilot did not disclose her movie plot to any of her co-pilots or friends, which might make the information "secret," there is no indication that the information she disclosed derives value from being maintained as a secret. *See* Uniform Trade Secrets Act (UTSA) § 1(4). In fact, the information will yield its ultimate value when it is later disclosed and shared with the public as part of a movie. More important, however, on these facts, is that even if this were otherwise trade-secret information, Pilot did not reasonably maintain the information as a secret when she provided her ideas and information to Screenwriter at a cocktail party, without advance promises of confidentiality from him. *See id.* And because she freely provided the information to him, his future use of the information was not misappropriation — he did not acquire the information "under circumstances giving rise to a duty to maintain its secrecy or limit its use," via a breach of confidence by another, or through improper means. *See* UTSA § 1(2).

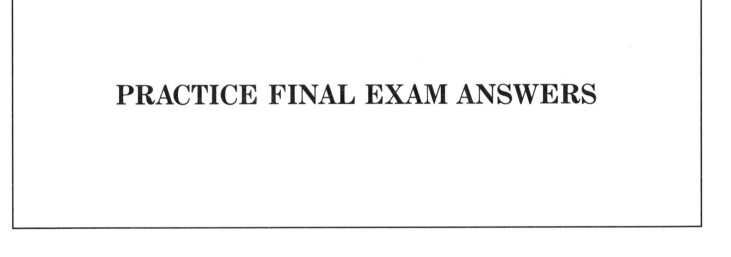

PRACTICE FINAL EXAM ANSWERS

1. The status of the "first to file" method for determining ownership of patents under United States law is that it is the law, with an important exception, for inventions whose applications were effectively filed on or after March 16, 2013. *See* U.S.C. § 102 (a) (2). Introducing a modified "first to file" system was the major feature of the America Invents Act, or AIA, which was enacted in September 2011. Inventions within applications containing only claims with effective filing dates before March 16, 2013, will continue to be evaluated for novelty, nonobviousness, and priority under prior law, which awarded priority to the first to conceive the invention, absent abandonment or suppression or lack of diligence.

    The above mentioned "important exception" in the AIA's modified "first to file" system is that priority will be awarded to an inventor who filed second, compared to a competing inventor of the same invention, if he or she publicly disclosed the invention *before* the first-to-file inventor filed his or her application (or publicly disclosed the invention). *See* 35 U.S.C. § 102 (b) (2) (B). The application must still, like all applications, be filed within a year of the inventor's disclosure, or it will be barred under section 102 (a). *See* 35 U.S.C. § 102 (a) and 102(b) (1).

2. **Answer (C) is correct.** Aesthetic or non-functional aspects of a product can be protected under design patent law — this is precisely the type of innovation that comes within the scope of design patent subject matter, the "ornamental design for an article of manufacture." 35 U.S.C. § 171 (a). Utility patents, on the other hand, protect useful features. Trade secret law is unsuited to protecting aesthetic features of a product, as by definition these features would be revealed to the consuming public and thus could not be maintained as a trade secret.

    Answer (A) is incorrect. As discussed above, utility patents protect useful features, not non-functional ones. *See* 35 U.S.C. § 101.

    Answer (B) is incorrect. As discussed above, trade secret law is unsuited to protecting aesthetic features of a product.

    Answer (D) is incorrect. Although design patents do protect non-functional features, trade secret law is unsuited to this task.

3. **Answer (A) is correct.** A lawfully purchased music CD can be resold based on the copyright law doctrine of first sale. The copyright owner's right of distribution is limited by the "first sale" doctrine enunciated in section 109(a) of the Copyright Act: "Notwithstanding the provisions of section 106(3), the owner of a particular copy or phonorecord lawfully made under this title, or any person authorized by such owner, is entitled, without the authority of the copyright owner, to sell or otherwise dispose of the possession of that copy or phonorecord." Although commercial rental of music CDs would be prohibited under § 109 (b), that provision does not restrain commercial or other resale.

Answer (B) is incorrect. The facts provide no evidence of misuse by the copyright owner.

Answer (C) is incorrect. The merger doctrine precludes copyright protection if an idea can only be expressed in one or a very small number of ways. It would not apply in this fact scenario.

Answer (D) is incorrect. Fair use is not the most directly relevant defense to this set of facts, given the clear defense provided by the first sale doctrine.

4.   **Answer (A) is correct.** An accounting system is not protected by copyright law. *See e.g., Baker v. Selden*, 101 U.S. 99 (1880).

Answer (B) is incorrect. Computer software is clearly protected under copyright law. Software code and user interfaces are protected as either a literary work or an audio-visual work, respectively. *See generally Justmed, Inc. v. Byce*, 600 F. 3d 1118 (9th Cir. 2010).

Answer (C) is incorrect. Sculptural works are expressly identified as a category of copyrightable subject matter. Section 102 of the Copyright Act states:

> Copyright protection subsists, in accordance with this title, in original works of authorship fixed in any tangible medium of expression, now known or later developed, from which they can be perceived, reproduced, or otherwise communicated, either directly or with the aid of a machine or device. Works of authorship include the following categories:
>
> (1) literary works;
>
> (2) musical works, including any accompanying words;
>
> (3) dramatic works, including any accompanying music;
>
> (4) pantomimes and choreographic works;
>
> (5) pictorial, graphic, and sculptural works;
>
> (6) motion pictures and other audiovisual works;
>
> (7) sound recordings; and
>
> (8) architectural works.

17 U.S.C. § 102 (a).

Answer (D) is incorrect. Architectural works are expressly identified as a category of copyrightable subject matter, as shown in the section 102 quote above.

5.   The minimum standard of originality for copyright protection, as announced in the Supreme Court's decision in *Feist Publications, Inc. v. Rural Telephone Service Co.*, 499 U.S. 340, 345 (1991), can be explained as follows:

> The *sine qua non* of copyright is originality. To qualify for copyright protection, a work must be original to the author. Original, as the term is used in copyright, means only that the work was independently created by the author (as opposed to copied from other works), and that it possesses at least some minimal degree of creativity.

The Court announced this rule in the context of a case involving a factual compilation — a "white pages" telephone directory. As the Court noted,

(1) facts are not copyrightable; and (2) compilations of facts generally are copyrightable. Each of these propositions possesses an impeccable pedigree. That there can be no valid copyright in facts is universally understood. The most fundamental axiom of copyright law is that "[n]o author may copyright his ideas or the facts he narrates."

Id. at 344–45. Most creative works, particularly non-factual works, easily satisfy this minimum standard for originality.

6.   **Answer (A) is correct.** The Visual Artists Rights Act of 1990 ("VARA") does not protect limited-edition or single-copies of films. VARA, at 17 U.S.C. § 106A, provides protections for a "work of visual art," a term of art defined in the Copyright Act as follows:

> (1) a painting, drawing, print, or sculpture, existing in a single copy, in a limited edition of 200 copies or fewer that are signed and consecutively numbered by the author, or, in the case of a sculpture, in multiple cast, carved, or fabricated sculptures of 200 or fewer that are consecutively numbered by the author and bear the signature or other identifying mark of the author; or

> (2) a still photographic image produced for exhibition purposes only, existing in a single copy that is signed by the author, or in a limited edition of 200 copies or fewer that are signed and consecutively numbered by the author.

17 U.S.C. § 101. Thus, painting, prints, and drawings are eligible for protection under VARA, but films are not. Moral rights laws in some foreign nations, such as France, do offer protection for films.

Answer (B) is incorrect. As noted above, paintings, prints, and drawings are eligible for protection under VARA.

Answer (C) is incorrect. As noted above, paintings, prints, and drawings are eligible for protection under VARA.

Answer (D) is incorrect. As noted above, paintings, prints, and drawings are eligible for protection under VARA.

7.   The Lanham Act defines a certification mark as a mark "used upon or in connection with the products or services of one or more persons other than the owner of the mark to certify regional or other origin, material, mode of manufacture, quality, accuracy or other characteristics of such goods or services." 15 U.S.C. § 1127. An example of a certification mark is the mark "UL Listed," which certifies that products sold by third parties meet certain safety standards set by Underwriter's Labs.

8.   **Answer (B) is correct.** A new mathematical algorithm cannot be protected as a utility patent under the Patent Act. The Patent Act offers protection for practical applications of ideas or concepts, but not for an abstract idea or concept standing alone. Thus, a mathematical algorithm would not be patentable subject matter. *See Diamond v. Diehr*, 450 U.S. 175 (1981).

Answer (A) is incorrect. A genetically modified animal — one not naturally occurring — such as a faster growing, bigger chicken, would be patentable subject matter. *See generally Diamond v. Chakrabarty*, 447 U.S. 303 (1980).

Answer (C) is incorrect. A process for producing a synthetic motor oil would be patentable subject matter as a "process." *See* 35 U.S.C. § 101.

Answer (D) is incorrect. An improved mousetrap would be patentable subject matter, *see* 35 U.S.C. § 101, although of course a *minor* improvement might not meet the section 103 requirement of nonobviousness.

9.   **Answer (A) is correct.** Reselling a used product covered by a patent is not an example of an infringement of a patent. Patent infringement does occur when a party makes, uses, sells, offers to sell, or imports the product into the United States. This is the "bundle of sticks" or collection of rights provided for in the Patent Act: "Except as otherwise provided in this title, whoever without authority makes, uses, offers to sell, or sells any patented invention, within the United States, or imports into the United States any patented invention during the term of the patent therefor, infringes the patent." 35 U.S.C. § 271(a). The resale of a used product still under patent, however, would not violate this patent based on the doctrine of first sale (also known as exhaustion of rights). *See, e.g., Keeler v. Standard Folding-Bed Co.*, 157 U.S. 659 (1895). The principle involved is that the patent owner has already received its reward from the original sale of the product.

Answer (B) is incorrect. Selling a product manufactured using a patented process would violate section 271(g).

Answer (C) is incorrect. Importation of a product covered by a patent would violate section 271(a), as set forth above.

Answer (D) is incorrect. Offering to sell a patented product would violate section 271(a), as set forth above, even if the product was not actually produced or sold by the defendant.

10.   **Answer (D) is correct.** An injunction in a trade secret case should last as long as it takes to reverse engineer the subject matter of the trade secret. A prevailing trade secret plaintiff is only entitled to an injunction lasting as long as the "head start" that the defendant received by usurping the trade secret. Thus, the injunction should remain in place for the time period that would have been needed to reverse engineer the product. *See Lamb-Weston, Inc. v. McCain Foods, Ltd.*, 941 F.2d 970 (9th Cir. 1991).

Answer (A) is incorrect. Allowing an injunction to continue indefinitely, as long as the requisite secrecy and competitive advantage exist, would require that the court engage in continuing supervision of the status of the trade secret. Courts are thus unlikely to grant this open-ended term for injunctive relief.

Answer (B) is incorrect. Although deterrence is an objective of trade secret law, a perpetual injunction would far exceed the likely time period in which an invention could be maintained as a trade secret.

Answer (C) is incorrect. There is no 20-year term in trade secret law. It is true that patent protection lasts for 20 years from the date of filing, and thus an injunction in a patent case might well be granted for the time remaining on a 20-year patent term.

11.   The level of secrecy required in order for information to be protected as a trade secret is that it must be sufficiently secret for its owner to derive an advantage, actual or potential, from the fact that the information is not generally known to others who might use it. Whether information qualifies as proprietary thus depends on the extent of secrecy of the information in the industry. If the information can readily be duplicated by those with general skills and knowledge in the field, it is not a protectable trade secret. *See Kewanee Oil Co. v. Bicron Corp.*, 416 U.S. 470 (1974). In comparison, the patent law standard of

novelty is considerably more demanding — the invention must be something new to the public and the marketplace. Section 102(a) of the Patent Act states: "A person shall be entitled to a patent unless — (i) the claimed invention was patented, described in a printed publication or in public use, on sale, or otherwise available to the public before the effective filing date of the claimed invention." It also bars a patent if the claimed invention was descried in a prior-filed patent application, even if the information was not public. *See* 35 U.S.C. § 102 (a) (2). Thus, while trade secret law requires that the information not be generally known, patent law requires that the invention not be known to the public at all.

12. **Answer (D) is correct.** The best way to protect a general idea for a new motion picture is through contracts and confidentiality agreements. An idea can be conveyed confidentially to third parties who expressly agree to be bound and who may agree to provide compensation for the conveyance of the idea. The enforceability of this type of agreement will depend on state law, which can vary by jurisdiction.

   Answer (A) is incorrect. As noted above, contracts and confidentiality agreements can be used to protect a general idea for a new movie.

   Answer (B) is incorrect. Trademark law cannot be used to protect a general idea for a new movie — trademark law requires use in commerce of a source-identifying word or other device.

   Answer (C) is incorrect. Copyright law cannot be used to protect a general idea for a new movie — only the expression used to convey that idea. As § 102(b) of the Copyright Act states: "In no case does copyright protection for an original work of authorship extend to any idea, procedure, process, system, method of operation, concept, principle, or discovery, regardless of the form in which it is described, explained, illustrated, or embodied in such work." 17 U.S.C. § 102(b).

13. **Answer (D) is correct.** Trade secret misappropriation can occur by either breach of confidence or use of improper means. These are the two fundamental ways in which a trade secret owner can show that proprietary information was taken unlawfully.

   Answer (A) is incorrect. As noted above, either a breach of confidence or use of improper means constitute impermissible means of obtaining a trade secret.

   Answer (B) is incorrect. As noted above, either a breach of confidence or use of improper means constitute impermissible means of obtaining a trade secret.

   Answer (C) is incorrect. Reverse engineering of a publicly available product is a permissible way to identify and replicate a trade secret.

14. **Answer (B) is correct.** The overall appearance and presentation of a restaurant can be protected as trade dress, as long as it is either inherently distinctive or has acquired distinctiveness (or secondary meaning). This was the holding of the Supreme Court's decision in *Two Pesos, Inc. v. Taco Cabana, Inc.*, 505 U.S. 763 (1992).

   Answer (A) is incorrect. The restaurant's appearance would be highly unlikely to satisfy the requirements of a utility patent of novelty, nonobviousness, and usefulness.

   Answer (C) is incorrect. The appearance of a restaurant would not quality as a certification mark, which focuses on the mark owner's vouching for the quality or characteristics of third parties' goods or services. *See* 15 U.S.C. § 1127 (definition of "certification mark").

Answer (D) is incorrect. By virtue of being publicly visible, the appearance of a restaurant could not qualify as trade secret subject matter.

15.   The merger doctrine in copyright law provides that "when there is essentially only one way to express an idea, the idea and its expression are inseparable, and copyright is no bar to copying that expression." *ATC Distribution Group, Inc. v. Whatever It Takes Transmissions & Parts, Inc.*, 402 F.3d 700 (6th Cir. 2005). Thus, the copyright owner cannot obtain exclusive rights to an idea when that idea cannot be expressed in sufficient alternative ways.

16.   **Answer (C) is correct.** A newly discovered human gene sequence useful in testing for certain types of leukemia, while newly discovered and useful, would not be patentable subject matter because it would not have been created or modified by the discoverer. For example, the human gene sequences that increased the probability of breast and other cancers — certain mutations of the BRCA1 and BRCA2 genes — were ruled to be unpatentable subject matter by the Supreme Court in *Association for Molecular Pathology v. Myriad Genetics, Inc.*, 133 S. Ct. 2107 (2013):

> Groundbreaking, innovative, or even brilliant discovery does not by itself satisfy the § 101 inquiry. . . . Myriad found the location of the BRCA1 and BRCA2 genes, but that discovery, by itself, does not render the BRCA genes "new . . . composition[s] of matter," § 101, that are patent eligible.
>
> . . . .
>
> Nor are Myriad's claims saved by the fact that isolating DNA from the human genome severs chemical bonds and thereby creates a nonnaturally occurring molecule. Myriad's claims are simply not expressed in terms of chemical composition, nor do they rely in any way on the chemical changes that result from the isolation of a particular section of DNA. Instead, the claims understandably focus on the genetic information encoded in the BRCA1 and BRCA2 genes.

133 S. Ct. at 2116–17. Thus, a naturally occurring gene sequence, or other naturally occurring composition of matter, will not be patentable subject matter.

Answer (A) is incorrect. A genetically modified plant is eligible for protection under the Plant Patent Act (if asexually reproduced) or by a traditional utility patent (if useful). *See J.E.M. Ag Supply, Inc. v. Pioneer Hi-Bred International, Inc.*, 534 U.S. 124 (2001).

Answer (B) is incorrect. A business method, such as a method of using computer automation to solve a complex accounting problem, would be patentable subject matter, although it might not meet the novelty or nonobviousness standards. *See generally Bilski v. Kappos*, 130 S. Ct. 3218 (2010) (rejecting an exclusion of "business methods" from patentable subject matter but holding that the particular patent in question (which involved a method for hedging against risk) was an abstract idea ineligible for patent protection).

Answer (D) is incorrect. An aesthetically pleasing design for an existing automobile battery would be protectable by a design patent, which does not require that the underlying article of manufacture be new, but only that the ornamental design for that article be new, original, and ornamental. *See* 35 U.S.C. § 171.

17.   **Answer (D) is correct.** The following statement most accurately describes the approach taken by federal patent law to questions of remedies: injunctive relief is frequently granted,

and money damages are generally available. Section 283 of the Patent Act states: "The several courts having jurisdiction of cases under this title may grant injunctions in accordance with the principles of equity to prevent the violation of any right secured by patent, on such terms as the court deems reasonable." Thus, injunctive relief is available based upon a four-factor equitable test. As noted in *eBay, Inc. v. MercExchange, L.L.C.*, 547 U.S. 388, 393–94 (2006), the patent holder must show:

> (1) that it has suffered an irreparable injury; (2) that remedies available at law, such as monetary damages, are inadequate to compensate for that injury; (3) that, considering the balance of hardships between the plaintiff and defendant, a remedy in equity is warranted; and (4) that the public interest would not be disserved by a permanent injunction.

The Court rejected the Federal Circuit's presumption that injunctions should be granted except in unusual cases. Injunctive relief is a very important remedy because it permits the patent holder to maintain its exclusivity in the marketplace, which is the essence of the patent reward. Section 284 of the Patent Act identifies damages recovery available to patent holders: "Upon finding for the claimant the court *shall award the claimant damages adequate to compensate for the infringement* but in no event less than a reasonable royalty for the use made of the invention by the infringer, together with interest and costs as fixed by the court." 35 U.S.C. § 284 (emphasis added). In cases of bad faith, section 285 of the Patent Act allows for the recovery of reasonable attorney's fees: "The court in exceptional cases may award reasonable attorney fees to the prevailing party." Enhanced damages are also available in cases of willful infringement.

Answer (A) is incorrect. As discussed above, damages are not presumed in patent cases, and injunctions are frequently issued to vindicate the patent owner's exclusive rights.

Answer (B) is incorrect. As discussed above, injunctive relief is not presumed in patent cases, and damages are frequently awarded to compensate the patent owner.

Answer (C) is incorrect. As discussed above, damages are frequently awarded to compensate the patent owner, even in the absence of bad faith or actual loss of profits — section 284 makes a "reasonable royalty for the use made of the invention by the infringer" the minimum monetary award.

18. **Answer (C) is correct.** If Congress wished to grant a perpetual copyright, the Intellectual Property Clause (Art. I, sec. 8, cl. 8) would expressly preclude such a law, and the Commerce Clause probably would not give Congress the power to circumvent the express limits of the Intellectual Property Clause. In *Eldred v. Ashcroft*, 537 U.S. 186 (2003), the Supreme Court held that Congress did not exceed its constitutional authority when it added 20 years to all existing and future copyrights. Justice Ginsburg found that "[t]ext, history, and precedent, confirm that the Copyright Clause empowers Congress to prescribe 'limited Times' for copyright protection and to secure the same level and duration of protection for all copyright holders, present and future." This holding, however, does not mean that Congress could enact a perpetual copyright statute, as that would be beyond its power under the Intellectual Property Clause, which gives Congress the power "[t]o promote the Progress of Science and useful Arts, by securing for limited Times to Authors and Inventors the exclusive Right to their respective Writings and Discoveries." U.S. Const. art. I, sec. 8, cl. 8. It seems unlikely that Congress could evade this express limit on its power by invoking the Commerce Clause to enact copyright legislation.

Answer (A) is incorrect. By its clear terms, the Intellectual Property Clause does not permit such a law.

Answer (B) is incorrect. As discussed above, it is highly unlikely that Congress could easily avoid the problem by relying upon the Commerce Clause.

Answer (D) is incorrect. Congress has not enacted any perpetual copyright legislation, including works of foreign authors. It restored foreign authors' copyrights to the statutory term in certain instances, *see* 17 U.S.C. § 104A, but the restoration of the remaining period of protection that was lost is not the same as a perpetual term. *See Golan v. Holder*, 132 S. Ct. 873 (2012).

19.   **Answer (A) is correct.** Assume that someone writes a new novel under a pseudonym in the year 2010. The current term of copyright protection for this work not published in the author's own name is 95 years from the date of publication or 120 years from the date of creation, whichever comes first. 17 U.S.C. § 302(c) ("In the case of an anonymous work, a pseudonymous work, or a work made for hire, the copyright endures for a term of 95 years from the year of its first publication, or a term of 120 years from the year of its creation, whichever expires first.").

Answer (B) is incorrect. As discussed above, the copyright term is 95 years from the date of publication or 120 years from the date of creation, whichever comes first.

Answer (C) is incorrect. Life plus 50 years was the term of copyright for works published in the author's own name prior to the copyright term extension.

Answer (D) is incorrect. Life plus 70 years is the term of copyright for works published in the author's own name. 17 U.S.C. § 302(c) ("Copyright in a work created on or after January 1, 1978, subsists from its creation and, except as provided by the following subsections, endures for a term consisting of the life of the author and 70 years after the author's death.") If the identity of the initially pseudonymous work is revealed in the registration records for the work during the term of copyright, then the term will change to "life plus seventy." *See* 17 U.S.C. § 302 (c).

20.   **Answer (D) is correct.** Your client wishes to use a copyrighted song and sound recording in a movie. This would require synchronization and master use licenses from the copyright owners. A synchronization (or "synch") license from the music publisher allows the moviemaker to place the musical work (the lyrics and melody) alongside the visual aspects of the movie. Assuming the moviemaker wishes to use a particular sound recording that has already been made by a performed, a master use license from the record company is needed to make use of this work. Two licenses are needed because there are two copyrights embodied in the recorded version of a song — the musical work copyright and the copyright in the sound recording.

Answer (A) is incorrect. Public performance rights from BMI, ASCAP, or SESAC do not cover synchronization of musical works. *See, e.g., Frank Music Corp. v. Metro-Goldwyn-Mayer, Inc.*, 772 F.2d 505 (9th Cir. 1985) (casino with a musical revue featuring copyrighted songs had ASCAP public performance license, which did not cover rights needed to set music to the theatrical production on stage).

Answer (B) is incorrect. A mechanical license allows a performer to record and sell "cover" versions (new sound recording) of a previously recorded musical work. It would not permit placing the song on a film or other audiovisual work without a synch license.

Answer (C) is incorrect. The right of distribution, standing alone, would not allow the use of the song on the film. The right to distribute the movie containing the musical work and sound recording is included in the synch license and master use license.

21. **Answer (C) is correct.** Assume that a professor at a private college copies a single news article from the local newspaper (to which he or she subscribes) and distributes these copies to her class the day following the initial publication. This action does not violate copyright law, in light of the fair use defense (and related educational copying guidelines). This appears to be a classic case of fair use under section 107, involving a single news article on a timely topic reproduced in limited quantity and immediately used a single time for educational purposes. It falls within the guidelines for classroom copying by educators and librarians. *See* http://www.copyright.gov/circs/circ21.pdf. These guidelines are not the law — section 107 is — but they can be helpful in discerning the likely reach of section 107 in certain educational settings.

Answer (A) is incorrect. As discussed above, this action does not violate copyright law, in light of the section 107 fair use defense (and related educational copying guidelines).

Answer (B) is incorrect. There can be secondary liability under various theories under the Copyright Act, but no copyright violation occurred on these facts.

Answer (D) is incorrect. The absence of profit by the professor and the college, though a factor in the fair use analysis, is not dispositive standing alone. Non-profit activities that exceed the scope of fair use based on a balancing of all relevant factors can violate the Copyright Act.

22. **Answer (A) is correct.** A company hires a freelance professional website designer to create and design its website. The website designer most likely owns the copyright to the work, absent an agreement to the contrary. An independent contractor who creates a copyrighted work for a client ordinarily owns the copyright to the work, even though the client pays for copies of the work and provides some input into its creation. A complete analysis of this question requires application of the common law agency standard set forth in the Supreme Court's decision in *Community for Creative Non-Violence v. Reid*, 490 U.S. 730 (1989). The case involved a homeless advocacy group, which hired a well-known sculptor to create a work depicting the homeless. The Court ultimately held that the sculptor owned the copyright to the work, even though the advocacy group owned physical sculpture itself. To determine whether a work is created by an independent contractor or whether it is a "work made for hire" by an employee (in which case the hiring party would own the copyright), the Court adopted the common law agency standard. This test involves analysis of the following factors:

> In determining whether a hired party is an employee under the general common law of agency, we consider the hiring party's right to control the manner and means by which the product is accomplished. Among the other factors relevant to this inquiry are the skill required; the source of the instrumentalities and tools; the location of the work; the duration of the relationship between the parties; whether the hiring party has the right to assign additional projects to the hired party; the extent of the hired party's discretion over when and how long to work; the method of payment; the hired

party's role in hiring and paying assistants; whether the work is part of the regular business of the hiring party; whether the hiring party is in business; the provision of employee benefits; and the tax treatment of the hired party.

Id. Applying this test on the present limited set of facts, it appears the web designer would be deemed an independent contractor and would be entitled to copyright ownership. The "specially ordered or commissioned" branch of the definition of a "work made for hire" will not apply here because a website, without more facts to alter the common understanding of that term, is not a work that will be used "as a contribution to a collective work, as a part of a motion picture or other audiovisual work, as a translation, as a supplementary work, as a compilation, as an instructional text, as a test, as answer material for a test, or as an atlas." 17 U.S.C. § 101 (definition of a "work made for hire"). Moreover, even commissioned works that are made for the uses listed above, are only works made for hire authored and owned by the hiring party if the parties agree in writing to such treatment. This conclusion would have serious implications for the company, particularly as to future modifications or use of the website. This result is, however, simply the default rule in copyright law and can be modified by agreement of the parties.

Answer (B) is incorrect. As discussed above, the web designer would be deemed an independent contractor and would be entitled to copyright ownership of a website.

Answer (C) is incorrect. Copyright law provides default rules in this situation, as discussed above. The outcome under the default rule can of course be modified by express agreement.

Answer (D) is incorrect. Without additional facts, it is highly unlikely that the company's contributions to the work were independently copyrightable or that the web designer ever intended a joint authorship arrangement. Section 101 of the Copyright Act defines a joint work as "a work prepared by two or more authors with the intention that their contributions be merged into inseparable or interdependent parts of a unitary whole." 17 U.S.C. § 101. As discussed in *Childress v. Taylor*, 945 F.2d 500 (2d Cir. 1991), two elements must be proven to form a joint work — (1) each author must make independently copyrightable contributions to the work and (2) there must be mutual intention that the contributions be combined into a unitary whole as a joint work. Thus, it is highly unlikely that the website was a joint work.

23. **Answer (B) is correct.** The general term of protection for a plant patent under the Plant Patent Act is 20 years from the date of patent filing. *See* 35 U.S.C. §§ 154 (a)(2) and 161. This is the same term as provided for utility patents. These patent terms were established in the Uruguay Round Agreements Act of 1994 ("URAA"), which established the term for patents sought after June 8, 1995.

    Answer (A) is incorrect. This does not correctly state the patent term, as noted above.

    Answer (C) is incorrect. This was the term for plant and utility patents under prior law, but the patent term was amended by the URAA, as noted above.

    Answer (D) is incorrect. This does not correctly state the patent term, as noted above.

24. **Answer (C) is correct.** The significance of a copyright notice under current law for a work first written and published in 2014 is that copyright notice is no longer required in light of the Berne Convention Implementation Act of 1988 ("BCIA"). Section 401(a) of the Copyright Act currently states:

> Whenever a work protected under this title is published in the United States or elsewhere by authority of the copyright owner, a notice of copyright as provided by this section *may* be placed on publicly distributed copies from which the work can be visually perceived, either directly or with the aid of a machine or device.

17 U.S.C. § 401(a) (emphasis added). A similar provision applies to phonorecords. *See* 17 U.S.C. § 402 (a). Notice can eliminate a defense of innocence, which could be used to mitigate damages. *See* 17 U.S.C. §§ 401(d) and 402(d). The elimination of a mandatory notice requirement applies to works published after March 1, 1989, when the BCIA took effect. *See* 17 U.S.C. § 405. The BCIA brought the United States into compliance with article 5(2) of the Berne Convention by eliminating the notice requirement for works published after its effective date. Article 5(2) of the Berne Convention states: "The enjoyment and the exercise of these rights shall not be subject to any formality." Mandatory copyright notice would be a prohibited "formality."

Answer (A) is incorrect. As discussed above, works published under current law are not subject to a mandatory notice requirement.

Answer (B) is incorrect. As discussed above, works published under current law are not subject to a mandatory notice requirement.

Answer (D) is incorrect. As noted above, the BCIA eliminated the notice requirement.

25. **Answer (A) is correct.** A law student prepares a written outline of a course based on the casebook readings and classroom discussion. The law student has a valid copyright on the outline because it is minimally creative and involves some judgment. The originality standard of *Feist Publications, Inc. v. Rural Telephone Service Co.*, 499 U.S. 340, 345 (1991), provides as follows:

> The *sine qua non* of copyright is originality. To qualify for copyright protection, a work must be original to the author. Original, as the term is used in copyright, means only that the work was independently created by the author (as opposed to copied from other works), and that it possesses at least some minimal degree of creativity.

The outline is independently created and has a minimal degree of creativity, based on the selection and arrangement of the material in the outline. Even though much of the content of the outline might be derived from the class lecture and casebook, the law student has an implied right to prepare notes from the class and from the readings, and fair use would be implicated as well. Of course, a verbatim reproduction of the class lecture or casebook that is used beyond the scope of section 107 fair use would raise copyright issues, but most student outlines do not fall into this category.

Answer (B) is incorrect. As noted above, there is an originality requirement, but the outline is very likely to satisfy the threshold for creativity.

Answer (C) is incorrect. This is the second-best answer. As noted above, although much of the content of the outline might be derived from the class lecture and casebook, the law student has an implied right to prepare notes from the class and from the readings. Of course, a verbatim reproduction of the class lecture or casebook that is used beyond the scope of section 107 fair use would raise copyright issues but most student outlines do not fall into this category.

Answer (D) is incorrect. As the Court made clear in *Feist*, factual works that meet the originality standard are copyrightable.

26. **Answer (B) is correct.** The primary source of Congress's authority to protect semiconductors (computer chips or mask works) in the Semiconductor Chip Protection Act is the Commerce Clause. Congress sought to avoid any issue as to whether the mask works constituted a "writing" under the Intellectual Property Clause by invoking the Commerce Clause power. *See* EDWARD C. WALTERSCHEID, THE NATURE OF THE INTELLECTUAL PROPERTY CLAUSE: A STUDY IN HISTORICAL PERSPECTIVE, 463 & n.132 (2002).

Answer (A) is incorrect. As discussed above, Congress sought to avoid any issue as to whether the mask works constituted a "writing" under the Intellectual Property Clause by invoking the Commerce Clause power.

Answer (B) is incorrect. The First Amendment is a limit on congressional power, not a general source of law-making authority.

Answer (D) is incorrect. The Impeachment Clause applies to matters related to statutory protection for mask works.

27. **Answer (B) is correct.** The best description of the role of proof of greater sophistication of purchasers in trademark cases is that increased purchaser sophistication weighs against a finding of likelihood of confusion analysis. A more sophisticated purchaser, such as a specialized or professional buyer or a procurement expert, is deemed less likely to suffer consumer confusion than would an ordinary consumer. Thus, if the relevant universe of purchasers is more sophisticated than an average consumer, then consumer confusion is less likely to take place. *See, e.g., In re N.A.D.*, 754 F.2d 996 (Fed. Cir. 1985) (taking into account purchaser sophistication in reversing refusal to register NARKOMED for anesthesia machines because of purported confusion with NARKO medical supply mark).

Answer (A) is incorrect. Purchaser sophistication, or a factor related thereto, is a factor in the likelihood of confusion analysis. *See, e.g., Polaroid Corp. v. Polarad Electronics Corp.*, 287 F.2d 492, 495 (2d Cir. 1961).

Answer (C) is incorrect. As discussed above, greater purchaser sophistication weighs against, not in favor of, a finding of likelihood of confusion analysis.

Answer (D) is incorrect. Greater purchaser sophistication is merely one factor in the likelihood of confusion analysis and certainly need not be proven in order for the trademark owner to recover.

28. **Answer (B) is correct.** The market for in-line skates is highly competitive, and Rollerblade is the leading brand (registered for many years). A new competitor wishes to make use of the name "Rychlak Rollerblades" and does not wish to use the more cumbersome term "in-line skates." Rychlak can use the name "Rychlak Rollerblades" if he can prove that it is or has become generic. If a term is proven to be generic, whereby its primary significance to consumers is to identify the product itself, then competitors are able to make use of it. *See King-Seeley Thermos Co. v. Aladdin Industries, Inc.*, 321 F.2d 577 (2d Cir. 1963). *See also* 15 U.S.C. §§ 1064 (3) and 1065 (4). There has been a dispute related to the Rollerblade trademark and its alleged genericness. *See* Rollerblade, Inc. v. CBNO & Ray Redican Jr., Case No. D2000-00427 (WIPO Arbitration & Mediation Center Admin. Panel Decision August 24, 2000) (*available at* http://www.wipo.int/amc/en/domains/decisions/html/2000/d2000-0427.html) (not finding the "Rollerblade" mark to be generic for skates but finding

that the registrant of rollerblading.com had not registered and used it in bad faith, due to third party use of "rollerblading" in a generic sense).

Answer (A) is incorrect. To prove a trademark fair use defense, a competitor must show (1) use of the term other than as a mark, (2) good faith, and (3) use of the term descriptively. Here the term "rollerblade" is being used too prominently to be "other than as a mark."

Answer (C) is incorrect. A mark can be challenged if it has become generic, even if the mark has attained incontestable status. The Lanham Act specifically states that "no incontestable right shall be acquired in a mark which is the generic name for the goods or services or a portion thereof, for which it is registered." 15 U.S.C. § 1065. (Moreover, long-term use must be accompanied by the filing of an affidavit of incontestability before the right to use the mark becomes incontestable. *See* 15 U.S.C. § 1065 (3).)

Answer (D) is incorrect. The test for whether a mark has become generic focuses on the primary significance to consumers, not on whether there are alternative words that can be used to identify the product.

29. **Answer (C) is correct.** The trademark term "Sun" for a bank is arbitrary. There is no connection at all between the sun and banking services, so the mark is arbitrary.

Answer (A) is incorrect. The term "Sun" does not describe characteristics of the bank.

Answer (B) is incorrect. The term "Sun" does not indirectly suggest something about the bank.

Answer (D) is incorrect. The term "Sun" was not coined to serve as a trademark.

30. **Answer (B) is correct.** The trademark term "Good Housekeeping Seal of Approval" is a certification mark. The mark is used to certify the goods or services of others (third parties other than Good Housekeeping itself).

Answer (A) is incorrect. There is no evidence that the trademark term "Good Housekeeping Seal of Approval" is used misleadingly or deceives consumers.

Answer (C) is incorrect. The trademark term "Good Housekeeping Seal of Approval" does not signify membership in an association or cooperative organization.

Answer (D) is incorrect. Good Housekeeping does not market services under the "Good Housekeeping Seal of Approval" mark.

31. **Answer (B) is correct.** The trademark term "Roquefort" for cheese originating in Roquefort, France — and meeting the production standard for that community's cured sheep's milk cheeses — is best characterized as a certification mark under these facts. The term signifies that this cured sheep's milk cheese meets the standards established for this variety of cheese, including having its origin in Roquefort, France. *See* 15 U.S.C. § 1127 (definition of "certification mark"). *See also Community of Roquefort v. William Faehndrich, Inc.,* 303 F.2d 494 (2d Cir. 1962).

Answer (A) is incorrect. This is a second best answer. Consumers can accurately connect "Roquefort" to Roquefort, France as the geographic origin of the goods, but because of the additional facts regarding the community's standards, the best answer is (B).

Answer (C) is incorrect. The term "Roquefort" does not signify membership in an association or cooperative organization.

Answer (D) is incorrect. The term "Roquefort" is not used to market services.

32.   **Answer (B) is correct.** The term "Dallas Steak Company" for a steak restaurant in Dallas, Texas is descriptive. It accurately identifies the geographic location of the restaurant and may be able to attain trademark status upon a showing of secondary meaning or consumer recognition.

Answer (A) is incorrect. Although many may think of Texas as a place synonymous with steak, "Dallas" does not identify a particular type of steak, so the term is not generic.

Answer (C) is incorrect. The term is not suggestive, as it does not have an indirect connection to the services (i.e., one that requires imagination to recognize).

Answer (D) is incorrect. There is no evidence that the term is used by persons other than the owner to signify the origin of goods or services. Instead, this mark, on these facts, is used to indicate a single source of goods or services — although the facts do not indicate that the mark has acquired the distinctiveness required for registration.

33.   **Answer (D) is correct.** A candy maker produces a new product which is made with synthetic chocolate flavoring and which it would like to call "Chocolaty Chompers." This mark is likely to be found deceptive if there is no real chocolate ingredient in it. Courts apply a three-part test to assess whether a mark is deceptive under the Lanham Act: "(1) Is the term misdescriptive of the character, quality, function, composition or use of the goods? (2) If so, are prospective purchasers likely to believe that the misdescription actually describes the goods? (3) If so, is the misdescription likely to affect the decision to purchase?" *In re Budge Manufacturing Co.*, 857 F.2d 773, 775 (Fed. Cir. 1988). Applying this test, the term falsely implies that chocolate is an ingredient, purchasers are likely to believe this statement, and it is likely to affect the purchasing decision. Deceptive marks are barred from registration. *See* 15 U.S.C. § 1052 ("No trademark by which the goods of the applicant may be distinguished from the goods of others shall be refused registration on the principal register on account of its nature *unless it* (a) *consists of* or comprises immoral, *deceptive*, or scandalous *matter*; or matter which may disparage or falsely suggest a connection with persons, living or dead, institutions, beliefs, or national symbols, or bring them into contempt, or disrepute . . .") (emphasis added).

Answer (A) is incorrect. The term in question does not identify a category of candy.

Answer (B) is incorrect. The term in question does appear to describe a feature of the candy. Thus, if the statement were true, this term probably would be descriptive. Given its falsity in this case, however, it would be deceptive and thus barred from registration under the Lanham Act.

Answer (C) is incorrect. The term in question is not suggestive. Instead, it falsely describes the goods and is likely to be found deceptive.

34.   **Answer (A) is correct.** An automobile parts manufacturer develops a revolutionary new engine. The process of manufacturing the engine and the engine itself both involve significant improvements over existing automobile technology. The best legal advice in this situation is that the manufacturer should seek only patent protection for the engine itself and weigh its options on whether trade secret or patent law offers the best form of protection for its new manufacturing process. The engine is patentable subject matter, and it likely meets the novelty and nonobviousness standards on these bare facts. It would be

susceptible to reverse engineering, which would render trade secret protection undesirable. The manufacturing process, on the other hand, could either be maintained as a trade secret or could be the basis for a process patent. The alternatives in this instance should be carefully weighed.

Answer (B) is incorrect. The manufacturer can maintain the process as a trade secret once it obtains patent protection for the engine. As long as it fully discloses the claimed features of the new engine, the firm can still maintain the production process as a trade secret.

Answer (C) is incorrect. As discussed above, the engine appears to be patentable and would be susceptible to reverse engineering, which would render trade secret protection undesirable.

Answer (D) is incorrect. This statement incorrectly assumes that the engine itself could be maintained as a trade secret and that the best way to protect the process is through disclosure and patenting. The best advice is the direct opposite of this statement, as discussed above.

35.   A transformative use is an important consideration in analysis of copyright infringement cases, particularly in the determination of fair use. Transformative use was given particular emphasis in the Supreme Court's decision in *Campbell v. Acuff-Rose Music Inc.*, 510 U.S. 569 (1994). That case involved a Two Live Crew rap parody version of the copyrighted song "Oh Pretty Woman." Analyzing whether the parody was a fair use under the Copyright Act, the Court emphasized the need to analyze each fair use situation on a case-by-case, fact-specific basis. In addressing the first factor, the character of the use, the Court found that it was transformative in nature, which mitigated the effect of the commerciality of the use. More specifically, the Court noted that Two Live Crew substantially altered the original Roy Orbison song. In particular, the lyrics of the Two Live Crew song are substantially different from the original and convey a very different message. The transformative nature of the use weighs in favor of fair use.

36.   **Answer (C) is correct.** The best form of intellectual property protection for a certain clothing design feature or fabric design is likely to be a copyright. *See Wal-Mart Stores, Inc. v. Samara Bros., Inc.*, 529 U.S. 205 (2000) (rejecting trademark claim for clothing design because of lack of secondary meaning, but not addressing successful copyright claim based on graphical features appliqued onto the articles of clothing). As commentators have noted, clothing designs have often failed to attain *any* form of protection. *See* Kal Raustiala & Christopher Sprigman, *The Piracy Paradox: Innovation and Intellectual Property in Fashion Design*, 92 VA. L. REV. 1687 (2006); Julie P. Tsai, *Fashioning Protection: A Note on the Protection of Fashion Designs in the United States*, 9 LEWIS & CLARK L. REV. 447, 447 (2005). Nonetheless, there have been instances in which some features of clothing design (particularly graphic design features or fabric patterns, but not the shape or overall "look" of the garment) have been found to be copyrightable.

Answer (A) is incorrect. Design patent law is ill-suited to protecting fashion designs, particularly given the high threshold for patentability (i.e., novelty and non-obviousness). The cost and time involved in patent protection are also unfavorable.

Answer (B) is incorrect. As discussed above, a copyright claim is likely to be more successful than a trademark claim as to certain clothing design features and fabric patterns. *See, e.g., Wal-Mart Stores, Inc. v. Samara Bros., Inc.*, 529 U.S. 205 (2000) (rejecting trademark claim for clothing design because of lack of secondary meaning, but not addressing successful copyright claim based on graphical features appliqued onto the articles of clothing).

Answer (D) is incorrect. This answer is second-best, as there is an argument that no current form of intellectual property protection adequately protects clothing designs. As noted above, however, designers have had success in protecting fabric patterns under copyright law. Particular nonfunctional handbag designs have also occasionally gained trade dress protection. There have been proposals to offer copyright-like protection for clothing designs, such as the Design Piracy Prohibition Act, H.R. 5055, 109th Congress, 2d Session. To date, however, no fashion design bill has been enacted in the U.S.

37.   **Answer (D) is correct.** The trademark term "Xerox" for photocopy machines and other office equipment is fanciful. Xerox is a coined term, which is deemed fanciful in trademark taxonomy (and therefore is the inherently strongest type of mark).

       Answer (A) is incorrect. The trademark term "Xerox" does not describe a feature of photocopy machines and other office equipment.

       Answer (B) is incorrect. The trademark term "Xerox" does not have an indirect connection to photocopy machines and other office equipment that requires some imagination to recognize.

       Answer (C) is incorrect. The trademark term "Xerox" is a coined term, not a term or word that previously existed.

38.   **Answer (A) is correct.** Injunctive relief is usually granted to successful patent owner plaintiffs, and actual damages can be recovered as well. Section 284 of the Patent Act sets forth the types of damage recoveries available to patent holders: "Upon finding for the claimant the court shall award the claimant damages adequate to compensate for the infringement *but in no event less than a reasonable royalty for the use made of the invention by the infringer*, together with interest and costs as fixed by the court." (Emphasis added).

       Answer (B) is incorrect. Lost profits are recoverable under section 284 as part of the "damages adequate to compensate for the infringement," but the floor or minimum recovery is a reasonable royalty. In other words, if the lost profits exceed a reasonable royalty, the patent owner can recover the higher amount.

       Answer (C) is incorrect. As noted above, under section 284, the minimum recovery is a reasonable royalty.

       Answer (D) is incorrect. Statutory damages are not available in the Patent Act; they can be recovered in certain instances in copyright law.

39.   **Answer (C) is correct.** Nonobviousness can be best described as a showing that the invention involves an inventive step, i.e., a departure from the prior art that would not be apparent to a person having ordinary skill in the art (PHOSITA). Section 103 of the Patent Act states: "A patent may not be obtained notwithstanding that the claimed invention is not identically disclosed as set forth in section 102, if the differences between the claimed invention and the prior art are such that the claimed invention as a whole would have been obvious before the effective filing date of the claimed invention to a person having ordinary

skill in the art to which the claimed invention pertains. Patentability shall not be negated by the manner in which the invention was made." *See Graham v. John Deere Co.*, 383 U.S. 1, 17–18 (1966) ("Under § 103, the scope and content of the prior art are to be determined; differences between the prior art and the claims at issue are to be ascertained; and the level of ordinary skill in the pertinent art resolved. Against this background the obviousness or nonobviousness of the subject matter is determined.").

Answer (A) is incorrect. This statement is relevant to novelty, not nonobviousness, under the Patent Act. *See* 35 U.S.C. § 102(a).

Answer (B) is incorrect. This statement is not relevant to either novelty or nonobviousness under the current Patent Act. Under pre-AIA patent law, there was some relevance to prior knowledge by others before the date of invention, but current law does not utilize the date of invention.

Answer (D) is incorrect. This standard focuses on the applicant-inventor rather than section 103's person having ordinary skill in the art.

40. **Answer (A) is correct.** The changes to sections 102 and 103 of the Patent Act enacted as part of the America Invents Act (AIA) took effect on March 16, 2013, and they affect the validity of all patents containing claims with an effective filing date on or after March 16, 2013. The novelty and nonobviousness of inventions within applications containing only claims with effective filing dates before March 16, 2013 will continue to be judged under the pre-AIA sections 102 and 103.

Answer (B) is incorrect. As stated above, the standards of novelty and nonobviousness of patents existing on March 16, 2013, or of inventions within applications containing only claims with effective filing dates before that date, will continue to be judged under the pre-AIA sections 102 and 103 — regardless of the context in which their validity is examined, including reexamination.

Answer (C) is incorrect. As stated above, the standards of novelty and nonobviousness of patents existing on March 16, 2013, or of inventions within applications containing only claims with effective filing dates before that date, will continue to be judged under the pre-AIA sections 102 and 103 — regardless of the context in which their validity is examined, including later invalidity challenges during infringement litigation.

Answer (D) is incorrect. Answer (A) is the only correct answer.

41. **Answer (A) is correct.** A work was published without proper copyright notice in 1970. Under present law, this work is likely in the public domain. Copyright notices were required under the 1909 Act and works published without the copyright notice fell into the public domain. Later amendments did not change this result, unless this was a foreign work whose copyright was restored under 17 U.S.C. § 104A. These facts do not allude to foreign authorship or first publication in a foreign country.

Answer (B) is incorrect. This statement is true as to works that were not published prior to the effective date of the 1976 Copyright Act, January 1, 1978, but were published before March 1, 1989. Thus, the work in question is still governed by the strict rule of the 1909 Act, unless restored under section 104A. *See above.*

Answer (C) is incorrect. This statement is only true as to works that were not published prior to the effective date of the Berne Convention Implementation Act, which is March 1,

1989. The work in question is still governed by the strict rule of the 1909 Act. *See above.*

Answer (D) is incorrect. The Sonny Bono Copyright Term Extension Act did not address the copyright notice issue.

42.   **Answer (D) is correct.** In most states, misappropriation of a trade secret is governed by the Uniform Trade Secrets Act (UTSA). As of late 2013, 47 states had adopted the UTSA either in whole or with only slight modifications. Under section 1 of the UTSA, "misappropriation" includes both of the following: obtaining another's trade secret, when the acquirer knows or has reason to know that the information was acquired by improper means; and either disclosing or using another's trade secret without the other's express consent, when the discloser or user either used improper means to obtain the information or knows or has reason to know that the information had been either obtained by improper means or had been obtained as a result of a breach of confidence or outside the scope of permitted use.

Answer (A) is incorrect. Obtaining a trade secret, when the acquirer knows or has reason to know that the information was acquired by improper means, does constitute misappropriation, but using and disclosing the trade secret are also potential acts of misappropriation.

Answer (B) is incorrect. Using a trade secret of another without the other's express consent does constitute misappropriation when the user either used improper means to obtain the information or knows or has reason to know that the information had been either obtained by improper means or had been obtained as a result of a breach of confidence or outside the scope of permitted use. Both obtaining the secret and disclosing the secret are, however, also potential acts of misappropriation.

Answer (C) is incorrect. Disclosing a trade secret of another without the other's express consent does constitute misappropriation when the discloser either used improper means to obtain the information or knows or has reason to know that the information had been either obtained by improper means or had been obtained as a result of a breach of confidence or outside the scope of permitted use. Both obtaining the secret and using the secret are, however, also potential acts of misappropriation.

43.   **Answer (B) is correct.** An ordinary citizen (who is not a famous celebrity) has her name and image used to sell products without her consent. Her best claim is a violation of the right of publicity under applicable state law. It is a common misconception that only celebrities or famous persons have a right of publicity action, as their endorsements tend to have far greater commercial value. But as long as the elements of a right of publicity claim are met, an ordinary person can bring a claim as well. *See* RESTATEMENT (THIRD) OF UNFAIR COMPETITION § 46 ("One who appropriates the commercial value of a person's identity by using without consent the person's name, likeness, or other indicia of identity for purposes of trade is subject to liability for the relief appropriate under the rules stated in §§ 48 and 49."). Those elements appear to be met on these facts.

Answer (A) is incorrect. Common law copyright, which protects unfixed expressive works, would not apply to these facts. See the answer to Question 5 in Topic 1 for more on state common law copyright protection.

Answer (C) is incorrect. Although proposals have been put forward, there is currently no federal cause of action for violation of the right of publicity.

Answer (D) is incorrect. As discussed above, ordinary citizens can have a cause of action for violation of their right of publicity. Ordinary citizens whose image would not lead a consumer to believe that the citizen depicted was endorsing the product or service would not, however, have success with a claim of false endorsement under the Lanham Act. *See, e.g., Albert v. Apex Fitness, Inc.*, 1997 U.S. Dist. LEXIS 8535 (S.D.N.Y. June 12, 1997).

44.   **Answer (D) is correct.** Section 504 of the Copyright Act sets forth the types of damage recoveries available from a copyright infringer, but it does not provide a minimum damage award, as does the Patent Act. (*See* above answer to practice exam question 38.) With respect to actual damages and profits, the Copyright Act requires proof that the owner's damages were the "result of the infringement" before they may be recovered, and it allows recovery of the infringer's profits, but only to the extent that they were "attributable to the infringement." 17 U.S.C. § 504(b). Statutory damages are addressed below.

Answer (A) is incorrect. The owner's lost profits are recoverable to the extent that they were the "result of the infringement," but that proof can be difficult, *see, e.g., Frank Music Corp. v. Metro-Goldwyn-Mayer, Inc.*, 772 F.2d 505 (9th Cir. 1985), and a court may decline to award any amount as actual damages if the court believes the evidence offered is too speculative.

Answer (B) is incorrect. The Copyright Act does not provide for damages for harm to the reputation of the copyright owner of a literary work. *Cf.* 17 U.S.C. § 106A (protecting additional, non-economic interests of the author of a work of visual art).

Answer (C) is incorrect. Although statutory damages are available in the Copyright Act, this is not the best answer because those statutory damages do not serve as a minimum recovery for all copyright owners. Statutory damages are only available to most copyright owners if the work either was registered before the infringement commenced or was registered within three months of first publication of the work, if the infringement commenced after that publication and before registration. *See* 17 U.S.C. § 412.

45.   **Answer (C) is correct.** Section 284 of the Patent Act provides that: "Upon finding for the claimant, the court shall award the claimant damages adequate to compensate for the infringement, but in no event less than a reasonable royalty for the use made of the invention by the infringer. . . . " The minimum award is thus a reasonable royalty, but if the plaintiff patent owner can prove lost profits on its own competitive product that were caused by the infringement, those would be recoverable as reasonably foreseeable damages. *See, e.g., Rite-Hite Corp. v. Kelley Co., Inc.*, 56 F.3d 1538 (Fed. Cir. 1995).

Answer (A) is not correct. Section 284 does not provide for recovery of the defendant infringer's own profits, nor does any other portion of the Patent Act. The minimum damage award of a reasonable royalty could take into account, in assessing what royalty is *reasonable*, the amount of profit earned by the defendant as a result of the infringement.

Answer (B) is not correct. Under section 285, an award of attorney's fees is permitted only in "exceptional cases." 35 U.S.C. § 285. While fees may be awarded in cases where infringement was not willful, the defendant would generally need to have engaged in some sort of misconduct, such as frivolous filings or vexations litigation conduct, taking the case outside the typical case of unintentional infringement.

Answer (D) is not correct. *See above.*

46. **Answer (C) is correct.** If your client owns a trademark that has been used from 2006 to the present in North and South Carolina but never registered anywhere, you can advise the client that it may have a civil action against an infringer under both the state common law of unfair competition and under section 43(a) of the Lanham Act, which does not require federal registration by a trademark plaintiff, as long as the requisite nexus with "commerce" (defined in the Act as coextensive with Congress's commerce power) is present. *See* 15 U.S.C. § 1125(a)(1)(A). Although the facts specify that there is no federal diversity jurisdiction between the client and the infringer, you could file the claims in either federal or state court. Federal district courts have original, but not exclusive, jurisdiction over Lanham Act claims. *See* 28 U.S.C. § 1338(a). And under 28 U.S.C. § 1338(b), federal district courts have original jurisdiction over civil claims of unfair competition "when joined with a substantial and related claim under the . . . trademark laws." Most trademark owners prefer to bring trademark claims in federal court, because of those courts' greater familiarity with trademark law.

     Answer (A) is incorrect. Although your client would indeed be able to bring its claims in state court — even its Lanham Act claims — it can also bring them all in federal court, as explained above.

     Answer (B) is incorrect. Although your client would indeed be able to bring its claims in federal court — even its state unfair competition claims, if joined with its Lanham Act claim — it can also bring them all in state court, as explained above.

     Answer (D) is incorrect. Your client can bring claims in either state or federal court.

47. **Answer (C) is correct.** If your client owns a trademark that has been used from 2006 up to present in North and South Carolina and was registered in 2014 with the U.S. Patent & Trademark Office, you can advise the client that it may have a civil action against an infringer under both the state common law of unfair competition and under section 32 of the Lanham Act. Section 32, unlike section 43(a), requires federal registration of the mark being asserted. Your client could also, for good measure, assert a claim under section 43(a), particularly if its use-based rights in the mark might arguably be broader than the rights reflected in the registration. *See* 15 U.S.C. §§ 1114(1) & 1125(a)(1)(A). Although the facts specify that there is no federal diversity jurisdiction between the client and the infringer, you could file the claims in either federal or state court. Federal district courts have original, but not exclusive, jurisdiction over Lanham Act claims. *See* 28 U.S.C. § 1338(a). And under 28 U.S.C. § 1338(b), federal district courts have original jurisdiction over civil claims of unfair competition "when joined with a substantial and related claim under the . . . trademark laws."

     Answer (A) is incorrect. Although your client would indeed be able to bring its claims in state court — even its Lanham Act claim or claims — it can also bring them all in federal court, as explained above.

     Answer (B) is incorrect. Although your client would indeed be able to bring its claims in federal court — even its state unfair competition claims, if joined with its Lanham Act claim or claims, it can also bring them all in state court, as explained above.

     Answer (D) is incorrect. Your client can bring claims in either state or federal court.

48. **Answer (C) is correct.** Inventor B is likely to receive the patent rights. Inventor A conceived of an invention and reduced it to practice in the year 2001, but did not proceed to seek patent

protection. Inventor B independently conceived of the same invention in December 2009. She reduced it to practice in March 2010. Learning of B's efforts, A applied for a patent in May 2010. B applied for a patent in June 2010. Although pre-AIA United States patent law ordinarily gives priority to the "first to conceive" an invention, this rule does not apply if that inventor suppresses the invention, conceals it, or acts with a lack of diligence. Pre-AIA section 102(g) of the Patent Act states:

> A person shall be entitled to a patent unless — . . . (1) during the course of an interference conducted under section 135 or section 291, another inventor involved therein establishes, to the extent permitted in section 104, that before such person's invention thereof the invention was made by such other inventor and not abandoned, suppressed, or concealed, or (2) before such person's invention thereof, the invention was made in this country by another inventor who had not abandoned, suppressed, or concealed it. In determining priority of invention under this subsection, there shall be considered not only the respective dates of conception and reduction to practice of the invention, but also the reasonable diligence of one who was first to conceive and last to reduce to practice, from a time prior to conception by the other.

Thus, the first inventor could lose priority if that inventor failed to exercise reasonable diligence in reducing the invention to practice or if he or she abandoned, suppressed, or concealed the invention. As noted in *Paulik v. Rizkalla*, 760 F.2d 1270, 1275 (Fed. Cir. 1985):

> The decisions applying section 102(g) balanced the law and policy favoring the first person to make an invention, against equitable considerations when more than one person had made the same invention: in each case where the court deprived the de facto first inventor of the right to the patent, the second inventor had entered the field during a period of either inactivity or deliberate concealment by the first inventor. Often the first inventor had been spurred to file a patent application by news of the second inventor's activities. Although "spurring" is not necessary to a finding of suppression or concealment, the courts' frequent references to spurring indicate their concern with this equitable factor.

Here, Inventor A appears to have failed to act diligently and was "spurred" into seeking patent protection by learning of the inventive efforts made by Inventor B.

Answer (A) is incorrect. Inventor A does not appear to have acted diligently in seeking patent protection, as discussed above.

Answer (B) is incorrect. As discussed above, the first to conceive of the invention received the patent rights under pre-AIA patent law, but not if there was a failure to act diligently, which can be shown in this case.

Answer (D) is incorrect. Joint inventors are required to work together in at least some way — there is no collaboration on these facts.

49.   **Answer (C) is correct.** An ornamental feature of a useful device is eligible for protection under either copyright or design patent law. Section 171 of the Patent Act states: "Whoever invents any new, original, and ornamental design for an article of manufacture may obtain a patent therefor, subject to the conditions and requirements of this title." And as long as the ornamental feature is either physically or conceptually separable from the utilitarian aspects of the device, it will also be eligible for copyright protection, as further explained in the answer to Question 14 in Topic 1.

Answer (A) is incorrect. Both forms of protection are available. The creator of such an ornamental design or feature is not required to elect one form of protection over the other. *See, e.g., Application of Richard Q. Yardley,* 493 F.2d 1389 (C.C.P.A. 1974) (noting that there is an area of overlap between copyright and design patent subject matter, and rejecting the argument that an author-inventor must elect between the two available forms of protection).

Answer (B) is incorrect. As noted above, both forms of protection are available.

Answer (D) is incorrect. As noted above, both forms of protection are available.

50. **Answer (C) is correct.** A consumer buys a copyrighted print and scans it onto a digital file and then posts a full-size image of the print on the Internet. The consumer has violated both the right of reproduction and the right of public display. By scanning the photo to create the digital file, the consumer has reproduced the work in a copy in violation of section 106(1). There is no "exception" for a private copy (and these bare facts alone do not support fair use). The consumer has also publicly displayed the work. To display a work "publicly" includes, under section 101, transmitting a display to members of the public. *See* 17 U.S.C. § 101 (definition of "publicly"). Section 101 of the Copyright Act also provides that to "display" a work "means to show a copy of it, either directly or by means of a film, slide, television image, or any other device or process or, in the case of a motion picture or other audiovisual work, to show individual images nonsequentially." Posting a work on the Internet is considered a public display. *See, e.g., Kelly v. Arriba Soft Corp.,* 280 F.3d 934 (9th Cir. 2002). The first-sale protection for public displays only applies when the display is to viewers present at the place where the lawful copy is located, not to transmissions of displays. *See* 17 U.S.C. § 109(c). Thus, both rights are likely to be violated on these facts.

Answer (A) is incorrect. As discussed above, both the right of reproduction and the right of public display are violated on these facts.

Answer (B) is incorrect. As discussed above, both the right of reproduction and the right of public display are violated on these facts.

Answer (D) is incorrect. The first sale doctrine does not apply since the consumer has not transferred or displayed the original, lawful copy of the work and has instead violated other rights of the copyright owner.

51. **Answer (D) is correct.** A teenage computer hacker develops software code to enable anyone receiving streaming video, such as a movie watched via the Internet from Netflix, to be able to download a permanent copy onto a computer. The hacker posts the code onto the Internet, with the announcement — "I am king of the world. Anyone can download movies for free now. Have at it, people!" The hacker most likely has violated rights under the Digital Millennium Copyright Act ("DMCA") and committed secondary copyright infringement by contributory infringement or inducement. The DMCA prohibits trafficking in anti-circumvention devices. *See* 17 U.S.C. 1201(a)(2) ("No person shall manufacture, import, offer to the public, provide, or otherwise traffic in any technology, product, service, device, component, or part thereof, that — (A) is primarily designed or produced for the purpose of circumventing a technological measure that effectively controls access to a work protected under this title; (B) has only limited commercially significant purpose or use other than to circumvent a technological measure that effectively controls access to a work protected under this title; or (C) is marketed by that person or another acting in concert with that person with that person's knowledge for use in circumventing a technological measure that

effectively controls access to a work protected under this title."); *Universal City Studios, Inc. v. Reimerdes*, 111 F. Supp. 2d 294 (S.D.N.Y. 2000), *aff'd sub nom. Universal City Studios, Inc. v. Corley*, 273 F.3d 429 (2d Cir. 2001). As for secondary liability, it is likely that the hacker can be found to have intentionally encouraged others to violate copyright law and to have provided the tools by which to do so (inducement). *See MGM Studios, Inc. v. Grokster, Ltd.*, 545 U.S. 913 (2005).

Answer (A) is incorrect. The facts show no direct violation of these rights.

Answer (B) is incorrect. As discussed above, the hacker has most likely committed secondary copyright infringement and violated the DMCA.

Answer (C) is incorrect. As discussed above, the hacker has most likely committed secondary copyright infringement and violated the DMCA.

52. The factors considered under the common law agency standard for defining a "work made for hire" by an employee under copyright law are set forth in *Community for Creative Non-Violence v. Reid*, 490 U.S. 730 (1989):

> In determining whether a hired party is an employee under the general common law of agency, we consider the hiring party's right to control the manner and means by which the product is accomplished. Among the other factors relevant to this inquiry are the skill required; the source of the instrumentalities and tools; the location of the work; the duration of the relationship between the parties; whether the hiring party has the right to assign additional projects to the hired party; the extent of the hired party's discretion over when and how long to work; the method of payment; the hired party's role in hiring and paying assistants; whether the work is part of the regular business of the hiring party; whether the hiring party is in business; the provision of employee benefits; and the tax treatment of the hired party.

If a hired party is deemed an employee under this agency standard, then authorship vests in the employer. On the other hand, if the hired party is found to be an independent contractor, then that individual has authorship rights.

53. **Answer (A) is correct.** Record Co. sells its copyrighted songs worldwide. It licenses a British company to make and sell CDs in the United Kingdom but not to import them into the United States. The British company makes CDs in a factory in England. One of its wholesale distributors sells them to a U.S. distributor, which sells them to buyers in the U.S., resulting in a copyright suit by Record Co. against the U.S. distributor. Record Co. will likely lose because of the first sale defense. *See* 17 U.S.C. § 109(a) ("Notwithstanding the provisions of section 106(3) [the right of distribution], the owner of a particular copy or phonorecord lawfully made under this title, or any person authorized by such owner, is entitled, without the authority of the copyright owner, to sell or otherwise dispose of the possession of that copy or phonorecord."). In *Kirtsaeng v. John Wiley & Sons, Inc.*, 133 S. Ct. 1351 (2013), the Supreme Court ruled that a copy or phonorecord owned by a distributor or reseller could be "lawfully made under this title" and subject to section 109(a), even if made abroad, as long as it was made under the authority of the copyright owner and would therefore be a lawful copy of phonorecord if U.S. law had governed its making.

Answer (B) is incorrect. The first sale defense applies to lawful copies of works, including musical works.

Answer (C) is incorrect. As discussed above, the Supreme Court has rejected this argument.

Answer (D) is incorrect. The fair use defense is not the best defense on these facts, as shown above.

54. **Answer (C) is correct.** The type of patentable subject matter having the shortest term (14 years) is the design patent. The term for design patents is 14 years from the date of issuance. Section 173 of the Patent Act states: "Patents for designs shall be granted for the term of fourteen years from the date of grant." In contrast to utility and plant patents, the design patent term was not extended under the Uruguay Round Agreements Act of 1994, and is thus still governed by the prior law regarding the patent term. The design patent term is therefore keyed to the issuance date of the patent, rather than to the application date.

    Answer (A) is incorrect. Utility patents have a term of 20 years from the filing of the patent application.

    Answer (B) is incorrect. Plant patents have a term of 20 years from the filing of the patent application.

    Answer (D) is incorrect. As shown above, only the design patent is given the 14-year term.

55. **Answer (B) is correct.** The following statement most accurately describes the current importance of a copyright notice for a work first published in 1982 — copyright notices are required and works published without the copyright notice fall into the public domain unless "cured" under the Copyright Act of 1976. The Copyright Act of 1976 provisions in effect in 1982 essentially still apply to this work because it was published in that year. The 1976 Act ameliorated the harsh effect of the copyright notice requirement under the 1909 Copyright Act, under which a work published without notice fell into the public domain. The 1976 Act continued to require copyright notice, but it allowed for a cure of or excuse for the omission of the notice in some circumstances. Specifically, it provided for cure of the omission in some cases. The cure provision continues to be relevant even though current law no longer requires copyright notice for new copies of a work published after March 1, 1989. Section 405(a) of the Copyright Act, which would govern the work in question, states:

    (a) Effect of Omission on Copyright.— With respect to copies and phonorecords publicly distributed by authority of the copyright owner before the effective date of the Berne Convention Implementation Act of 1988, the omission of the copyright notice described in sections 401 through 403 from copies or phonorecords publicly distributed by authority of the copyright owner does not invalidate the copyright in a work if—

    (1) the notice has been omitted from no more than a relatively small number of copies or phonorecords distributed to the public; or

    (2) registration for the work has been made before or is made within five years after the publication without notice, and a reasonable effort is made to add notice to all copies or phonorecords that are distributed to the public in the United States after the omission has been discovered; or

    (3) the notice has been omitted in violation of an express requirement in writing that, as a condition of the copyright owner's authorization of the public distribution of

copies or phonorecords, they bear the prescribed notice.

17 U.S.C. § 405(a). *See generally Hasbro Bradley, Inc. v. Sparkle Toys, Inc.*, 780 F.2d 189 (2d Cir. 1985) (applying 1976 Act notice requirement and cure provisions).

Answer (A) is incorrect. As discussed above, a strict notice requirement applied prior to the effective date of the Copyright Act of 1976, but was modified by that statute for works published on or after that date — January 1, 1978.

Answer (C) is incorrect. This rule only applies to works published after March 1, 1989, when the Berne Convention Implementation Act of 1988 took effect.

Answer (D) is incorrect. As noted above, the BCIA eliminated the notice requirement for works published after March 1, 1989. The Sonny Bono Copyright Term Extension Act made a number of modifications to copyright law, but it did not address the notice requirement.

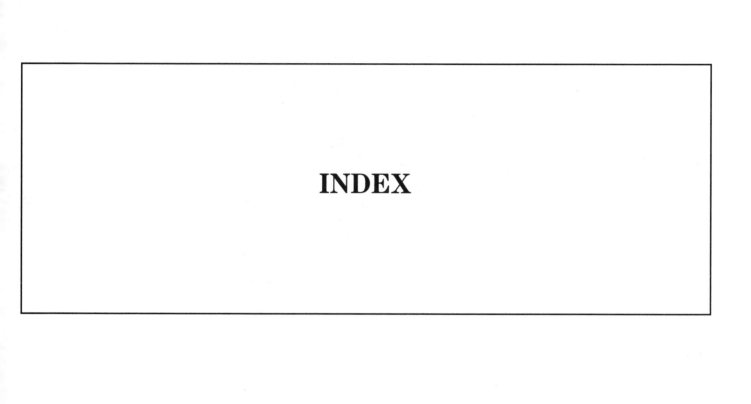

INDEX

INDEX

The letter "P" prior to a question number indicates that the question is found in the "Practice Exam" section of this text.